LITERATURE, PHILOSOPHY, AND THE SOCIAL SCIENCES

ESSAYS IN EXISTENTIALISM AND PHENOMENOLOGY

by

MAURICE NATANSON

Department of Philosophy, University of North Carolina

MARTINUS NIJHOFF / THE HAGUE / 1962

THESE ESSAYS ARE DEDICATED
TO THE MEMORY OF MY MOTHER,
KATE NATANSON
AND MY UNCLE,
ALEXANDER G. SCHEER

Foreword

A collection of one man's essays in book form tends to be viewed today with some suspicion, if not hostility, by philosophical critics. It would seem that the author is guilty of an academic sin of pride: causing or helping to cause separately conceived articles to surpass their original station and assume a new life, a grander articulation. It can hardly be denied that the essays which follow must face this sullen charge, for they were composed at different times for different sorts of audiences and, for the most part, have already been published. Their appearance in a new form will not allay commonplace criticisms: there are repetitions, certain key terms are defined and defined again in various places, a few quotations reappear, and, beyond this, the essays are unequal in range, depth, and fundamental intent. But it is what brings these essays together that constitutes, I trust, their collective merit. Underlying the special arguments that are to be found in each of the chapters is a particular sense of reality, not a thesis or a theory but rather a way of seeing the world and of appreciating its texture and design. It is that sense of reality that I should like to speak of here.

Philosophy stands in a paradoxical relationship to mundane existence: it is at once its critique and one of its possibilities. Why there should be an ordered, coherent (if tortured) reality rather than nothing at all, to paraphrase Heidegger's version of the metaphysical question, is as trying a problem as its alternative formulation: why there should be philosophy instead of the straightforward acceptance of daily life. The reflexive act which is the initial starting point of philosophical activity must be accepted as a primordial choice of the living agent. Whatever its causal conditions, its historical antecedents, its psychological motives, philosophical wonder is a phenomenon *sui generis*. Its valence for the life of the person can be measured only by its givenness, its magical irruption in the life of consciousness. To speak of "choice" here is to suggest something less than sifting among alternatives and something more than volition. To wonder is to transcend what is problematic about this or that aspect of experience and to come to a thematic awareness of experience as such, problematicity as such, and the uniqueness of one's own being confronted with reality in the adventure of a single and solitary existence. In wonder the strain of being thrust into a world reveals itself as a possibility, a condition for self-illumination. Choice is a fundamental predicate attaching to the self, a subscript in search of its proper integer.

It is in a phenomenologically conceived existentialism that I find the surest approach to the sense of reality as the cardinal issue of philosophy. The phenomenologist is concerned with the magical modes of existence as well as with their epistemological delineation. Terror is as much a part of the problem of intersubjectivity as love, and the student of social life must come to terms with both if he is to understand in what sense it is possible for men to share a world. Similarly, the distance between aesthetics and social science is shortened by the same concern. Art as an uncovering of the Real is a mode of its presentation, not a surrogate. The epistemological question the artist asks (implicitly, most often) is analogous to that posed by the phenomenologist of the social sciences: What are the essential conditions for there being a world? As Wallace Stevens conceives of the poet as the "orator of the imagination," so we may think of the philosopher as the spokesman of wonder. The problems of literature and the social sciences that are discussed in these pages turn upon the philosophic concern with the sense of "what there is" as the most splendid datum. Accordingly, literature and the social sciences are taken as moments in a philosophic dialectic.

The names that recur so often in this book are perhaps an index of my indebtedness to other thinkers and writers: Husserl and Sartre, Dostoievski and Kafka, Max Weber and Alfred Schutz. Of this distinguished company it was my privilege to know one man in living directness, the late Alfred Schutz. I hope that what is best in these essays reflects something of his teaching, encouragement, and phenomenological brilliance. Undoubtedly, Schutz would have disagreed with a number of my ideas and disapproved of many of my formulations. I would like to think that there is one generic point upon which agreement would have been reached: it is the task of the philosopher to capture, in rigorous form, the essential meaning of man's experience in the Life-world without denying the complex ambiguity of that world and without robbing it of its warmth and cunning. For whatever else it is, philosophy is also the discipline of passion.

Chapel Hill, N.C.   M.N.
June 13, 1961

AUTHOR'S ACKNOWLEDGMENT

Most of the essays which comprise this volume were originally published as articles in journals or as chapters in books: "Phenomenology: A Viewing," *Methodos*, Vol. X, 1958; "Phenomenology and Existentialism," *Modern Schoolman*, Vol. XXXVII, 1959; "The Empirical and Transcendental Ego" in *For Roman Ingarden: Nine Essays in Phenomenology*, Martinus Nijhoff, 1959; "Being-in-Reality," *Philosophy and Phenomenological Research*, Vol. XX, 1959; "Jean-Paul Sartre's Philosophy of Freedom," *Social Research*, Vol. XIX, 1952; "Toward a Phenomenology of the Aesthetic Object," (in Spanish) *Notas y Estudios de Filosofia*, Vol. III, 1952; "Phenomenology and the Theory of Literature" and "Existentialism and the Theory of Literature" in *The Critical Matrix* (edited by Paul R. Sullivan), Georgetown University, 1961 ("Existentialism and the Theory of Literature" also appeared in *Forum*, Fall 1959, under the title "Sartre and Literature"); "Existential Categories in Contemporary Literature," *Carolina Quarterly*, Vol. X, 1958; "The Privileged Moment: A Study in the Rhetoric of Thomas Wolfe," *Quarterly Journal of Speech*, Vol. XLIII, 1957; "Albert Camus: Death at the Meridian," *Carolina Quarterly*, Vol. XI, 1960; "A Study in Philosophy and the Social Sciences," *Social Research*, Vol. XXV, 1958; "History as a Finite Province of Meaning," (in Spanish) *Convivium*, Vol. II, 1957; "History, Historicity, and the Alchemistry of Time," *Chicago Review*, Vol. XV, 1961; "Causation as a Structure of the Lebenswelt," *Journal of Existential Psychiatry*, Vol. I, 1960; "Death and Situation," *American Imago*, Vol. XVI, 1959. I thank the editors and publishers of these publications for permission to reprint my writings. Also, I wish to thank Mr. G. H. Priem of Martinus Nijhoff for his editorial aid. My wife, Lois Natanson, has helped to bring all of my efforts to their best stylistic form. Where inadequacies remain it is because of my obstinacy. My gratitude to Lois is as profound as my indebtedness.

Table of Contents

PART ONE

PHILOSOPHICAL FOUNDATIONS

1. Phenomenology: A Viewing

⟨I⟩

I wish to begin and end with an irrelevancy. In the autobiographical statement that appears in the recent volume in the Library of Living Philosophers devoted to his thought, Karl Jaspers contrasts his experience living the life of a physician (he began as a psychiatrist) with that of his life as a philosopher. Regarding his colleagues in both professions, he writes:

> The memory of the intellectual fellowship of our hospital in Heidelberg has accompanied me throughout my entire life. My later work was quite independent and was undertaken at my own risk ... without contact with any professional group. The comparison enabled me to measure how diffused, artificial, and unreal is the professional association of teachers of philosophy, no matter how often its representatives may meet each other in congresses or express themselves in journals and books.[1]

The point at issue is the existential commitment or lack of commitment of the professional philosophers to philosophy. It is one thing to master a jargon and develop a stock-in-trade of questions, answers, arguments, parries and thrusts; it is quite another thing to have philosophy as your ultimate concern, to learn to know, in Husserl's language, "the despair of one who has the misfortune to be in love with philosophy." To be existentially involved in philosophy is to confront oneself and others in a dialogue that goes beyond both chatter and conversation. Such dialogue requires the listening that transcends hearing and the seeing that is never synonymous with looking. Philosophy is an act of imaginative extrapolation founded on existential commitment, quite independent of particular standpoints and regardless of concrete results. At least part of the silence that has greeted Husserlian pheno-

---

[1] *The Philosophy of Karl Jaspers* (ed. by Paul Arthur Schilpp), New York, 1957, 24.

menology in Anglo-American philosophy for the past half century is, I would suggest, the function of a root suspicion of commitment in general and existentialism in particular. At the center of this silence is a paradox that brings us directly to the issues of this paper.

Perhaps the most striking feature of Anglo-American and continental philosophy at mid-century is the disparity of sources and aims. The major impact of analytic and neo-positivistic philosophy in England and America, on the one hand, is sharply at odds with the leading motive and theme of French and German thought, the phenomenology of Edmund Husserl.[2] The paradox of contemporary philosophy, then, is that of the dominance of phenomenology abroad, the quiescence of phenomenology at home. What explains the situation of world philosophy in which phenomenology can either be taken for granted as a starting point in technical discussions or else require the most elementary set of explanations and distinctions for discussion even to be possible? As Merleau-Ponty points out,[3] fifty years after the first works of Husserl, it is still necessary to ask, What is phenomenology?

There are a variety of reasons which may be cited to explain the lack of understanding or, worse, the misunderstanding of phenomenology today in so many quarters. Some of these reasons are clear cut and limited, others are more subtle. The lack of adequate translations into English of much of phenomenological literature is an obvious source of trouble. More generally, however, phenomenology is written in European style, and its language is strange-sounding to ears accustomed to Russell and Moore, Carnap and Quine. Finally, the "geography" of problems explored by phenomenologists – phenomenological reduction, the intentionality of consciousness, the transcendental ego – is unearthly terrain. One is reminded of the New Yorker's map of the United States: here is, of course, New York City, toward the eastern bottom of the country is Miami, in the middle is Chicago, and to the far west is Los Angeles. And in between these notables is a vast, mysterious swampland into which no intelligent traveller ever voyages. On a comparable map, phenomenology lies somewhere in between California and Florida, at best a potentially rich fossil preserve.

But the misunderstandings of phenomenology are more important

    [2] Wild, J., "Is There a World of Ordinary Language?" *Philosophical Review*, LXVII, 1958, 460–476.
    [3] Merleau-Ponty, M., "What is Phenomenology?" (translated by John F. Bannan), *Cross Currents*, VI, 1956, 59–70. Original: avant-propos of *Phénoménologie de la perception*, Paris, 1945.

matters for our attention. The list is imposing.[4] Phenomenology is taken as a kind of introspectional psychology, as a subjectivism, as a kind of phenomenalism, as a mysticism whose central concern is a dark realm of essences, as an intuitionism of a Bergsonian order, as an anti-scientific doctrine, or as a philosophy that denies the reality of the world by bracketing out existence. Add to this the complex historical relationship between the work of Husserl and that of Heidegger and Sartre, and you see infinite possibilities for still further absurdities. But there are other types of misunderstandings or possibilities for confusion which relate to the very complexity of the historical development of phenomenology. First of all, in addition to the phenomenology of Husserl, there are the phenomenologies of Scheler, Hartmann, and still other investigators whose methods differ in important ways from that of Husserl. Secondly, even the work of Husserl is far from completely known. Great parts of his philosophical writings are now being edited and published. And during Husserl's own lifetime, his thought underwent important developments. The reader of Husserl's *Logical Investigations* who failed to study the philosopher's volume *Ideas* would have an abortive notion of phenomenology.

For all of these reasons, some valid, others rather sickly, misunderstandings of Husserl's method and outlook are the rule rather than the exception in Anglo-American circles. But there is a totally different kind of reason for the failure to understand and appreciate phenomenological philosophy which I wish to explore in some detail, and that is the rootedness of both common sense and most non-phenomenological philosophy in what Husserl calls the "natural attitude." The central effort of phenomenology is to transcend the natural attitude of daily life in order to render it an object for philosophical scrutiny and in order to describe and account for its essential structure. Common sense and those philosophies which share its fundamentally naive, realistic view of the world are defined, phenomenologically, by their urgent yet implicit protest against such an examination. The world

[4] Ames, V. M., "Mead and Husserl on the Self," *Philosophy and Phenomenological Research* XV, 1955, 320–331.

Natanson, M., "Phenomenology from the Natural Standpoint: A Reply to Van Meter Ames," *ibid.*, XVII, 1956, 241–245.

Ames, V. M., "Reply to Maurice Natanson's Reply," *ibid.*, XVII, 1956, 246–247.

Williams, F., "Doubt and Phenomenological Reduction: An Appendix to the Natanson-Ames Controversy," *ibid.*, XVIII, 1958, 379–381.

Zilsel, E., "Concerning 'Phenomenology and Natural Science,'" *ibid.*, II, 1941, 219–220.

Cerf, W., "In Reply to Mr. Zilsel," *ibid.*, II, 1941, 220–222.

may be taken apart piecemeal as in the dismemberment of a completed jigsaw puzzle, but the inquiry into the very sense of reality, into the meaning of there being a reality of which each piece is a part – such an investigation is suspended in its very genesis by the natural attitude itself: the doxic belief in the real existence of a world *out there* which holds each one of us forever in its epistemic embrace.

By the natural attitude Husserl understood the fundamental un-stated thesis underlying the situation of man in the daily public world which holds that there is a real external existent world which persists in space and time and which is much the same for all men. Doubts, fears, anxieties, questions, hypotheses all presuppose the thesis of the natural attitude because, in varying ways, they all take for granted the being of the world-totality of which some special part arises to be questioned, doubted, interrogated. But the doubting, inquiring, researching is itself within the world investigated and the investigation is always *into* something. The natural attitude is not merely a deeply rooted prejudice or presupposition; it is an implicit metaphysical com-mitment which lies at the heart of our worldly experience. And just as important, it constitutes the central metaphysical assumption of the natural sciences, especially of psychology. The clue to phenomenology is the appreciation of the natural attitude. Husserl's own description is valuable.

I find continually present and standing over against me the one spatio-temporal fact-world to which I myself belong, as do all other men found in it and related in the same way to it. This 'fact-world' as the word already tells us, I find *to be out there*, and also *take it just as it gives itself to me as something that exists out there*. All doubting and rejecting of the data of the natural world leaves standing the *general thesis of the natural standpoint*. 'The' world is as fact-world always there; at the most it is at odd points 'other' than I supposed, this or that under such names as 'illusion', 'hallucination', and the like, must be struck *out of it*, so to speak; but the 'it' remains ever, in the sense of the general thesis, a world that has its being out there. To know it more comprehensively, more trustworthily, more perfectly than the naive lore of experience is able to do, and to solve all the problems of scientific knowledge which offer themselves upon its ground, that is the goal of the *sciences* of *the natural standpoint*.[5]

The central and ultimate difficulty in seeing what phenomenology is trying to do relates directly and inevitably to the rootage of all non-phenomenological attitudes in the natural standpoint. This I take to be the true basis for so much misunderstanding of phenomenology.

[5] Husserl, E., *Ideas: General Introduction to Pure Phenomenology* (translated by W. R. Boyce Gibson) London, 1931, 106. Original: *Ideen zu einer reinen Phänomenologie und phäno-menologischen Philosophie* (ed. by W. Biemel), Haag, 1950.

It is not so much a matter of this or that phenomenological idea, concept, or principle that is viewed in a wrong way as it is a failure to grasp the very style of phenomenological concern. Perhaps one suggestive way of exploring the phenomenological critique of the natural attitude is to turn to a brief account of the historical development of Husserl's thought, particularly with regard to his reaction to the naturalistic psychology of the late nineteenth century.

<II>

Biographically, Husserl's early interests were in the natural sciences, first astronomy, later mathematics. He studied under Weierstrass and took his doctorate in mathematics with a dissertation on the calculus of variations. In 1891 he published the first volume of a Philosophy of Arithmetic with the subtitle, Psychological and Logical Investigations. The major theme of this work was the subjective ground of mathematical operations, and it was developed in concurrence with the reduction of logic and mathematics to psychological processes urged in the work of Sigwart, Lipps, Wundt, and Mill. Although there are pre-phenomenological or proto-phenomenological themes and insights contained in this early work, Husserl at this stage had yet to reach the threshold of phenomenology and had, in the main, been positively influenced by psychologism. It was partly as a result of a review of his book by Frege that Husserl came to be persuaded that logic cannot be properly reduced to psychological operations, that, indeed, the central terms and structure of both logic and mathematics are ideal objects, meaning-unities, whose status is precisely independent of the concrete activities of mind and of thinking in its neurological aspect. Logic is not, as Lipps had proclaimed, the physics of thought; and with this turn against psychologism (which was to reach its fulfillment in Husserl's refutation of psychologism in his Logical Investigations) is to be seen the phenomenological reaction not only against a particular view of logic but, more generally, against a naturalistically oriented theory of consciousness. Historically, it was his study with Brentano which occasioned this decisive advance in Husserl's thought.

In his Psychology from an Empirical Standpoint (Vol. I, Book II) Brentano distinguishes between psychic and physical phenomena. The latter are the terms, objects, or events of sensory awareness which have as their specific differentia spatial localization. As examples of physical phenomena Brentano cites: a color, a figure, heat, cold, etc. Psychic phenomena, on the other hand, involve sensory or imaginative representation to consciousness. And by representation, Brentano writes, he means the act of representing and not that which is represented. Psychic phenomena have as their cardinal differentia intentional structure. That which characterizes all psychic phenomena, Brentano argues, is what the scholastics had called intentional presence or what he prefers to term relatedness to a content or direction toward an object or immanent objectivity. Directionality means that in representation something is represented, in judgment something is admitted or rejected, in love something is loved, in hate something is hated, in desire something is desired. Intentionality is unique to psychic phenomena. "Thus" Brentano writes (Vol. I, p. 125), "we are able to define psychic phenomena in saying that they are the phenomena which intentionally contain an object in them."

Although Husserl ultimately rejected Brentano's theory of intentionality (for reasons that will be presented later), it provided him with a thematic insight into the nature of consciousness which pervades the phenomenological conception of intentionality. Together with the acceptance of the ideality of logic, the turn to an intentional theory of consciousness may be seen as a leading motive in the historical evolution of Husserl's philosophy. Fully developed, they provide a basis for understanding Husserl's reaction against a naturalistic psychology and a naturalistic theory of mind. In his *Logos* article, Husserl writes: "Characteristic of all forms of extreme and consistent naturalism, from popular naturalism to the most recent forms of sensation-monism and energism, is on one hand the *naturalizing of consciousness*, including all intentionally immanent data of consciousness, and on the other the *naturalizing of ideas* and consequently of all ideals and norms."[6] For Husserl naturalism meant the general philosophical orientation which treated the total range of mental activity as essentially causally conditioned by and, in the final analysis, a part of the events of nature. The paradigm for philosophical understanding is taken, in the naturalistic persuasion, as causal explanation. Finally, naturalism is defined by its insistence on locating the primary problems of philosophy *within* a continuum of inquiry whose ideal form is that of scientific method. The crucial difficulty with this, for Husserl, is that natural science and its methodology begin with a set of major philo-

[6] Husserl, E., "Philosophy as a Strict Science," (translated by Quentin Lauer), *Cross Currents*, VI, 1956, 231. Original: "Philosophie als strenge Wissenschaft," *Logos*, I, 1910.

sophical presuppositions and implicit metaphysical commitments which vitiate its application to a philosophy of mind. This is most clearly seen in the case of psychology. Husserl writes:

> All natural science is naive in regard to its point of departure. The nature which it will investigate is for it simply there. Of course *there are* things, as things at rest, in motion, changing in unlimited space, and temporal things in unlimited time. We perceive them, we describe them by means of simple empirical judgments.[7]

For psychology as a natural science, the psychical does not constitute an independent realm; rather "it is given as an ego or as the experience of an ego ... and this sort of thing reveals itself empirically as bound to certain physical things called bodies. This, too, is a self-evident pre-datum." And, Husserl continues, "even where psychology – the empirical science – is oriented toward the determination of mere events of consciousness and not toward those which depend on the psycho-physical in the ordinary narrower sense, still these events are thought of as those of nature, i.e., as belonging to human or animal consciousness, which for their part have a self-evident connection with human and animal bodies, along with which they are grasped."[8] Naturalistic psychology and naturalism as a whole remain within the natural attitude; there is a "commonsensism" which informs their very being. The only way out, for Husserl, is a procedure which seeks in the most radical way to examine consciousness directly, to appreciate its contents and structures quite apart from prior scientific commitments or from philosophical pre-judgments, and which strives, above all, to regain the immediate experiential world we have forgotten, denied, or bartered away. Phenomenology purports to offer such a way out, and it is now possible to examine its claims.

⟨III⟩

As a preliminary definition, we may say that phenomenology is the logos of the phenomenon, the discipline concerned with the descriptive delineation of what presents itself to consciousness as it presents itself and in so far as it presents itself. Obviously, the central term here is "consciousness," and it is necessary to explore the Husserlian theory of the intentionality of consciousness before this definition can make

[7] *ibid.*, 233–234.
[8] *ibid.*, 234.

sense. But we must first be clear about the "phenomenon." For Husserl, the phenomenon is not the Kantian appearance which points back necessarily to a noumenal reality. The Husserlian phenomenon has no *ding an sich* behind it; rather, the phenomenon is taken as that which gives itself directly through the acts of consciousness. Again, before this can be fully clarified, it is necessary to explore Husserl's conception of the intentional character of consciousness. Postponing such an account for the time being, we may say that phenomenology is at least negatively defined by its refusal to turn to an account of presentations which either assumes their status as real entities within a space and time world or takes for granted the causal connections such presentations bear to the natural order. Phenomenology is in this sense an epistemologically neutral instrument for the inspection of the presentations of consciousness. Later I shall reformulate this working definition of phenomenology; for the present, I shall restrict myself to formulating a list of general theses and goals phenomenology establishes and sets for itself.

(1) Phenomenology seeks to found and develop itself as a "presuppositionless" philosophy.

(2) Phenomenological theory is itself phenomenologically conceived and, ideally, phenomenologically realized.

(3) Phenomenology demands, in Husserl's phrase, a "return to the things themselves" of immediate experience.

(4) Phenomenology attempts to clarify the meanings of the fundamental terms, basic concepts, and essential categories of all special or higher level disciplines, including the natural sciences.

(5) Phenomenology is concerned with the location and clarification of the *a priori* structure of all so-called "regional ontologies."

(6) Phenomenology returns to the Cartesian and Leibnizian ideal of a *mathesis universalis* but tries to reconstruct its character both with regard to a point of departure and an ultimate goal for a fully realized science of man.

(7) Phenomenology continues the essential style of transcendental philosophy involved in the *Critique of Pure Reason* but at the same time may be interpreted as both criticism of Kantianism and as an advance beyond Kant.

(8) Phenomenology seeks to reconstruct the total range of the life of consciousness in terms of its underlying eidetic structure from the standpoint of transcendental subjectivity.

(9) Phenomenology explores the genesis of meaning in both nature and history and endeavors to describe the "sedimentations" of meaning that lie within the evolution of our experience.

(10) Phenomenology, finally, seeks the reconstruction of the *Lebenswelt*, the life-world within which each one of us is born, exists, and dies.

Out of these mutually related theses and aims arise a number of major philosophical innovations which lead us to the very ground of Husserl's thought:

(1) Phenomenology presents a unique method for pursuing its special ends. More specifically, it develops a theory of *epoché* and of reductions.

(2) Phenomenology presents a radical theory of consciousness, that of intentionality.

(3) Phenomenology expresses a new theory of meaning, one intimately bound up with Husserl's doctrine of essence.

(4) Phenomenology requires and presents a special theory of evidence,[9] one developed in terms of "self-givenness."

(5) Finally, phenomenology articulates a theory of transcendental consciousness in terms of which the "constitutive" activity of the transcendental ego emerges as the sovereign theme.

Within our present limits it is clearly impossible to go into a detailed examination of all of the terms, concepts, and theories just outlined. Instead, I propose to turn to a study of those elements of phenomenological method and theory which are in some sense fundamental and necessary to grasp the style of Husserl's general problematic, to say it Germanically. These elements I take to be phenomenological method, the theory of intentionality, and the transcendental ego. I will devote myself, then, to a statement of their meaning and purpose in the matrix of Husserlian thought.

(1) Phenomenological method: Concerned as it is with an immediate confrontation with what is presented in experience, phenomenology obviously cannot take over the methods of natural scientific inquiry or of any philosophy which begins within the natural attitude. Descartes comes closest to the radical mode of scrutiny with which Husserl

---

[9] Spiegelberg, H., "Phenomenology of Direct Evidence," *Philosophy and Phenomenological Research*, II, 1942, 427–456.

wishes to commence his philosophizing. Yet, for reasons that will be evident presently, a qualitative step beyond Descartes is needed. Such an advance is possible, according to Husserl, if the phenomenologist starts with the explicit methodological decision to attend only to what presents itself to him in the full range of his perception *as* it presents itself. He can not, then, assume that his presentations are of real things or that they are occasioned by real events or that they are psychic events having neurological accompaniments or that they are part of the real world or that there is an external world outside his perceptual stream of awareness within which or somehow in contrast with which his presentations arise. In order to assure the neutrality of givenness, the phenomenologist begins, therefore, by setting in abeyance his common-sense belief in the existence of the real world. It is exactly at this point that so many typical misunderstandings of phenomenological method arise. Our problem is to see what Husserl means by the methodological suspension of what he terms the "general thesis" of the natural standpoint.

When I suspend or place in abeyance my common-sense belief in reality, I merely decide to make no use of the thesis which ordinarily guides our total cognitive and conative life; but this thesis is not to be understood as a proposition or a formulated article of faith. Rather, it is the unstated, utterly implicit theme of our common-sense relatedness to reality. Husserl writes:

> The General Thesis according to which the real world about me is at all times known not merely in a general way as something apprehended, but as a fact-world *that has its being out there*, does *not* consist of course *in an act proper*, in an articulated judgment about existence. It is and remains something all the time the standpoint is adopted, that is, it endures persistently during the whole course of our life of natural endeavour.[10]

Phenomenological suspension or, to use Husserl's term, *epoché*, consists in making explicit to consciousness the thesis which unconsciously underlies every individual judgment made within ordinary life about reality. Suspension means first of all coming into awareness of the very meaning of the natural attitude itself. Negatively put, suspension of the General Thesis of the natural standpoint most certainly does not include or signify a denial of the reality of the external world or of the validity of our ordinary experience within it. Rather, as phenomenologist I place in phenomenological doubt (which is not psychological

---

[10] Husserl, E., *Ideas*, 107.

doubt) my traditional common-sense taking for granted of the very reality of the world within which things and events are noted and appraised. Suspension, then, involves a shift in modes of attention. The same reality I took for granted in typical fashion in naive attitude I now re-view in phenomenological attitude. The real world, everyday existence, etc., do not mysteriously vanish under *epoché*; they are merely seen in terms of a perspective hitherto unimagined and even unimaginable in common-sense terms. Husserl's own description of phenomenological *epoché* may now make sense:

> *We put out of action the general thesis which belongs to the essence of the natural standpoint*, we place in brackets whatever it includes respecting the nature of Being: *this entire natural world therefore* which is continually 'there for us,' 'present to our hand,' and will ever remain there, is a 'fact-world' of which we continue to be conscious, even though it pleases us to put it in brackets. If I do this, as I am fully free to do, I do *not* then *deny* this 'world,' as though I were a sophist, I *do not doubt that* it is there as though I were a sceptic; but I use the 'phenomenological' *epoché*, which *completely bars* me *from using any judgment that concerns spatio-temporal existence.*[11]

Epoché is the necessary condition to all other phenomenological procedures, for it guarantees the freedom of a starting point which refuses to remain within the metaphysical orientation of common sense. And further, *epoché* is the clue to phenomenological method to the extent that it points to the kind of descriptive neutrality phenomenology encourages. Presentations and not interpretations become the central object of concern. Dorion Cairns makes a careful statement of the principle to which all of this leads:

> The fundamental methodological principle of phenomenology may ... be initially formulated as follows: *No opinion is to be accepted as philosophical knowledge unless it is seen to be adequately established by observation of what is seen to be itself given 'in person.' Any belief seen to be incompatible with what is seen to be itself given is to be rejected. Toward opinions that fall in neither class – whether they be one's own or another's – one is to adopt an 'official' philosophical attitude of neutrality.*[12]

And here as well is the clue to the meaning of a "presuppositionless" philosophy in Husserl's specific sense. A presuppositionless philosophy does *not* mean a philosophy without presuppositions; instead, what is involved is a philosophy which attends phenomenologically to any com-

---

[11] *ibid.*, 110–111.
[12] Cairns, D., "An Approach to Phenomenology," in *Philosophical Essays in Memory of Edmund Husserl* (ed. by Marvin Farber), Cambridge, Mass., 1940, 4.

mitment, however profound and primal, which may be delineated in its
own procedure. Presuppositions are rendered explicit through phenomenological inspection and so neutralized to whatever extent neutral-
ization is possible in rational operations. The interesting thing is that
phenomenological method is reflexive in nature and intent: phenomenological method is itself phenomenologically derived.

(2) Intentionality: With *epoché* methodologically effected, the next
step in phenomenological procedure involves a series of "reductions."
We may distinguish two particular stages in reduction which are of
paramount importance, though it should be borne in mind that these
are by no means the only reductions. First, there is what Husserl calls
the "eidetic reduction." This consists in moving from matters of fact
to essences, from empirical to essential universality. The *epoché*
fulfills an essentially negative function,[13] it prepares us for the appreciation of a purified field of consciousness; the eidetic reduction, on
the other hand, has a more positive role to play. It is concerned with a
residuum presented in the phenomenological orientation; it is the
status of the elements of the residuum which is now of interest. The
eidetic reduction is a method by means of which the phenomenologist
is able to attend to the character of the given, setting aside that which
is contingent and secondary and noting that which shows itself as
universal. Although it is not possible at this point to explain what
Husserl means by "essence," an example of the sort of thing he has in
mind might be helpful.

Euclidean geometry might be considered as an example of an eidetic
science. It is concerned with essences rather than with particulars; the
distinction between token and type is central to its meaning. However
carefully drawn, an illustration of a triangle is never to be confused
with what it is supposed to illustrate. Strictly speaking, a triangle
cannot be drawn at all, it can only be represented. In looking at *this*
particular examplar of triangle I draw on the blackboard, I may, in
eidetic attitude, reduce away the particularity of this concrete token
and *see* the triangle it represents no longer as *this* triangle but simply
as triangle. For Husserl, seeing the essence triangle does not mean
merely knowing the definition of a Euclidean triangle as, say, a plane
figure bounded by three straight lines which intersect. The definition
expresses the essence; the essence is not constructed by stipulation.

[13] Lauer, J. Q., *The Triumph of Subjectivity: An Introduction to Transcendental Phenomenology* (with a preface by Aron Gurwitsch), New York, 1958, 50.

But essences are not, of course, restricted to the domain of mathematics. The child who learns to recognize the typical figure of the dog is able to point out this or that kind of dog as being a dog. Whatever jest of evolution is responsible for borzois and dachshunds both being dogs does not interfere with the child's immediate grasp of their both being dogs. And even if a particular child does as a matter of fact judge that some cats are more dog-like than are some dogs or what purport to be dogs, still he recognizes cats and dogs to be kinds of animals, and he *sees* the difference between members of the class animal and the generic properties of the class.

But it is with the second stage, that of transcendental reduction, that the full meaning of both *epoché* and eidetic reduction becomes clear and that the Husserlian theory of the intentionality of consciousness finds its statement and rationale. At the same time, it is necessary to realize that the meaning of transcendental reduction is perhaps the part of the phenomenological procedure most difficult to comprehend precisely because it shows most vividly the phenomenologist's methodological transcension of the mundane sphere. As Husserl writes, "What makes the appropriation of the essential nature of phenomenology, the understanding of the peculiar meaning of its form of inquiry, and its relation to all other sciences (to psychology in particular) so extraordinarily difficult, is that in addition to all other adjustments *a new way of looking at things* is necessary, one that contrasts *at every point* with the natural attitude of experience and thought."[14] The movement from the interpretive attitude of daily life to that of phenomenological attitude is fundamentally a reorientation in perceptual experience which transforms perceptual immersion in the object perceived in naive attitude into a reflexive concern with the very activity of consciousness. Instead of seeing, hearing, tasting, touching things or objects, I now turn my attention to my seeing, my hearing, my tasting, and my touching. Instead of "living in my acts," in Husserl's phrase, I make my acts the explicit object of phenomenological inspection. Such a reflexive procedure leads us directly to the intentionality of consciousness, but it is still necessary to establish the status of the transcendental reduction before we can treat intentionality explicitly.

In eidetic reduction the phenomenologist is still a being in the world in whose stream of conscious acts essences present themselves. The

---

[14] Husserl, E., *Ideas*, 43.

subjectivity involved in eidetic description is still a worldly subjectivity, having an individual temporality and an historical biography. What is now needed for ultimate phenomenological purification is a reduction which brackets the very worldliness of the ego and returns the phenomenologist to the pure stream of consciousness as such. Such a return is the object of transcendental reduction. The transcendental phenomenologist reduces the residuum gained in eidetic attitude to the ultimate ground of the transcendental ego in whose constitutive activity his world arises. Through transcendental reduction, Husserl writes:

I no longer survey my perception experiences, imagination-experiences, the psychological data which my psychological experience reveals: I learn to survey transcendental experience. I am no longer interested in my own existence. I am interested in the pure intentional life, wherein my psychically real experiences have occurred. This step raises the transcendental problem ... to its true level. We have to recognize that relativity to consciousness is not only an actual quality of our world, but, from eidetic necessity, the quality of every conceivable world. We may, in free fancy, vary our actual world, and transmute it to any other which we can imagine, but we are obliged with the world to vary ourselves also, and ourselves we cannot vary except within the limits prescribed to us by the nature of subjectivity. Change worlds as we may, each must ever be a world such as we could experience, prove upon the evidence of our theories and inhabit with our practice. The transcendental problem is eidetic. My psychological experiences, perceptions, imaginations and the like remain in form and content what they were, but I see them as 'structures' now, for I am face to face at last with the ultimate structure of consciousness.[15]

What arises from all of these complex procedures is the basis for understanding the very nature of consciousness itself. *Epoché* and the reductions make sense only if seen in relationship to the theory of mind they are intended to disclose. It is now possible to turn directly to Husserl's theory of the intentionality of consciousness.

All conscious acts, for Husserl, have a fundamental directional character: they point toward some object, whether objectively real or not. Thus, all thinking is thinking *of* or about something, all remembering is remembering *of* something, all imagining is imagining *of* something, all willing is willing *of* something. All consciousness, then, is consciousness *of* something. Consciousness is intentional in the sense that it has as its essential character this projective or directional activity. The term "intentional," it must be remembered, does not mean planned or purposeful thought in the sense in which we say that Mulholland intentionally tripped Auerbach as the latter was walking down the aisle. Intentionality in Husserl's sense refers primarily to the

[15] Husserl, E., article on Phenomenology in *Encyclopedia Britannica*, 14th edition, 701.

phenomenological structure of the acts of perception, in the broad Cartesian sense of that term. But if intentionality has such directional form, what is it that is intended and what does it mean to intend? And what, to begin with, do we mean by an "act" in this context?

Acts of intentionality are *not* psychological events; they are not to be confused with apprehensions of any order. It is the underlying eidetic character of all apprehension which concerns Husserl. The structure of intentionality is necessarily purely *a priori*, and this means that a phenomenologist is interested in getting at the pure form, in general, of any concrete example of an intentional act. Moreover, Husserl's task is to transcend the dualism of subject and object which he thinks is the historical source of the failure of both traditional realisms and idealisms to give an adequate account of mind. As psychological events, as happenings in consciousness, mental acts have subjects – persons who perform them – and objects – things designated in the world. However, as phenomenological structures, acts are "experiences of meaning,"[16] they are themselves the initial terms of consciousness. Consciousness is not so much composed of acts as it is itself the texture of continuous and interrelated acts bound together in the unity of inner time. In this sense, "act" no more implies an "actor" than consciousness implies a "consciousness-er." Acts do have grounding and generic origin, for Husserl, in the constitutive activity of the transcendental ego. Finally, intentionality is seen phenomenologically as foundationally given; it is neither deduced from other elements of consciousness or experience nor postulated from observed elements. Consciousness *is* intentionality, and should this turn out to be a tautology, the task of the phenomenologist is to make the most of it.

Let us now take a closer look at the structure of intentional acts. The "object" intended, for Husserl, is "real" only in so far as it is taken or meant as real, i.e., in so far as, in hyphenated language, it is real-for-me. The objective status of the thing to which the intention may or may not correspond becomes a phenomenological problem when we consider the intentional structure involved in assertive judgments, not otherwise. Within the structure of the intentional act, Husserl recognizes two polar though interrelated aspects: a subject and an object dimension. The former he calls the noetic aspect of intentionality, the latter the noematic aspect. Noesis and noema correspond to subjective and objective sides of intentional experience, and

[16] Farber, M., *The Foundation of Phenomenology: Edmund Husserl and the Quest for a Rigorous Science of Philosophy*, Cambridge, Mass., 1943, 333.

by means of this distinction Husserl is able to open up for examination
the phenomenological geography of these dimensions. The most important location made in this exploration, for our present purposes,
is Husserl's treatment of the noema, the object-aspect of the intentional
act, for it is the noematic aspect of intentionality which turns out to
be the clue to the phenomenological theory of essence and the "intu-
ition" of essence.

The noema is the intentional meaning presented by way of the
act or acts which intend it. The noema as the *meant* correlate to the
act which intends it is that which presents itself immediately or, in
Husserl's language, "originarily" to consciousness. But the noematic
object is not a particular, though in some sense it may be occasioned
by a particular in actual experience. The particular is always "irrealized" in transcendental reduction so that the phenomenologist is
always concerned with noematic unities as non-realities. The phenomenologist's attention is drawn to *this* object only in so far as it is "irrealized" as *this* and rendered object as such. *This* object as meant,
this object as intended, are when transposed in phenomenological attitude precisely noematic unities, or, we may now say, essences. The
Husserlian essence is the noema understood as an originary meaning-
unity presented in person within transcendentally reduced consciousness by way of the acts of intentionality. Since all of this discussion
of essence and meaning is necessarily condensed, a substantial illustrative quotation from Husserl may be permitted at this point:

Let us suppose that we are looking with pleasure in a garden at a blossoming
apple-tree, at the fresh young green of the lawn, and so forth. The perception
and the pleasure that accompanies it is obviously not that which at the same time
is perceived and gives pleasure. From the natural standpoint the apple-tree is
something that exists in the transcendent reality of space, and the perception as
well as the pleasure a psychical state which we enjoy as real human beings.
Between the one and the other real being ... the real man or the real perception
on the one hand, and the real apple-tree on the other, there subsist real relations.
Now in such conditions of experience and in certain cases, it may be that
the perception is a 'mere hallucination' and that the perceived, this apple-
tree that stands before us, does not exist in the 'real' objective world. The
objective relation which was previously thought of as really subsisting is now
disturbed. Nothing remains but the perception; there is nothing *real* out there
to which it relates.

Let us now pass over to the phenomenological standpoint. The transcendent
world enters its 'bracket'; in respect of its real being we use the disconnecting
epoché. We now ask what there is to discover, on essential lines, in the nexus of
noetic experiences of perception and pleasure-valuation. Together with the
whole physical and psychical world the real subsistence of the objective relation
between perception and perceived is suspended; and yet a relation between

perception and perceived (as likewise between the pleasure and that which pleases) is obviously left over, a relation which in its essential nature comes before us in 'pure immanence,' purely, that is, on the ground of the phenomenologically reduced experience of perception and pleasure, as it fits into the transcendental stream of experience. This is the very situation we are now concerned with, the pure phenomenological situation. It may be that phenomenology has also something to say concerning hallucinations, illusions, and deceptive perceptions generally, and it has perhaps a great deal to say about them; but it is evident that here, in the part they play in the natural setting, they fall away before the phenomenological suspension. Here in regard to the perception, and also to any arbitrarily continued nexus of such perceptions ... we have no such question to put as whether anything corresponds to it in 'the' real world. This posited (*thetische*) reality, if our judgment is to be the measure of it, is simply not there for us. And yet everything remains, so to speak, as of old. Even the phenomenologically reduced perceptual experience is a perception *of* 'this apple-tree in bloom, in this garden, and so forth,' and likewise the reduced pleasure, a pleasure in what is thus perceived. The tree has not forfeited the least shade of content from all the phases, qualities, characters *with which it appeared in this perception, and 'in' this pleasure proved 'beautiful,' 'charming,' and the like.*

From our phenomenological standpoint we can and must put the question of essence: What is the *'perceived as such'? What essential phases does it harbour in itself in its capacity as noema?* We win the reply to our question as we wait, in pure surrender, on what is essentially *given*. We can then describe 'that which appears as such' faithfully and in the light of perfect self-evidence.[17]

It is now possible to see that for Husserl the central terms of phenomenological discourse are all bound to each other, imply each other, and require each other for a meaningful interpretation of the method and task of phenomenological philosophy. Intentionality, meaning, noema, essence – these are all intersecting moments of one schema whose ultimate foundation is the transcendental ego. And this will be the last stage in our phenomenological journey.

(3) The Transcendental Ego: The evolution of Husserl's thought was very far from a smooth and simplistic progression. Each major work by Husserl was an endeavour to return to root problems, to reconceive the whole structure of his work, to reconstruct the fundament of his philosophy. There is one historical transformation from the Husserl of the *Logical Investigations* to the Husserl of *Ideas* which requires special attention, and that is his theory of the nature of the ego. At the time of *Logical Investigations* Husserl held to what is sometimes termed a "non-egological" conception of consciousness, i.e., he treated consciousness as completely contained and fulfilled in and through intentional acts. More specifically, he deemed it unnecessary to posit some ground or container or source of intentionality. There is no ego

[17] Husserl, E., *Ideas*, 258–260.

at the basis of intentional acts; the ego is nothing more than the concatenated intentional acts located in experience. The "I" appears only
after acts of reflection; it is never to be found prior to reflection, for
it is no proper part of the *a priori* structure of pre-reflective or, in
other terms, non-positional consciousness. A brief excursion into
Sartre's critique of Husserl's theory of the ego may clarify what is at
issue here.

Claiming to follow the Husserl of *Logical Investigations* and to avoid
the fundamental error he thinks is involved in Husserl's later theory of
the transcendental ego, Sartre states his case:

For most philosophers the ego is an 'inhabitant' of consciousness. Some affirm
its formal presence at the heart of *Erlebnisse*, as an empty principle of unification.
Others – psychologists for the most part – claim to discover its material presence,
as the center of desires and acts, in each moment of our psychic life. We should
like to show here that the ego is neither formally nor materially *in* consciousness:
it is outside, *in the world*. It is a being of the world, like the ego of another.[18]

Consciousness in these terms fulfills itself in its very directionality,
and it is only with reflective thought, acts concerned with prior acts,
that an ego arises. My original being in the world is intentional prior
to any thetic or positing act:

When I run after a streetcar, when I look at the time, when I am absorbed in
contemplating a portrait, there is no I. There is consciousness *of the streetcar-
having-to-be-overtaken*, etc., and non-positional consciousness of consciousness.
In fact, I am then plunged into the world of objects; it is they which constitute
the unity of my consciousness; it is they which present themselves with values,
with attractive and repellent qualities – but *me*, I have disappeared; I have
annihilated myself. There is no place for *me* on this level. And this is not a matter
of chance, due to a momentary lapse of attention, but happens because of the
very structure of consciousness.[19]

Now in the *Ideas* Husserl changes position radically and insists on the
necessity for a transcendental ego as the ground from which radiate all
intentional acts. Sartre, for reasons we cannot discuss here, considers
the change not only unnecessary but positively injurious to phenomenological theory.[20] In any event, it is clear that Husserl considered the
full development of his phenomenology to be bound up necessarily
with a transcendental idealism in which pure consciousness as the

---

[18] Sartre, J.-P., *The Transcendence of the Ego: An Existentialist Theory of Consciousness*
(translated by Forrest Williams and Robert Kirkpatrick), New York, 1957, 31. Original: "La
Transcendance de l'Ego: Esquisse d'une description phénoménologique," *Recherches Philo-
sophiques*, VI, 1936–37, 85–123.

[19] *ibid.*, 48–49.

[20] Gurwitsch, A., "A Non-Egological Conception of Consciousness," *Philosophy and
Phenomenological Research*, I, 1941, 325–338.

phenomenological residuum gained by means of *epoché* and transcendental reduction is the rock bottom of all phenomenological inquiry. And this transcendental ego is, for Husserl, consciousness as such, in its ultimate generality, revealed as the very condition for the possibility of individual empirical egos and ultimately, their world. Thus, there are not transcendental egos, but The Transcendental Ego, which is the phenomenological ground and source for the individuated consciousnesses within empirical reality. Phenomenology as an eidetic science is possible in virtue of the discovery and disclosure of the transcendental sphere. In Husserl's words: "Consciousness in itself has a being of its own which in its absolute uniqueness of nature remains unaffected by the phenomenological disconnexion. It therefore remains over as a 'phenomenological residuum,' as a region of Being which is in principle unique, and can become in fact the field of a new science – the science of Phenomenology."[21]

In contrast with the Kantian transcendental ego, Husserl's conception does not involve a purely formal judgmental unity, the "I think" which, according to Kant, accompanies all of our judgments as a necessary condition for the unity of consciousness. Further, the Husserlian ego is essentially constitutive in nature, since it is the source of intentional acts. Although there is a fundamental similarity between Kant and Husserl at this point (especially regarding the very meaning of transcendental method), the difference arises precisely in terms of the doctrine of intentionality. However one may be able to translate and interpret the relationship between Kantian appearances and what they are "of," the full force of an intentional theory of consciousness is not to be found in Kant. Furthermore, the formalism of the Kantian "I think" involves an essentially constructive rather than descriptive procedure. Kantian deduction is very different from Husserlian "seeing." The former is an effort to characterize the given in terms of a cognitive apparatus that can explain it; the latter consists in attending to the phenomena and appreciating them in their intentional unfolding. For Husserl the court of final appeal is what he calls "the things themselves," the noematic unities originarily given to a transcendentally purified consciousness and possessed of an immanent sovereignty.[22]

A final note comparing Husserl's theory of consciousness with that of Descartes and Brentano is relevant. In his *Cartesian Meditations*

---

[21] Husserl, E., *Ideas*, 113.
[22] Husserl, E., *Formale und transzendentale Logik*, Halle, 1929, section 59.

Husserl indicates both his indebtedness to Descartes as well as the points of vital disagreement he has with the author of the earlier *Meditations*. The points of difference are of primary interest here. First, Husserl argues[23] that Descartes failed to recognize and to elucidate the meaning of *epoché*. Doubt remains a psychological procedure in Descartes' way of doing things. Second, Descartes stopped short of entering the entire domain of transcendental consciousness. His concern with certitude limited itself to argument and demonstration and failed, accordingly, to see the infinite range of transcendental experience.[24]

Husserl's relationship to Brentano can be clarified at this point. Indebted as he was to his teacher for the generic concept of intentionality, Husserl felt that there was a radical difference between Brentano-intentionality and his own. The difference was this: psychic acts for Brentano are still permeated with the sensationism and naturalism of the natural standpoint, and intentionality has not worked itself free from psychologism. Despite its positive value for both philosophy and psychology, Husserl finds it necessary to reject Brentano's psychology of intentionality since it "remains fettered to this inherited naturalism."[25] Husserl can be satisfied only with a theory of consciousness which is founded on the methodological transcension of the natural standpoint and of every naturalism which permeates those disciplines naively rooted in the mundane sphere.

Let us return to the problem of defining phenomenology and see if our early working definition of phenomenology as the discipline concerned with the description of the phenomena cannot now give way to a more sophisticated formulation, one which will sum up the results of our exposition. Phenomenology is an essentially descriptive examination of the noetic and noematic structure of intentional acts as grounded in transcendental subjectivity; and its concern is with a total reconstruction of consciousness, in terms of which science will achieve its rationale, art and religion their validation, and philosophy its own consummation. That a programmatic philosophy of such massive proportion and difficulty should have been so profoundly misconstrued and so wildly misinterpreted is perhaps, upon reflection, not as surprising as it appears. Yet Husserl would be justified in saying with

[23] Husserl, E., *Cartesianische Meditationen und Pariser Vortäge* (ed. by Stephan Strasser), Haag, 1950, section 13.
[24] Fulton, J. S., "The Cartesianism of Phenomenology," *The Philosophical Review*, XLIX, 1940, 285–308.
[25] Husserl, E., *Ideas*, 24.

Kierkegaard: "People understand me so little that they do not even understand when I complain of being misunderstood."[26]

⟨IV⟩

Important as the phenomenological movement is on the Continent, it is far from being a univocal expression of orthodox Husserlian philosophy. Even excepting the radical developments of Heidegger and Sartre, those phenomenologists who were the original students of Husserl are far from standing in agreement with each other on points of major significance. There is hardly a follower of Husserl today who would accept all of his pronouncements, and there is hardly a major follower of Husserl who has not put forward serious criticisms of phenomenological philosophy. Although these criticisms are immanent, internal arguments, it would be false to dismiss them as trifling family quarrels. I take it to be a sign of the vitality of phenomenology that it can not only tolerate serious internal criticism but that it can avoid hagiolatry. Certainly no philosopher was ever harder on himself than was Husserl, and few academicians today would, I think, have the intellectual courage Husserl showed in withdrawing a completed work from the printer's table because he felt not fully satisfied with his formulation. When the tense is the present such an act is rare; in the subjunctive we can all be heroes.

The central lines of internal criticism raised by present-day phenomenologists move toward a cluster of central problems: Husserl's theory of intersubjectivity, the nature of transcendental constitution, the entire question of ontology. The feeling is generally that these, among other issues, form the focus for present phenomenological investigation. And the quality as well as amount of research and publication now going on in phenomenological circles is great. In addition to work in philosophy proper, there is also considerable activity in sociological, psychological, and psychiatric fields of inquiry. On the American scene, the work of Aron Gurwitsch[27] in phenomenology of perception and of Alfred Schutz[28] in phenomenology of the social sciences is especially noteworthy. The recently published volume *Existence*[29] which contains important translations into English of the

[26] *The Journals of Søren Kierkegaard* (ed. by A. Dru), London, 1943, 25.
[27] Gurwitsch, A., *Théorie du champ de la conscience*, Paris, 1957.
[28] Schutz, A., *Der sinnhafte Aufbau der sozialen Welt*, Vienna, 1932.
[29] *Existence: A New Dimension in Psychiatry and Psychology* (ed. by Rollo May, Ernest Angel, Henri F. Ellenberger), New York, 1958.

work of such phenomenologically influenced psychiatrists as Ludwig Binswanger, Eugene Minkowski, and Erwin W. Straus brings to a focus the convergence of phenomenology and existentialism and their import for psychiatry – all of this presented to a potential American audience reared in a naturalistic and behavioristic tradition. Such investigators and such works point to a possible breakthrough of phenomenology into the Anglo-American intellectual scene. Whether such a breakthrough does or does not come is not so much connected with the understanding of phenomenology as a collection of principles, concepts, and procedures as it is with appreciating what I have called the style of phenomenological concern. In the beginning as well as in the end the real question at issue is the phenomenologist's sense of reality.

It has been said that phenomenology is above all a *method*, that in principle it may, as a neutral instrument, be utilized by a philosopher of any persuasion. Theoretically, perhaps this is true. More realistically and more honestly, I feel, it is quite mistaken. For phenomenology is above all a way of seeing, a way of grasping the world and of articulating experience. Rather than some esoteric or mystical realm of essences, it is the common everyday reality with which the phenomenologist is ultimately concerned. His mode of concern is radically different from that of the common-sense man, but the object of his inquiry is the daily world seen in its uncontaminated givenness. To this daily world of which we are forever a part Husserl gives the name "Lebenswelt," the "Life-world," and it is the *Lebenswelt* which became the final theme of his phenomenological life.[30] It is here that the "style" of phenomenological philosophy is manifest.

To be a phenomenologist is to see the world in its givenness as perpetually and repeatedly bearing the universal in its slightest, most ephemeral aspects. But the essential here does not turn out to be a divinely ordered realm; it is instead the gift of subjectivity and the genius of consciousness. That each one of us constitutes for himself language and a coherent world is the miracle of man's existence. Phenomenology seeks to disclose by description and analysis the miracle of daily life, and the phenomenologist is defined, in Fink's phrase, by his "astonishment before the world."[31] It is in this sense that Sartre is able to write: "The phenomenologists have plunged man back into the world; they have given full measure to man's agonies and

[30] Husserl, E., *Die Krisis der europäischen Wissenschaften und die transzendentale Phänomenologie*, Haag, 1954, part three.
[31] Fink, E., "Die phänomenologische Philosophie Edmund Husserls in der gegenwärtigen Kritik (Mit einem Vorwort von Edmund Husserl)," *Kant-Studien*, XXXVIII, 1933, 319–383.

sufferings, and also to his rebellions."[32] In short, phenomenology has given back to philosophy its existential commitment. And this returns us to the point of our beginning in this paper and to the promise of a final irrelevancy.

It seems to me that quite apart from whether he is persuaded by phenomenology, naturalism, logical positivism, ordinary language analysis, Thomism or anything else, the student of philosophy today is faced with the personal decision of whether to commit himself fundamentally to his work or whether to play his role, advance his professional prospects, and leave the anguish to somebody else. His choice may decide his attitude, but another way of seeing the problem is to suggest that what he finds may define his attitude, that philosophy may define the philosopher. To adapt a remark of Kierkegaard's to my own purpose, the student of philosophy today is much like the wanderer in the city who chances by a store which has in its window display a sign reading "PHILOSOPHY DONE HERE." Our friend rushes in eager for illumination only to learn from the storekeeper that the sign itself is for sale.

---

[32] Sartre, J.-P., *The Transcendence of the Ego*, 105.

2. *Phenomenology and Existentialism*

HUSSERL AND SARTRE ON INTENTIONALITY

Heraldry and genealogy are cognate disciplines; the former often leads to exciting emblems, the latter sometimes to family embarrassments. An exploration of some central roots of existentialism certainly leads back to phenomenology, and following the line of Sartrean thought brings us quickly to Husserl's philosophy. Whether the results are more embarrassing than exciting may be decided later. Right now the problem is the nature of the family relationship. I will begin by suggesting that this relationship has as its ground Husserl's doctrine of the intentionality of consciousness and that Sartre's existentialism derives from a problematic critique and transformation of that doctrine. I will end by suggesting that Sartre's inadequacies illuminate Husserl's achievements.

The prime character of consciousness, for Husserl, is its implicit directionality. All consciousness is consciousness *of* something; all acts of consciousness intend some object. The ontological status of the intended object is neutralized by phenomenological reduction, so that the question of whether the object intended is real, illusory, hallucinatory, imaginary, independent, subsistent, or transitory is set aside for purposes of description. Whether the intended object is veridical has nothing to do with its status as intended. The task of the phenomenologist, then, is to investigate phenomena as correlates of the acts which intend them. Just as phenomenological reduction neutralizes the ontological placement of the object, so it sets in abeyance the belief in personal identity, history, and empirical reality of the individual making phenomenological descriptions. The central terms of the phenomenological enterprise are within the structure of intentionality; real object and real person are no proper part of that structure.

Instead, they may appear only as intentional concerns; that is, they may be considered as meant or intended objects of consciousness.

Some critics of phenomenology have taken this conception of intentional consciousness as a paradigm case of subjectivism or some kind of solipsism. They have suggested that Husserl has abandoned the real world, that his procedure of phenomenological reduction leaves the phenomenologist in epistemic isolation, and that, consequently, there is no way of ever achieving objective confirmation of phenomenological reports. An indirect but interesting answer to these complaints is found in Sartre's interpretation of intentionality, for the whole point of his positive reaction to phenomenology is that he found in Husserl's early writings a deliverance from subjectivism, an escape from the egocentric predicament. The overwhelming importance of intentionality for Sartre was what he took to be Husserl's insistence on a view of consciousness which transcended the subject-object dualism, which overcame the traditional debates of idealism and realism, and which opened up for the first time a view of consciousness which placed the self in the world, in the midst of life, in direct confrontation with being. Through phenomenology a return to "the things themselves" had taken place. What Quentin Lauer has called phenomenology's "triumph of subjectivity" was initially, for Sartre, a triumph over subjectivism. But victor and vanquished must be examined more closely.

What impresses Sartre in the phenomenological theory of intentionality is the nonegological conception of consciousness developed in Husserl's *Logical Investigations*. Intentionality in this perspective does not derive from a subject pole which is the condition for its activity. At this stage there is no transcendental ego to serve as the dynamic matrix for intentional acts. The emphasis, then, is necessarily on the noematic side of the intentional stream. Consciousness brings us face to face with reality as the correlate of intentional acts. Instead of an ego building its world, constituting its experiential façade, consciousness is thrust into reality and locates its egological nature after the encounter. The ego arises with experience; it has no status prior to experience. It is at this point that Sartre seizes on the nonegological conception of consciousness and announces its existential possibilities. For if the ego is not an original resident of consciousness, consciousness reveals itself as translucent, as a nothingness which fulfills itself purely in its intentional activity. What for Husserl began as an emphasis on the noematic aspect of the phenomena is radically transposed by Sartre into a theory of consciousness in which the nonbeing of the ego is the prime phenomenological datum. Husserl's nonegological theory of consciousness becomes transformed into a philosophy of nihilation.

Although Sartre's essay "The Transcendence of the Ego" is the first major statement announcing his transformation of Husserl's doctrine, his fascination with the possibilities of the phenomenological doctrine of intentionality can be seen more dramatically perhaps in his note entitled "A Fundamental Idea of the Phenomenology of Husserl: Intentionality," published in 1939.[1] Here Sartre interprets Husserl as insisting on the co-givenness of object and consciousness. Consciousness and the world are given simultaneously. And consciousness is an irreducible fact which we can only characterize through metaphors that suggest its thrusting, volatile nature. Knowing is like exploding; mind is centrifugal; consciousness is a vortex; awareness is like combat. Here Sartre is struggling to rid epistemology of the metaphysical incubus of knowledge as possesssion. For Sartre, one does not *have* knowledge; one bursts out in the acts of knowing toward the object known. Consciousness fires itself toward its mark. These strange metaphors (some of which are Sartre's and some of which are mine) support each other in suggesting a conception of consciousness as a nonsubstantial presence to the world. Sartre writes:

Knowledge cannot, without dishonesty, be compared to possession. ... consciousness is purified, it is clear like a great wind, it no longer has anything in it, except a movement to avoid itself, a gliding beyond itself; if, against all impossibility, you were to enter "into" a consciousness, you would be seized by a vortex and thrown out ... because consciousness has no "inside"; it is nothing but the outside of itself, and it is that absolute flight, that refusal to be substance which constitutes it as consciousness.[2]

Here, then, is the nexus between Sartre and Husserl, between existentialism and phenomenology. For Sartre the phenomenological doctrine of the intentionality of consciousness not only leads to but *is* an existential theory. Instead of the rather staid conception Husserl presented, Sartre sees in intentionality the full drama of the life of consciousness.

Imagine [he writes] a linked series of explosions which wrench us from ourselves ... which throw us on ... the dry dust of the world, on the rough earth, among things; imagine that we are thus rejected, forsaken by our very nature in an indifferent, hostile and restive world; you would then know the profound

[1] Originally published in *Nouvelle revue française*, January 1939; reprinted in Jean-Paul Sartre's *Situations I*, Paris, 1947, 31–35. Our references are to the latter edition.
[2] *ibid.*, 32–33.

meaning of the discovery that Husserl expresses in that famous phrase: "All consciousness is consciousness of something." [3]

On the basis of this existentialized conception of intentionality Sartre builds his world. All of the structures of man's being that he explores – the body, concrete relations with other selves, the emotions, imagination – are comprehensible only in terms of their intentional foundation. Perhaps one way of viewing this procedure is to suggest that perception, understood in the broad Cartesian sense, possesses a cognitive dimension. Feeling, sensory awareness, emotionality are meaning-laden aspects of human experience, for their nature is grounded in intentional consciousness. Meaning here is not designative or referential; it is precisely that which is presented as the correlate of intentional activity. This approach to meaning becomes clearer if we turn to a further point of connection between phenomenology and existentialism.

Husserl and Sartre agree in their rejection of a naturalistic or scientistic *Weltanschauung*. Physics and mathematics are not accepted as disciplines whose methodological form is paradigmatic for all other intellectual enterprises. Rooted and remaining in the natural attitude, science commits the sin of pride if it insists on projecting its naive realistic vision of the world on to the concrete and unique problems of philosophy and the social sciences. The rejection of scientism is not a rejection of natural science. Rather, phenomenology and existentialism hold to a common front in their insistence on facing phenomena in their givenness, quite apart from causal and genetic considerations. The liberation of logic from physics and psychology in the late nineteenth and early twentieth century must be matched by a liberation of epistemology from neurological and behavioristic grounds. This is the whole point of Husserl's refutation of psychologism. And implicit in Sartre's position is the same root dissatisfaction with psychologistic theories. Phenomenology and existentialism are thus bound to each other as much by negative as by positive agreements. The common denominator of intentionality is matched by a mutual disenchantment with the explanatory categories of naturalism.

Yet despite all sympathetic connecting bonds, there are still differences between Husserl and Sartre which are more than family quarrels. There are two points of basic conflict, and they center about Sartre's rejection of the phenomenological reduction and the transcendental ego. His radicalization of Husserl's doctrine of intentionality appears to require the abandonment of the central instrument of phenom-

[3] *ibid.*, 33.

enological method as well as the whole grounding of conscious life in a transcendental subject. Sartre's reasons for moving in this direction are complex. In addition to an early invocation of Occam's razor against the transcendental ego in his essay "The Transcendence of the Ego," Sartre goes on later in *Being and Nothingness* to protest against Husserl's idealistic reduction of the phenomenon to the noema as an irrealized object. Sartres writes:

It is futile to attempt, by a sleight of hand, to found the *reality* of the object on the subjective plenitude of impressions and its *objectivity* on non-being; the objective will never come out of the subjective nor the transcendent from immanence, nor being from non-being. But, we are told, Husserl defines consciousness precisely as a transcendence. In truth he does. This is what he posits. This is his essential discovery. But from the moment that he makes of the *noema* an *irreal*, a correlate of the *noesis*, a noema whose *esse* is *percipi*, he is totally unfaithful to his principle.[4]

Phenomenological reduction and the transcendental ego rob intentionality of its genius by relinquishing the immediate world seized through intentional consciousness. What Sartre calls the transphenomenality of being is lost in the reduction. Now, this criticism relates to, but is not synonymous with, the argument that Sartre rejects the reduction because it brackets out precisely what the existentialist is most concerned with: existence. It is a distortion of Husserl's theory of reductions to accuse the phenomenologist of disregarding or of being unable to regard concrete existence as a philosophical problem. But the misunderstanding appears to me to be compounded by those who suggest it, since neither Husserl nor Sartre, in my opinion, makes this claim or is necessarily involved in such an interpretation. Sartre's attack against the reduction rests immediately on his conviction that the irrealized noema lacks transphenomenal being, that the whole purpose, therefore, of Husserl's doctrine of intentionality has been undermined. Instead of consciousness transcending itself toward the objects of reality, consciousness falls back upon itself. Sartre does not argue, however, that the phenomenologist's concept of existence is somehow a shadow of the real thing, that existence in its givenness as phenomenon is a surrogate for flesh and blood reality. Indeed, it might be suggested at this point that Sartre's rejection of the reduction is based partly on phenomenological considerations, upon a common refusal with Husserl to take what is called concrete existence at face value. Those who insist on a distinction between the object as intended

---

[4] *L'Être et le néant*, Paris, 1943, 28. The present translation is my revision of Hazel E. Barnes's translation, *Being and Nothingness*, New York, 1956, lxiii.

or meant and the real honest-to-goodness object itself presuppose a
theory of *action* in which the term "real" operates as a predicate of
force, displacement, and material efficacy. One major consequence of
the alignment between Sartre and Husserl, I submit, is the interpretation of action as an intentional category. The real honest-to-
goodness thing is the thing interpreted as honest and good, and interpretation becomes the signal moment of action. Sartre's break with
Husserl is not to be found along these lines. It is not a question of
existence but of transcendence. Phenomenological reduction and the
transcendental ego, according to Sartre, draw us away from the reality
which intentionality not only promised but gave. The Husserlian
cogito remains trapped in immanence. Sartre writes:

If Husserl's *cogito* is first given as instantaneous, there is no way to get outside it
... Husserl for the length of his philosophical career was haunted by the idea of
transcendence ... But the philosophical techniques at his disposal removed from
him any way of accounting for that transcendence; his intentionality is only the
caricature of it. Consciousness, as Husserl conceived it, can not in reality
transcend itself either toward the world or toward the future or toward the
past.[5]

Sartre believes that he has liberated the lonely ego and delivered
Husserl's theory of intentionality from the essential misunderstanding
of its creator. It is now time to examine Sartre's good works.

Although the radicalization of intentionality requires the rejection
of the transcendental ego, what is gained carries with it the impact of
what is lost. Sartre is now faced with the problem of accounting for
the unity and continuing identity of the ego. If the ego is, as Sartre
maintains, "a being of the world, like the ego of another," if it arises
only through reflection, then how is it possible to account for the ego
as being *mine*? How is it that I do not confuse my ego with that of
the other? Sartre answers these questions by appealing to a certain
intimacy which attends my ego, to transverse intentions which
spontaneously bind together the ego as object of reflection. The result,
he says, is that "my I, in effect, is *no more certain for consciousness
than the I of other men*. It is only more intimate." [6] But this spontaneously personal ego constitutes itself as mysteriously as any transcendental ego. Moreover, a circle in explanation results. A phenomenology of intimacy is invoked to account for personal identity when

---

[5] *Being and Nothingness*, 109.
[6] *The Transcendence of the Ego*, 104.

the very recognition of the ego presupposes a recognizing agent. Recognizer and recognized are reconciled in the assertion that "my I ... is no more certain for consciousness than the I of other men." And this, I am suggesting, is reconciliation at the price of circularity. Giving up the transcendental ego deprives Sartre of a constitutive ground for the unity and identity of the self.

Coeval with the rejection of the transcendental ego is the apparent though problematic repudiation of the phenomenological reduction. Sartre argues[7] that Husserl cannot account for the transposition from the mundane to the phenomenological attitude of the individual who begins, as we all do, in the natural attitude. He interprets the natural attitude itself as a kind of objectification of the ego, an instance of "bad faith" in which consciousness seeks to escape from itself. A miracle becomes necessary for the individual in the natural attitude to perform the *epoché*. On Sartrean grounds, however, consciousness is perpetually confronted with *epoché* not as an intellectual method but, in Sartre's words, as "an anxiety which is imposed on us and which we cannot avoid." [8] Phenomenological reduction, then, is really transposed by Sartre rather than simply repudiated. But in his efforts to avoid the idealistic implications of the reduction, Sartre fails to acknowledge his profound debt at this point to Husserl's method. It is, rather, Merleau-Ponty who makes explicit the indebtedness of existentialist philosophy to phenomenological reduction. He writes:

The philosopher ... is a perpetual beginner. This means that he holds nothing as established which the popular majority or the scientists believe they know. It also means that philosophy cannot consider itself as definitively established in any of the truths which it can utter, that it is a renewed experience of its own beginning, and that it consists entirely of a description of this beginning. It means, finally, that this radical reflection is consciousness of its own dependence upon a non-reflective life which is its initial, constant and final situation. Far from being, as one might think, the formula for an idealistic philosophy, the phenomenological reduction is that of an existentialist philosophy.[9]

Reduction, then, opens up for phenomenological appreciation the full drama of consciousness and its initial placement in the *Lebenswelt*. And rather than Sartre, it is Husserl who should be credited with seeing the full depth of his methodological creation. Here as elsewhere,

---

[7] *ibid.*, 102 ff.
[8] *ibid.*, 103.
[9] Merleau-Ponty, M., *Phénoménologie de la perception*, Paris, 1945, lx. The present translation is my revision of John F. Bannan's translation of the "Avant Propos" which appears in *Cross Currents*, VI, Winter 1956, 59–70, under the title "What is Phenomenology?" The quotation cited appears on 64–65.

Sartre's efforts to correct Husserl's "mistakes" miscarry, and this miscarriage is our final theme.

Sartre sees in most of the major principles of phenomenology implicit clues to existential philosophy; he believes that he is carrying out the vital impulse of Husserl's discoveries. This attitude and its consequences are at once suggestive and misleading. More than anything else, Sartre's advances beyond Husserl illuminate the full range of insights achieved in traditional phenomenology. Husserl's original doctrine of the intentionality of consciousness is not "liberated" through Sartre's radicalization; it merely includes the existential dimension as one of its possibilities; phenomenological reduction is not positively transposed in Sartre's analysis, for the existential possibilities were there all along; and finally, Sartre's rejection of the transcendental ego ignores its existential implications.[10] Here Sartre's determination to rescue Husserl from himself blinds him to the very subjectivity existentialism seeks. It is in this sense that Sartre's inadequacies illuminate Husserl's achievements.

If Sartre's existentialism cannot be examined without some concern for Husserl's phenomenology, it is no less the case today that Husserl is being looked at suspiciously because of Sartre's exploits. Professor Herbert Spiegelberg in a recent paper[11] warns us that phenomenology should not sell its birthright for a mess of existentialist pottage. I would suggest instead that this warning should be the occasion for self-examination rather than embarrassment, and self-examination is the first principle of Husserl's philosophizing. Most, if not all, of the results of Sartre's technical contributions will have to be reexamined phenomenologically to separate the responsible from the purely spectacular, but there is no doubt in my mind that something responsible as well as original is there to be sifted. Talk of "existentialist pottage" may give comfort to those who have little patience with either existentialism or phenomenology but who are willing to admit that Husserl, at least, is respectable. If there is any conclusion to these considerations it is that Sartre stole much of his existential fire from Husserl. Or to put the same thing differently, the lesson to be learned from Husserl is that a responsible philosopher may also be a conceptual terrorist.

[10] *ibid.*

[11] "Husserl's Phenomenology and Existentialism," paper read as part of a symposium on phenomenology and existentialism held by the Western Division of the American Philosophical Association on April 30, 1959, at Madison, Wisconsin.

3. *Phenomenology and the Natural Attitude*

At first glance it would appear that Husserlian phenomenology and ordinary language analysis have little in common. At second glance, however, it seems that these positions are so violently opposed to each other that their representatives do not even share a universe of discourse. In a recent and provocative article entitled "Is There a World of Ordinary Language?,"[1] John Wild has taken a third glance at these rivals and has come forth with the suggestion that there are some fundamental points of contact between them, that, in fact, they have a good deal in common. I wish to take some of his remarks as a point of departure for considering the relationship between phenomenology and analytic philosophy. The focus for discussion will be Husserl's conception of the "natural attitude," the fundamental belief in the existence and validity of our common sense experience. The point is to clarify what I take to be the differences that set apart the philosophical enterprises being carried on by analysts and phenomenologists. Such a clarification is the necessary condition for meaningful contact between what is happening now in Anglo-American philosophy and what is happening on the Continent.

For John Wild, the positive bond between analysis and phenomenology turns, first of all, on an implicit agreement about what is the wrong way of philosophizing. Both positions reject transcendent objects and problems; both reflect what Wild calls "a similar distrust of transcendent, unobservable objects, and of the artificial problems engendered by such assumptions."[2] In different terms, one might say that the bias of both analysis and phenomenology is against meta-

1 *Philosophical Review*, LXVII, October 1958, 460–476.
2 *ibid.*, 461.

physical speculation and in favor of a radical empiricism. "One also finds," Wild writes, "a similar urge towards empiricism, a respect for what is called *fact*, and finally a similar recognition of the depth and fertility of that ordinary language which is presupposed in all the artificial constructions and abstract modes of speech which grow out of it. These similarities," Wild continues, "led me to reflect on the mistrust and suspicion which is so openly expressed on both sides of the English Channel, and to wonder if this is not somehow based on avoidable misunderstandings and misconceptions. ... Are not phenomenology (in the current broad sense) and linguistic analysis both approaching the same thing (concrete experience) from different angles?" [3] Professor Wild says that an affirmative answer is possible, although some important preliminary distinctions must be made. He recognizes that there are, of course, differences between the camps, but his point is to make the analyst realize that these differences, if probed in the right way, reveal an underlying unity of intention and outlook. My present purpose is not to reply to Wild's article, but rather to continue the exploration he has begun. I think he is right in suggesting that there is an underlying connection between analysis and phenomenology, but my reasons for believing this are not his reasons. Concomitantly, I agree with him that there are differences involved – crucial ones, I think – but again the differences I find are not the ones Wild stresses. In short, we find ourselves docked at the same port but on different vessels.

In order to explore the similarities and differences between analysis and phenomenology, it might be helpful to get before us some central issue which both positions must, in some sense, confront. I recommend that we consider Husserl's conception of the "natural attitude." Suppose we begin with Husserl's own statement of the problem. "I find continually present and standing over against me," Husserl writes, "the one spatio-temporal fact-world to which I myself belong, as do all other men found in it and related in the same way to it. This 'fact-world,' as the word already tells us, I find to *be out there*, and also *take it just as it gives itself to me as something that exists out there.* All doubting and rejecting of the data of the natural world leaves standing the *general thesis of the natural standpoint.* 'The' world is as fact-world always there; at the most it is at odd points 'other' than I supposed, this or that under such names as 'illusion,' 'hallucination,' and the like,

[3] *ibid.*, 461–462.

must be struck *out of it*, so to speak; but the 'it' remains ever, in the sense of the general thesis, a world that has its being out there." [4] To live in the natural attitude, then, is to live "believingly" in the world, to have the massive content of experience unfold not only as part of the world but as inevitably given within a tacitly accepted frame of reality. It is not an act or a judgment which founds such belief; rather all predication presupposes it. And even when we have cause to doubt the status of an event within the world, that doubt arises within an undoubted relationship between the event in question and the ground of reality over against which it appears as doubtful. Moreover, along with what Husserl calls this "doxic" belief in the existence of the world, there is an unsophisticated commitment to its intersubjective character. This is, above all, *our* world, and *we* must come to terms with it. The event in question is questionable, in principle, for you as well as for me, and reasonable doubt means precisely that others, fellow men, will view the event as doubtful in much the same way and for much the same reason as I do. The historical, cultural, scientific, and religious interpretations of the world largely presuppose the epistemic involvement of the individual with a range of experience we call the common-sense world. Whatever interpretation is given that world, it remains the universally acknowledged base in terms of which our daily lives are oriented. The phenomenologist is concerned with the examination of the world of daily life and the implicit epistemic commitment of men to it. At this point we might ask how this rough sketch of Husserl's approach to the natural attitude squares with the analyst's idea of the common sense world.

Philosophers have so many things to apologize for that it is unnecessary to confess at this point that of course the term "analyst" and the phrase "ordinary language analysis" are mean shorthands for positions or movements of some complexity not all of whose adherents agree with each other and whose embrace includes quite different sub-orientations. To a lesser degree but still with justification, the same may be said of "phenomenology." Later I hope to examine aspects of these differences I must now pass by. For the time being, I'm limited to shorthand, but even so a general account may be given of what I think would be the analytic response to Husserl's theory of the natural attitude. First of all, assuming the analyst could get over the initial giddiness Husserl's language may occasion, he might agree that there is some justification in saying that men in ordinary life seldom have

[4] *Ideas*, 106.

cause to doubt the veridical character of experience in general and that, in this sense, they take the existence of the world for granted. The balk might well arise over the epistemic concept of what Husserl has termed "the general thesis of the natural attitude." Second of all, the analyst might well find sense in the suggestion that each of us experiences the world as intersubjectively valid, but again the snag might come in understanding the phenomenologist's way of explaining the genesis of intersubjectivity. Finally, the analyst could hardly fail to welcome a philosophy that turns its critical attention toward the structure of the common-sense world, but the real question would be whether the "common" of common sense and the "ordinary" of ordinary language are truly equivalent or even fundamentally related to Husserl's natural attitude or his theme of the *Lebenswelt*. Here then are three strata of the problem: the world as believed in, the intersubjectivity of that world, and the world of lived experience, the *Lebenswelt*. The delineation of differences and similarities between analysis and phenomenology will hinge on the examination of these issues.

The phenomenologist has as his prime task the examination of the natural attitude, and by this is meant a reflective inquiry which takes as the object of its inspection the very believing in the world, a "believing" identified with the general thesis of the natural attitude. The complex methodological apparatus phenomenology develops, its theory of reductions, is generated in order to overcome the difficulty of securing a neutral description of the root belief in the existence and validity of the world. It is not so much the world that is evasive as the subtle and unsaid commitment to it which is the quarry here. Phenomenology tries to render the naive believing in the world an object for philosophical inspection through an act of methodological restraint. The world is not denied or, in one sense, even doubted. We continue to be common-sense men living our lives in the intersubjective world of daily life; but in the phenomenological attitude this taken for granted thematic commitment to the world is put into relief, rendered evident through the very act of designating it an object for descriptive examination. My believing in the world is a proto-logical commitment, a pre-rational involvement which I discover at any moment as already implied in the predications I make about the world. It becomes clear that it is methodologically impossible to approach such a theme in terms of any philosophy which begins by assuming that we are already in a world, that communication of course is not only possible,

but exists, and that fellow men with whom we communicate share the
general features of a "normal" world, that they experience things in
much the same way we do. The philosophical starting point is crucial
here because the whole point of phenomenology is to reconstruct the
world in terms of consciousness, without presupposing precisely those
problems which are philosophically at issue here: world, communication, and intersubjectivity.

If the phenomenologist cannot presuppose the general thesis of the
natural attitude as a philosophical starting point, no more can he
begin with a world of common, shared experience.

Intersubjectivity remains the root problem of philosophy for those
who follow Husserl. The phenomenologist cannot properly begin by
saying "we"; he must speak for himself. That so many critics of
phenomenology have seized on the problem of error, the question
of how one phenomenologist can verify the findings of another, has
always struck me as odd, assuming that the critic understands that
there is no issue of "subjectivism" here, for is it not the case that every
act of philosophical verification is ultimately a *seeing* by the self for
itself? If, in this sense, we may say that seeing is believing, the phenomenologist must see for himself, and his enterprise involves getting
clear, rigorously clear, about the logic of seeing. Not "we" but "I,"
then, must be the point of departure for phenomenology. But the
hallmark of the natural attitude is that this common world we live in is
taken as *our* world, the world *we* inhabit and engage in our joint
pursuits. The phenomenological task here is complex and may be
fulfilled at different levels. Among other things, the phenomenologist
is interested in the constitution of intersubjectivity, that is, the
phenomenological uncovering of its genesis in the activity of consciousness. Such an interest can be satisfied only by the pursuit of a
transcendental phenomenology which seeks to trace the constitution
of an intersubjective world from the ground of the transcendental ego.
But there is a more humane and less dark aspect of the problem. At
another level phenomenology is interested in a descriptive account
of the essential features of the world taken as intersubjective within the
natural attitude. What Husserl referred to as a phenomenological
psychology would have as part of its task the location, ordering, and
illumination of what Alfred Schutz has called the "typifications" of
common sense. These basic assumptions of daily life are distinctively
different from the constructions and formal typifications or models
utilized by natural scientists and form the basis for a radical distinction

between the intersubjective world of daily life and the artificial worlds of scientific inquiry. The difference between these worlds leads to the phenomenological theory of the *Lebenswelt*.

By the *Lebenswelt*, or Life-world, the phenomenologist understands the concrete reality of the individual's lived experience in contrast to the interpretation of that reality within the context of models or types constructed for particular purposes by the scientist. My immediate living, being in the world, my awareness of what is about me now, my fresh or indistinct memories of my past, my lively or vague anticipations of my future, my existential relations to home and family and friends, my situation in life and its problems for me, my life and my death, are all elements or themes of the *Lebenswelt*. The phenomenologist believes that not only is the structure of this world as complex and rich in philosophical implications as the world of natural science but that the latter is ultimately founded on the experiences rooted in the former. The *Lebenswelt* is the underlying matrix of our lives, and its full exploration would mean the fulfillment of a phenomenology of the natural attitude. The elements or essential structures of the *Lebenswelt* would include the spatio-temporal location of the self within its Life-world, the incarnation of the self and the ways in which the body is an instrumentality for the discovery and articulation of experience, the *situation* of the self, understood as the complex of attitudes, projects, and interpretations which form the ground for the emergence of any problem, and, finally, the action of the self as an agent in reality whose self-interpretation of the meaning of its acts is the paradigm for what may be termed meaning in the *Lebenswelt*. The self is at once situated, involved, and continuously interpreting its world within the horizon of criteria, values, norms, and goals which are both conceived and realized in *Lebenswelt* terms. Death remains the only full escape from the natural attitude.

The implicit distinction between what I have said about the phenomenological approach to the natural attitude and the position of analytic philosophy must now be made explicit, and this will be the condition as well for locating whatever sympathies these movements truly share. Boldly, and therefore inadequately stated, what distinguishes one from the other is first that intentionality is missing from the analyst's scheme of consciousness and that as a consequence a completely different conception of meaning arises for both camps; second, that there is a behavioristic thesis or bias to which analysis is tied; third, that there is a residue of the earlier therapeutic positivism which remains in analysis; and fourth, that it lacks an existential dimension. I take the first claim about intentionality to be crucial, the rest symptomatic. But each point deserves fuller treatment.

By intentionality, I understand, of course, Husserl's definitive conception of the directional character of all acts of consciousness as well as the intimately related distinction between the activity of consciousness and the objects posited by that activity. If we are considering contemporary phenomenology, as we have been throughout, a phenomenology which had no commitment to the intentionality of consciousness would be a contradiction in terms. What is so central about the doctrine of intentionality is that the entire phenomenological conception of meaning is generated out of and sustained by its special treatment of the stream of consciousness. The primary locus of meaning is not the linguistic instrument which is the vehicle for the expression of meaning but rather the activity of an intentional consciousness in whose dynamic operation unities are constituted. Even before the predications expressed in linguistic form are possible or given, there is a pre-predicative range of experience within which unities of meaning are primordially grasped. All of this, I think, is at a far remove from the concern of analytic philosophy, which begins with the world of common-sense experience and the ordinary language we use to express the meanings we locate there and wish to communicate to each other. The "ordinary" and the "common" are, for phenomenology, constituted by the activity of consciousness, and are sedimented deposits of meaning realized progressively though the intentional activity of consciousness. For the analyst, the world about us is simply and beyond any real question *familiar;* but I do not believe that he would recognize *familiarity* to present a cardinal or even distinctive philosophical problem. On the contrary, for phenomenology, the familiar is not only a central issue, it is one which can be handled properly only by a methodology which neutralizes and so sets in relief the general thesis of the natural attitude. Where the analyst might wish to turn to psychology for help in explaining the nature and origin of familiarity, the phenomenologist insists that the problem is an intentional one, that psychology or any other naturalistically oriented discipline cannot be brought in without hopelessly prejudicing the case. Stated another way, we might suggest that the ordinary, the familiar is the experiential surface of a philosophical domain whose depth and constitutive structure the phenomenologist tries to uncover. This seems to me alien to the concern of the analyst.

The other differences must be given summary treatment. The lack of an intentional theory of consciousness in analysis is not accidental; it is related directly to an implicit psychological commitment in an opposite direction, that of behaviorism. The analytic philosopher is primarily an observer; he shares with the natural scientist a professional distrust of first-person reports. And to the extent that he is true to this orientation, he adopts a view of mind which is necessarily antagonistic to phenomenology. Behaviorism and phenomenology are irreconcilable terms. Next, I maintain that there remains in analysis a residue of the early therapeutic positivism with its insistence on treating the metaphysician as a disturbed person, philosophy itself becoming transformed into a therapeutic enterprise. There are still signs of such practioners going about their rounds, and the language of phenomenology is surely enough to excite their blood.

Finally, I suggest that analysis lacks an existential dimension, and by this I mean only to point to what must be evident to everybody – that phenomenology has moved beyond logical investigations into a concern with the life and death of the monad, and with the texture of the *Lebenswelt* as the locus of ambiguity and cross-purposes, of metaphysical defeat no less than of office memoranda and business contacts. To say, in the end, that the analyst and phenomenologist are trying to describe the same world from different vantage points can only be considered, at this level, the inevitable triumph of an eclecticism which is determined at all costs to award everybody prizes.

It is at this point that my argument must be reformulated, for it is clear that the license taken at the beginning to use the terms analysis and analyst in some generic sense cannot possibly be maintained at this stage. I propose to step out over these usages now and to disregard the scaffolding that has enabled us to paint a total sketch of the relationship involved between phenomenology and analytic philosophy. Such a liberation will, at the same time, provide the basis for determining the positive connection which we have been anticipating. Again, only a summary statement is possible. I suggest that there are two related but qualitatively different strands in the fabric of analysis. The first is represented by such figures as Ryle and Austin; the second by Strawson and Hampshire. The adjectives that qualify the first grouping are behavioristic, psychologistic, and lexicographical; those for the other group are egological, descriptive, and in a sense still to be specified, phenomenological. In terms of publications the clearest representatives of the different modes of analysis are Ryle's *Concept of Mind* and Hampshire's *Thought and Action*. An indication of what I find in Hampshire's book which I would call phenomenological may be the best way to point to the positive nexus between analysis and phenomenology.

What I take to be Hampshire's central view in *Thought and Action* is this: the individual human being is seen as a person caught up in a social world in which his actions define his experience. The center of this world is the individual to whom experience is given in his particular temporal and spatial location, but that individual is at the same time an actor, an agent operating in reality, transforming his experience. Here Hampshire is reacting against the older empiricism which thought of mind as a kind of receptacle into which experience dropped its marks, and a view of the self as standing simply over and against other things in reality which act as stimuli to which the self responds. Thought and action, for Hampshire, are integrally related aspects of the unity of the world of human experience. It is noteworthy that Hampshire speaks of *intention* as the fundamental character of both thought and action. That he does not mean by intention what Husserl means by it is not as important as the realization, which I think is fully justified, that Hampshire is approaching a theory of mind which is basically continuous with phenomenology. I can merely suggest at this point that Hampshire's analysis of thought and action is an analytic counterpart, independently developed, to the kind of phenomenology of the natural attitude so brilliantly carried out in the writings of Alfred Schutz. It is Hampshire's sensitivity to the essential ambiguity and darkness of intentional consciousness which I have found so lacking in much of recent analytic philosophy; and if I interpret Hampshire correctly, that lack was not endemic to analytic philosophy as such, but rather to the behavioristic and lexicographical versions of it I find exemplified in the work of Ryle and Austin.

This positive note, however, must be sustained on just grounds. It would be as unavailing as it would be deceitful to argue at this point for some sort of rapprochement between analysis and phenomenology. Neither camp would stand to gain very much from an artificial synthesis or effort toward reconciliation. But the kind of dialogue between them which John Wild calls for is a possibility, although a rather distant one at the moment. To return to our point of departure, Professor Wild concludes his article by asking analysts to attend seriously to the contributions of phenomenology for a philosophy of the *Lebenswelt*. "Is it not true," he asks, "that ordinary language is concerned with facts of a different order from those of science? Is there not a world of ordinary language?" [5] And is it not the case that the contributions of analysts and phenomenologists to the study of this world are not opposed but mutually supplementary? This paper has been an effort to show the slippery terrain on which these very meaningful questions are posed and the still frozen depths in which the answers are locked.

[5] *op. cit.*, 476.

4. The Empirical and Transcendental Ego

> "We are talking now of summer evenings in Knox-
> ville, Tennessee in the time that I lived there so
> successfully disguised to myself as a child ... After a
> little I am taken in and put to bed. Sleep, soft smiling,
> draws me unto her: and those receive me, who
> quietly treat me, as one familiar and well-beloved in
> that home: but will not, oh, will not, not now, not
> ever; but will not ever tell me who I am."
>
> James Agee

Psychologists have often distinguished between the ego and the self,
taking ego as subject and self as object of thought. So, for example,
George H. Mead's distinction of the "I" and "me" aspects of the self
points, at one level at least, to the "I" as the subject and the "me" as
the object of any act. More explicitly, William James in the first
volume of his *Principles of Psychology* distinguishes between the self
and the ego. But James is quick to establish a distinction between what
he calls the "empirical self" and the "pure ego." "The Empirical Self of
each of us," he writes, "is all that he is tempted to call by name of
me," [1] but the pure ego refers to a "pure principle of personal identity"
and leads ultimately to considerations of transcendental philosophy.

Contemporary psychologists have not been as ready to allow for
such demarcations within the province of psychology; but more
interesting, I think, they have missed the clue to James's contribution
to philosophical psychology. He entitles his famous chapter on the self
"The *Consciousness* of Self," [2] for his theory of the nature of the self is
really a theory of the nature of consciousness and is the logical as well
as the chronological continuation of his previous chapter on "The
Stream of Thought." The self, for James, is incomprehensible apart
from the structure of consciousness. An inquiry into either the psychological or philosophical aspects of the self is therefore necessarily, at
bottom, an inquiry into the genetic or transcendental structure of consciousness.

I propose here to consider a certain conception of the ego. The
framework for my remarks consists of chapters from the history of

---

[1] James, W., *Principles of Psychology*, Vol. I, New York, 1893, 291.
[2] Italics mine.

act psychology, particularly Brentano, Husserl, and Sartre. The focus will be on Husserl's theory of the intentionality of consciousness. The distinction we have to begin with, however, is not that between self and ego, but between two conceptions of the ego, both of which logically antecede the self and are keys to its interpretation. I refer to the empirical and the transcendental ego.

By the empirical ego I understand the actually existent stream of perceptual acts – thinking, remembering, imagining, etc. – realized in the life of a concrete individual. By an "actually existent" perceptual stream I mean one in which the elements are unique spatio-temporal events having a neurological ground in a body. The present events of my conscious life, the actual stream of my awareness, are particulars, distinctively *mine*. Thus, the empirical ego has a neural history conjoined with a personal biography of unique events of consciousness which renders individual consciousness a natural object within the spatio-temporal world of nature.

The transcendental ego, on the other hand, is the pure stream of consciousness, freed from the causal conditions that occasion psychic events and independent of the concrete character of any elements within the stream. Rather, the transcendental ego is the pure *a priori* structure of consciousness understood as a noetic matrix of intentional acts. By intentionality here, I mean the doctrine first adequately expressed by Brentano and renovated and reconstructed by Husserl which holds that there is a directional character to the entire range of perceptual life. All thinking is thus thinking *of* something, all remembering is remembering *of* something, all imagining is imagining *of* something. Intentionality is the prime feature of consciousness, and the transcendental ego may now be understood as the pure intentional stream of perceptual acts.

In moving from the empirical to the transcendental ego it would appear that the unique individualized character of events of consciousness is transcended, so that the content of the stream of transcendentally purified consciousness is no longer "mine" in the sense in which the events of empirical consciousness are mine. How can the "mine" be expressed at all in terms of the transcendental ego? Within the phenomenological tradition two radically different answers have been suggested. The first is that the transcendental ego is itself the ground for the unity of experience, for there being "my" world. Experience is "mine" because it comes to articulation within the constitutive activity of the transcendental ego. Just as the Kantian "I think" is necessary for the coherence of experience, so the transcendental ego is the precondition, *a priori*, for there being world at all and for there then being "my" world.

The other answer to the question, How can the "mine" be expressed in terms of the transcendental ego? is found in the earlier writings of Husserl and has been, more recently, refurbished and advanced with considerable force by Jean-Paul Sartre in his essay on "The Transcendence of the Ego." The position here involves nothing less than an abandonment of the concept of a transcendental ego. The radical claim is, then, that the "mine" need not be expressed at all through a transcendental ego, that a non-egological conception of consciousness is adequate to the task of describing and understanding the phenomena of conscious life. This idea will be clearer if we return for a moment to Husserl's doctrine of intentionality.

To say that consciousness is always consciousness *of* something means that the objects of intentional acts are merely *meant* and are not held to be ontologically real in nature. The ontological status of the object as real or illusory, as veridical or hallucinatory is held in abeyance. But the "meant" object is always taken as the correlate of the act which intends it. If this is so, the life of consciousness is the life of intentionality and all that is given in and through consciousness is the intentional stream itself. The "I" that does the intending is not given in the intentional activity, but is rather a reflective addition made possible only after the intentional act is rendered an object of inspection. Thus, rather than speaking of "my" consciousness of chair, it is proper, phenomenologically, to speak of there being "consciousness-of-chair." Indeed, rather than say "I am conscious of chair," it would be proper to say "I am consciousness of chair." The "I" enters the scene of consciousness only after the drama is underway. "The ego," Sartre writes, "is neither formally nor materially *in* consciousness: it is outside, *in the world*. It is a being of the world, like the ego of another." [3]

The examples Sartre offers by way of illustration of this so-called "non-positional" consciousness are interesting. "When I run after a street car," he writes, "when I look at the time, when I am absorbed in contemplating a portrait, there is no I. There is consciousness of the streetcar-having-to-be-overtaken, etc., and non-positional consciousness of consciousness. In fact, I am then plunged into the world of

[3] Sartre, J.-P., *The Transcendence of the Ego*, 31.

objects; it is they which constitute the unity of my consciousnesses; it is they which present themselves with values, with attractive and repellent qualities – but me, I have disappeared; I have annihilated myself. There is no place for *me* on this level. And this is not a matter of chance, due to a momentary lapse of attention, but happens because of the very structure of consciousness." [4] The ego, then, according to Sartre, is found after or upon the act of self-conscious objectification; it is not any original ground for intentional acts. The transcendental ego is not only surplus baggage for a phenomenological theory of consciousness; it is inimical to the very essence of such a theory. "The transcendental I," Sartre writes, "is the death of consciousness." [5]

We have before us now two phenomenological conceptions of the nature of consciousness: one position maintains that intentionality presupposes a transcendental ego as its absolute ground; the other that it does not and, indeed, cannot. I would now like to sketch an outline of a phenomenological approach to consciousness which argues for the necessity of a transcendental ego but which allows for the non-positional character of intentionality as Sartre describes it. Quite apart from the adequacy of my proposal in phenomenological terms, I hope that it will help to illuminate the relationship between the psychological and phenomenological approaches to consciousness. [6]

My approach is built upon the following theses: first, that the decisive feature of consciousness is intentionality; second, that intentionality is a non-natural and purely *a priori* structure; third, that we may distinguish between the experiential givenness of intentionality and its transcendental presuppositions; fourth, that the direct experiential givenness is non-positional or, in other terms, presents no "I"; but fifth, that the transcendental presuppositions of intentionality do both require and, in some sense, present a transcendental ego; and sixth, that this transcendental ego is the pure possibility which metaphysically underlies and attends the actualization of any empirical ego in the world and which may then be understood as the interpretation of the role I choose to play in the drama of conscious life in which the *dramatis personnae* are announced, if at all, only at the conclusion of the performance. The transcendental ego in this sense is the condition of my being able to find out, through the performance of my life, who I am.

[4] *ibid.*, 48–49.
[5] *ibid.*, 40.
[6] See Aron Gurwitsch, "The Phenomenological and the Psychological Approach to Consciousness," *Philosophy and Phenomenological Research*, XV, March 1955, 303–319.

Now the first two theses are acceptable to both Husserl and Sartre and indeed constitute the minimum for any phenomenological theory of consciousness. The third thesis, however, that we may distinguish between the experiential givenness of intentionality and its transcendental presuppositions, is what I take to be the first differentiating point in my own approach. Some further explanation is required. The experiential givenness of intentionality refers to what is directly presented in the pure reflexive act of phenomenological inspection. When in phenomenological attitude I render my own intentional activity the object of investigation, I locate the qualitative stream of my intentional life. And to be sure, here I can locate no transcendental "I" in the immediacy of what is directly given. But there is a difference between what is phenomenologically given and the transcendental structures which are the ultimate presuppositions for what is given. The transcendental I is "presented" only as a horizonal theme, unifying and directing my conscious acts and rendering them, all along, concatenated fragments of *my* life.

The phenomenological problem at this point is to elucidate the relationship between the I as an empirical ego concretely and historically in the world and the transcendental ego as the pure possibility which metaphysically underlies and attends the actualization of the empirical ego. I suggest that at each moment in the becoming of empirical consciousness there is the actualization of the transcendental possibilities of the ego. Whether I conceive of this actualization through an image of self-realization is a psychological question, but that this image transcends the facets that point toward it and operates as a thematic unification of my conscious life is the essential feature for emphasis. My empirical existence is a projection out of the pure possibilities of consciousness as such toward the horizon of my life's completion. In this sense, my historical life is one realization of the infinite pure possibilities of the transcendental ego.

The relationship between empirical and transcendental consciousness may be reposed in Sartrean terms. The pre-reflective cogito (nonpositional or non-thetic consciousness) is a sheer spontaneity which stands phenomenologically prior to the actualization of the empirical ego: *before I am, there is*. The instantaneous spontaneity of the pre-reflective consciousness as *pour-soi* is, in Sartre's formulation, that which it is not and is not that which it is.[7] Each moment of its actualization is at once a collapse of its past, a presentiment of its future, and

---

[7] Cf. Sartre's *L'Être et le néant*, Paris, 1943, deuxième partie.

a restructuration in its present of these elements of the past and future. The Sartrean instantaneity is the moment at which the pre-reflective cogito causes there to be consciousness. Thus, "each instant of our conscious life reveals to us a creation *ex nihilo*. Not a new arrangement but a new existence." [8]

What may then be termed original presence to the world is made possible by the activity of the *pour-soi*, but reflection upon this activity is the burden of the ego as an empirical being actualized in the world. What is the relationship, then, between the *pour-soi* and the ego? What is the connection between the nihilating structure of pre-reflective consciousness and the self-reflective person who has a name, a unique biography, and a life? It is of decisive importance that Sartre never presents a satisfactory answer to these questions. And this is because there occurs in *L'Être et le néant* a magical transition, never philosophically explicated or justified, from the *pour-soi* as pre-reflective cogito to the *pour-soi* as self. How do I as a concrete being in this world ever come into connection with the *pour-soi*? In eliminating the transcendental ego, Sartre has given up the possibility of answering these questions or resolving the problems they announce.

The applications of Sartre's non-egological conception of consciousness are no less fraught with difficulties. Consider his example of the friend whose need is given as a quality of his being:

> I pity Peter, and I go to his assistance. For my consciousness only one thing exists at that moment: Peter having-to-be-helped. This quality of 'having-to-be-helped' lies in Peter. It acts on me like a force ... I am in the presence of Peter's suffering just as I am in the presence of the color of this inkstand; there is an objective world of things and of actions, done or to be done, and the actions come to adhere as qualities to the things which call for them.[9]

Now is it the case that "I am in the presence of Peter's suffering just as I am in the presence of the color of this inkstand?" The question is not, of course, whether Sartre is reducing felt experiences to the status of simple perceptions; rather, the sole question here is whether the qualitative presentations are, in truth, of the same order. I think they are not. Peter's suffering is never merely given; it is given to *me*. I encounter Peter-in-need-of-help in *my* encounter with him. His need is given only if it is recognized, and recognition is not an aspect of Peter's-having-to-be-helped but of my active awareness of his condition. It is

[8] *Transcendence of the Ego*, 98–99.
[9] *ibid.*, 56.

above all *I* who encounter Peter-in-need, and this I is not a reflective perceiver but an actor in the world.

If I say of this inkstand, "It is green," I note a quality of the object as it is for *an* observer. Its being green is something held to be true of the object in the sense that any observer, any *typical* observer, with normal color sensitivity will also perceive the object as green. The predication is on the side of the object. But in the case of Peter, I must admit that my pity may not be shared by others. Peter-in-need as I find him is not necessarily Peter as you encounter him. Need is not a quality on the object side exclusively; it is a function of the act of encounter in which a human being locates, sympathetically, a fellow man. The suffering, anguish, and desperation of fellow men may be encountered as objective qualities of their being only if I choose to divorce myself from the meaning of recognition as a human act. The condition and ground of such recognition is the ego as phenomenologically prior to the objects it encounters.

It is still possible, however, to interpret the Sartrean ego as an ideal noematic unity. Aron Gurwitsch writes:

The general result of Sartre's investigation may be formulated as follows. The ego exists neither *in* the acts of consciousness nor *behind* these acts. It stands *to* consciousness and *before* consciousness. It exists in the world as a worldly transcendent existent. This is true of my ego as well as that of other persons. Now a transcendent existent may be conceived only as an ideal noematic unity. Such is in fact the case of the ego; it turns out to be the noematic correlate of reflective acts.[10]

Taken in this way, the Sartrean ego presents itself as a totality only through particular dispositional aspects:

As the totality of the dispositions and actions the ego may not appear except as seen from this or that disposition or action, its self-presentation is necessarily one-sided. Every apprehension of the ego involves empty meanings and intentions bearing on dispositions and actions which, for the time being, are not given, i.e., do not appear through a correspondent conscious fact grasped by reflection; these empty meanings and significations may of course be filled out in further apprehensions.[11]

The problem here, I feel, is how we can interpret the ego as an ideal noematic unity without at the same time implying that this unity is a correlate of a noetic unity which is the polar ground and transcendental condition of reflections as noetic acts. Although the noematic unity

[10] Gurwitsch, A., "A Non-Egological Conception of Consciousness," *Philosophy and Phenomenological Research*, I, March 1941, 337.
[11] *ibid.*

may appear only through particular dispositions or actions, its very appearing in this modality must mean an appearing *to* consciousness. How can I recognize the transcendent ego as *mine* unless the individual acts of self-reflection are caught up in a thematic continuum of self-recognition? [12] Without an ego as the noetic condition for there being a continual recognition of acts of consciousness as *mine*, it is conceivable that I might come to associate the events of my life as being those of the other, of a fellow man. The curious upshot of this possibility is the reinvocation of the transcendental ego on the noematic side of experience. If I locate my ego in the same way that I have presented to me the ego of the other, I may take the ego of the other as mine. But what distinguishes my ego from that of my fellow man is precisely its being *mine*; i.e., its being grounded existentially as well as epistemically in the truth of *my* life.

A further possibility we may consider here finally is the interpretation of the "mine" as being merely the formal condition for the ego as a noematic unity. Sartre interprets the Kantian "I think" to be a transcendental condition for the unity of experience as a purely formal requirement. "The Critical problem being one of validity, Kant says nothing concerning the actual existence of the *I think*." [13] Here Sartre equivocates between two senses of modality in his interpretation of Kant's claim that "the I think *must be able* to accompany all our representations." [14] Sartre holds that because Kant says the I think *must be able* to accompany all our representations, he "seems to have seen perfectly well that there are moments of consciousness without the I." [15] This does not follow. "Must be able" means that the possibility of this accompaniment is a necessary possibility, not that it may or may not be fulfilled in fact. The choice in interpretation is not, as Sartre thinks, between a transcendental ego as purely formal and as substantivized or reified. "There is in contemporary philosophy," he writes, "a dangerous tendency ... which consists of making into a reality the conditions, determined by Criticism, for the possibility of

---

[12] Cf. the following criticism offered by Schutz: If Gurwitsch "says that there is no egological moment involved if I see my friend in adversity and help him and that what is given to me is just 'my-friend-in-need-of-aid' it must be stated that any single element of the hyphenated term 'my', 'friend,' 'need,' 'aid,' already refers to the ego for which alone each of them may exist." In: Alfred Schutz, "Scheler's Theory of Intersubjectivity and the General Thesis of the Alter Ego," *Philosophy and Phenomenological Research*, II, March 1942, footnote on 339.

[13] *Transcendence of the Ego*, 32.

[14] *ibid.*

[15] *ibid.*

experience." [16] An alternative interpretation is to treat the transcendental condition as formally required but at the same time as phenomenologically presented in the on-going activity of consciousness. Not only do I locate the "I think" as formally necessary, but as indeed realized in conscious life. It is not necessary to reify the constitutive activity of consciousness in order to locate the givenness of its structure and achievement. The transcendental ego is not directly presented in the immediacy of consciousness, but its formal character is not restricted to its "validity" or pure possibility; instead – and this is the whole point – the transcendental ego is continuously evident and given in the thematic recognition that shocks the entire range of experience into existence as *mine*.

Let me restate what I have in mind here in more humane terms. I am suggesting that when I look for a transcendental "I" in immediate and pure reflection, I find one only as a formal presupposition thematic to my life. But this "I" is the cardinal ground of there being *my* life as an on-going fulfillment of my possibilities. We may imagine the quality of a concrete human existence as the fulfillment in some modality of the possibilities *a priori* available to each of us. In these terms, an individual life is the concrete actualization of *the* transcendental ego, not "my" transcendental ego. It follows that far from the transcendental ego being, as Sartre claims, the "death of consciousness," it is, indeed, the metaphysical life of consciousness. The support for this view, however, requires that we look for the transcendental "I" not in the reflexive act but in the thematic ground of intentional life. The general understanding of this thesis, moreover, requires that we distinguish sharply between consciousness as a transcendental stream of pure intentional activity and consciousness as a neurological product. We must differentiate radically between a phenomenological and a psychological conception of consciousness. This is what I have been trying to do in this paper. The reinforcement of this distinction may serve as conclusion.

In comparing phenomenology and psychology, some psychologists have seen what they thought was a basic similarity between subjective or introspectional psychology and Husserlian phenomenology. This was true in Husserl's day and it is true in ours. The supposed similarity was based on the idea that phenomenology begins with the immediate data of the field of individual consciousness and then proceeds to a descriptive account of the content presented in that field. The report

[16] *ibid.*, 32–33.

is then a report of the private, first-person experience of the reporter. From such an introspectionism, it is held to follow, for phenomenology, that Husserl's method is a subjectivistic report of private experience which is then useless for scientific purposes and suspicious at best for philosophical psychology. In his own day, Husserl tried, perhaps in vain, to correct these total misunderstandings of phenomenological method. Unfortunately, the misunderstandings are still with us; they stem centrally from what Husserl called the "naturalization of consciousness" and are part of a "natural science about consciousness."

"It is to be expected beforehand," Husserl writes, "that phenomenology and psychology must stand in close relationship to each other, in so far as both are concerned with consciousness, even though in a different way, according to a different 'orientation.' What we should like to express thereby is that psychology is concerned with 'empirical consciousness,' with consciousness from the empirical point of view, as an empirical being in the ensemble of nature; whereas phenomenology is concerned with 'pure' consciousness, i.e., consciousness from the phenomenological point of view." [17] It follows for Husserl "that any psychologistic theory of knowledge must owe its existence to the fact that, missing the proper sense of the epistemological problematic, it is a victim of a presumably facile confusion between pure and empirical consciousness. To put the same thing in another way: it 'naturalizes' pure consciousness." [18]

The classical Husserlian refutation of psychologism has as its chief implication, I think, not merely the liberation of logic from the "physics of thought," but more important, the liberation of intentional consciousness from the assumptions of a naturalistic psychology. The following points emerge: first, pure or transcendental consciousness is not "in" the world; second, the content of the intentional stream of consciousness is not psychic in the sense of being composed of events which have space-time referents in the real world; third, the objects of intentional acts are purely *meant* unities and not "things"; fourth, traditional subject-object dualisms must all be called into radical question and set in methodological abeyance as far as intentional experience is concerned; fifth, what is opened up through phenomenological reduction is a domain of pure meanings which present themselves directly as essences which are the noematic correlates of intentional acts.

[17] Husserl, E., "Philosophy as a Strict Science," *Cross Currents*, VI, Summer 1956, 236.
[18] *ibid.*, 236–237.

Understood in this way, phenomenology is the logical ground and philosophical foundation for empirical psychology. It follows that a phenomenology of the ego is not only qualitatively distinct from a psychology of the ego but that any philosophically clarified theory of the empirical ego presupposes phenomenological investigation. The larger conclusion implicitly suggested here is that a theory of mind which gives full value to the range and subtlety of cognition is impossible in psychologistic terms. The naturalization of consciousness is the philosophical death of consciousness.

5. Being-in-Reality

⟨ I ⟩

In Joyce's *A Portrait of the Artist as a Young Man*, the boy here, we are told, "turned to the flyleaf of the geography and read what he had written there: himself, his name and where he was.

> Stephen Dedalus
> Class of Elements
> Clongowes Wood College
> Sallins
> County Kildare
> Ireland
> Europe
> The World
> The Universe"[1]

Self-placement through listings of this sort is common, and we may attach to them no more significance than the desire of the child to find a primitive order in his world, or, perhaps, to approach what transcends him by pointing to it. But the very ordering arrangement may be a clue to a still different problem: the location and realization of the primal situation of the self in reality. Tentatively, it might be suggested that the ordering procedure is a way of securing the self against the initial lack of placement, a way of avoiding the ranges of experience that defy full comprehension, and a way of establishing the self as knowable, comprehensible, and controllable in a world in which knowing, comprehending, and controlling are ultimately ambiguous and fragmentary structures.

Transposed to the adult and philosophical level, it might be suggested that each of Stephen Dedalus' regions or realms could be fully

[1] Joyce, J., *A Portrait of the Artist as a Young Man*, New York, 1956, 15–16.

explored in terms of a naturalistic position; that, for example, understanding of Stephen himself is possible through an empirical psychology developed to its mature form, that a thorough knowledge of
place and county and country may be achieved through a coalescence
of information gained from a dozen disciplines ranging from geography
to political science; that, finally, knowledge of "world" and "universe"
can be gained through the method of inquiry characteristic of the
sciences. If the kind of naturalism involved here be of a sort similar to
that of John Dewey, the underlying attitude might be summarized in
the familiar recommendation that there is a qualitative continuity
between the problems of the natural sciences and those of the cultural
sciences, that scientific method is adequate, in principle, to resolve the
problems of man and nature, and that progress is made through a
reasoned effort to advance the possibilities inherent in a rational,
scientific view of the world. Man, in this view, is fundamentally at
home in the natural world, able to control crucial aspects of his environment and advance his cause over the opposition of superstition,
ignorance, and prejudice.

Were this a full account of the matter, there would be little more to
what we are calling the problem of placement in the world than awaiting
definitive scientific answers to questions of a limited sort. But if there
is any truth in suggesting that the problem of placement in reality goes
beyond scientific questions and answers, then it is necessary to put the
naturalistic position in question in order to see our problem. Just as
Stephen Dedalus' primitive cosmology can be understood as a way of
finding himself in the labyrinth of the world, so the categories and
methods of naturalism may be treated as markers set up to map an
otherwise wild terrain. So long as mapping the world is an ongoing
affair, the original status of the mapper does not arise; so long as we
are doing, making, acting in the world, our being in the world is
unproblematic. Dewey's idea that a problem arises always within a
context which is unproblematic is completely germane here, for being
in the world, original placement in reality, is taken by the naturalist as
the unproblematic context of his actions in the world. As long as we
remain in the naturalist's standpoint, the very techniques of inquiry
predicate a world and man in that world, the fundamental character of
both being taken for granted, or, if placed in question, reduced to
piecemeal problems. We suggest that the very articulation of the
problem of being-in-reality requires a departure from the naturalistic
position, or more generally, a disconnection from what Husserl calls

the "natural attitude." The statement of our problem, therefore, requires a phenomenological transposition.

⟨ II ⟩

Within the natural attitude I act in a world which is real, a world that existed before I was born and which I think will continue to exist after I die. This world is inhabited not only by me, but also by my fellow men, who are human beings with whom I can and do communicate meaningfully. This world has familiar features which have been systematically described through the genetic-causal categories of science. The world of daily life is lived within this natural attitude, and as long as things go along smoothly and reasonably well, there arises no need to call this attitude into question. But even if I do occasionally ask whether something is "really real," whether the world is "really" as it appears to be, these questions are still posed in such a way that they are my questions about the natural world in which I live. I do not really scrutinize my natural attitude in any rigorous manner: I merely mark off a bit of it for more careful study. And so I continue to be a real being in the real world of real things sharing real experiences with other real companions and living a real life.

If I am questioned about my "identity" in my natural attitude, my answers are ready: I can give my name, validated by birth certificate, my age, place of birth, parents' names, address, occupation, and, if necessary, a list of my hobbies. These "vital statistics" summate my position within the natural attitude, though a full examination of that attitude would require an exhaustive analysis of common-sense reality. The problem of being-in-reality does not and cannot arise within the natural attitude for the essential reason that the natural attitude is at its root founded on the assumption that the individual is, *of course*, already in the world when we interrogate him about his history and interests. Being in reality here can mean no more than psychophysical presence. The person is in the world in much the same way that a marble is in the bag, that a cat is in the house, that a teacher is in the classroom. But it is at this point that a kind of rebellion takes place: the full reality of the individual is surely not exhausted in statistics, and the identity of the person demands an appreciation of *his* situation in the world as distinct from *one's* situation in the world. I am forced to the question of the true character of my placement in the world, of the signification of name, place, and realm, of the credentials of the natural

attitude itself. It is Kierkegaard who leads the revolt. He writes in
Repetition:

One sticks one's finger into the soil to tell by the smell in what land one is: I
stick my finger into existence – it smells of nothing. Where am I? Who am I?
How came I here? What is this thing called the world? What does this word
mean? Who is it that has lured me into the thing, and now leaves me there? Who
am I? How did I come into the world? Why was I not consulted, why not made
acquainted with its manners and customs ...? How did I obtain an interest in
this big enterprise they call reality? Why should I have an interest in it? Is it not
a voluntary concern? And if I am to be compelled to take part in it, where is the
director? I should like to make a remark to him.[2]

But to place the natural attitude in question is not only to declare in
favour of an existential awareness of reality; it is also, in phenomenological terms, to try to get the meaning or sense of that awareness.
Therefore, the disconnection from the natural attitude that leads in the
direction of existential philosophy may itself be examined and made
the object of scrutiny. A phenomenological description of being-in-
reality turns first of all to the initial disconnection from the natural
attitude that is at the root of existential awareness of what it means to
be in the world. What is the character of this disconnection? Unfortunately, the celebrated theory of reduction in Husserl's phenomenology
is a much misunderstood topic, and so it is not possible to answer our
question by merely invoking the procedure of "bracketing." It is first
necessary to clarify what is meant by phenomenological reduction.

"'The' world is as fact-world always there," Husserl writes, "at the
most it is at odd points 'other' than I supposed, this or that under such
names as 'illusion,' 'hallucination,' and the like, must be struck *out of it*,
so to speak; but the 'it' remains ever, in the sense of the general thesis, a
world that has its being out there."[3] The radical "alteration" of the
natural thesis requires a continuing procedure of disconnection or
bracketing which transposes the naively experienced world into the
intentional field of world-for-me. To bracket the world is neither to
deny its reality nor to change its reality in any way; rather, it is to
effect a change in my way of regarding the world, a change that turns
my glance from the "real" object to the object as I take it, treat it,
interpret it as real. Within the natural attitude I attend to the object;
in the phenomenological attitude I attend to the object as known, as
meant, as intended. The reality of the object is bracketed only in the
sense that I attend to what presents itself to me immediately, whether
really real or not, and seize the reality of the object as the object of my

2 Kierkegaard, S., *Repetition*, Princeton, 1941, 114.
3 Husserl, E., *Ideas*, 106.

intentional acts. The object continues to be in the real world, as I do, but what now interests me, phenomenologically, is my awareness, my sense of its being in the real world. The object I reflect upon in the reduced sphere is the real thing as I've taken it to be real. Thus, "the" world is replaced by "my" world, not in any solipsistic sense, but only in the sense that "mine" indicates an intentional realm constituted by my own acts of seeing, hearing, remembering, imagining, and so on.

If I wish, phenomenologically, to refer to "the" world, I must attend to the world I take to be "the" world, i.e., world taken as "the" world. Placement *in* "the" world in the natural attitude presupposes the nature of that "in" structure, and the presupposition is not self-consciously considered. Husserl writes, "The General Thesis according to which the real world about me is at all times known not merely in a general way as something apprehended, but as a fact-world *that has its being out there*, does *not* consist of course *in an act proper*, in an articulated judgment *about* existence. It is and remains something all the time the standpoint is adopted, that is, it endures persistently during the whole course of our life of natural endeavour."[4] The disconnection or bracketing in phenomenological reduction is an alteration of this General Thesis which, for methodological reasons, I suspend. My being in the natural attitude, of course, continues. I remain in the natural attitude at the very time I disconnect myself from it in terms of judgment and description. This means only that my being in the natural attitude becomes the theme of my phenomenological consideration, but that my physical bodily existence continues in commonsense fashion.

With the transposition to the intentional realm, my being in the world, or more generally, my being in reality, may now be expressed through the hyphenation given in the title of my paper: being-in-reality; and we understand by this hyphenation that disconnection from the natural attitude permits the originally taken for granted placement in the world to become the intentional object of phenomenological examination. Whereas unhyphenated being in reality is the unconscious basis of all our predications and actions, hyphenated being-in-reality involves the self-conscious reflection on the signification and structure of the General Thesis of the natural attitude. The relationship between the natural attitude and intentional consciousness may be restated in still a different way by referring back to our discussion of the Deweyan position.

To say, with Dewey, that every problem presupposes an unproblematic context within which, against which it arises, is to leave unexami-

4 *ibid.*, 107.

ned and unclarified the very meaning of "context." Whatever interpretation of "situation" Dewey presents is already founded on the
assumption that we have, are *in*, or find or locate such a context. This
assumption is proper to empirical science; in fact, it is its point of
departure. But if part of the task of philosophy is to consider the
foundational concepts and presuppositions of the sciences, it is necessary to start at the beginning and place in question what it means to
take something as unproblematic. To do this is to shift from the natural
standpoint to a reflective one; and to attempt to take the reflective
standpoint itself as the object of scrutiny is to search for phenomenological roots. The effecting of the transposition from the natural to
the phenomenological standpoint in no way alters or disregards any
structure located or experienced in the natural attitude; in placing the
natural attitude in suspension, the phenomenologist only tries to
comprehend the meaningful structure of the Life-world as it reveals
itself in intentional consciousness. Properly understood, then, there is
no disagreement between the natural attitude and the phenomenological standpoint or between natural science and phenomenological
philosophy; the latter is nothing more than a systematic, sustained,
but completely radical endeavour to illuminate our being-in-reality in
its full intentional structure.

⟨ III ⟩

We are now prepared for a closer examination of our theme. My being-
in-reality always presents itself to me within a horizon of relatedness to
more or less determinate surroundings. My "being-in" is in a more or
less circumscribed situation. Each concrete event in experience is,
Husserl says, "partly pervaded, partly girt about with a *dimly apprehended depth or fringe of indeterminate reality.*"[5] Every "this" is a "this"
within a context, clearly or dimly grasped, of a "more-than-this." And
if I follow the horizonal character of the presentation involved, I am
led to the vague "form" of a total inclusiveness. Husserl, describing the
movement from limitation to form, writes:

Determining representations, dim at first, then livelier, fetch me something out,
a chain of such recollections takes shape, the circle of determinacy extends ever
farther, and eventually so far that the connexion with the actual field of perception as the *immediate* environment is established. But in general the issue is a
different one: an empty mist of dim indeterminacy gets studded over with
intuitive possibilities or presumptions, and only the "form" of the world as
"world" is foretokened. Moreover, the zone of indeterminacy is infinite. The
misty horizon that can never be completely outlined remains necessarily there.[6]

[5] *ibid.*, 102.
[6] *ibid.*

When I move, then, from a "this" to the vague form of "world" surrounding and including that "this," I explore the phenomenological
horizon of my immediate placement in reality. The "in" of hyphenated
"being-in-reality" is then, I would suggest, the horizonal directedness
which attends and defines every act of placement. The "in" is therefore
not the "in" of class inclusion or of physical habitation, but the radically different and unique structure of horizonal projection; i.e., the
fluid movement from being "in" a concrete situation to being "in"
world as such. Reality, in this sense, is the form of the widest generality, the horizon of all horizons, the indeterminate penumbra that
surrounds our farthest reach of intention and presents itself as transcendence. To complete the clarification of terms, "being" may now be
understood as the life of consciousness involved and engaged in intentional activity. Fully translated now, the title of our paper comes
out from behind its hyphens: As a thinking, willing, perceiving, feeling,
imagining consciousness, my intentions are directed to the concrete
situations in which I live. The elements of these situations are not the
objective things of the natural attitude, but the phenomenological
objects of my intentional acts: I live within a world of my own attitudes
and interpretations. But each act of consciousness intends some object
within a concrete situation which itself finds placement in the world I
think is "out there." When I carry out my intention to its farthest
limit, I end with the strangeness, the uncanniness of reality taken as
transcendent. *Being-in-reality is consciousness moving toward a horizon
of transcendence.*

The suspension of the natural attitude alone makes possible the
exploration of our theme. As long as we start with man naively existent
in the world, the meaning of "man-in-the-world" cannot be explored.
Phenomenology is an effort to overcome this naturalistic impasse by
opening up for inspection the region of intentional consciousness. The
point of this paper has not been to attempt a phenomenological study
of "being-in-reality," but to try to show in what sense that structure is a
valid philosophical problem, and to indicate the *kind* of approach a
phenomenologist makes to such a root-problem. Since the very statement of the problem requires phenomenological disconnection from the
General Thesis of the natural attitude, it has been necessary to move
within the problem rather than commence with a direct statement of it.
Instead of beginning with definitions, I have tried to end with them.
But I think that this reflexive mode of thought, if circular, is not
vicious. As Husserl says, "Philosophy can take root only in radical
reflexion upon the meaning and possibility of its own scheme."

6. Jean-Paul Sartre's Philosophy of Freedom

> "I desire to speak somewhere without bounds ... for I
> am convinced that I cannot exaggerate enough even
> to lay the foundation of a true expression."
>
> Thoreau

It is now a commonplace in discussions of existentialism to distinguish between existentialism the fad, the darling of the Left Bank and of the sensation seekers, and existentialism the serious philosophical endeavor to explicate the categories and structure of man's existence in its unique and immediate being. Nevertheless, any discussion of the writings of Jean-Paul Sartre seems, like a tropistic reaction of a plant, to bend toward a confused admixture of ontology, ethics, psychology, literature, and publicity. It is beyond the scope of my present intentions to determine the reasons for the unclarified status of Sartre's thought, but that lack of clarification may be taken as a starting point for an examination into the meaning of Sartre's conception of existential freedom.

SARTRE AND HIS PHILOSOPHICAL POSITION

Who is this enfant terrible who is at once philosopher, psychologist, novelist, dramatist, commentator, editor, lecturer, and disturber of the peace? His personal history[1] is not of crucial importance to us here. After learning that one of his parents was Catholic and the other a Protestant, that his father died when Sartre was four years old, that Sartre's childhood was that of a constantly sick and ailing boy, that he ultimately went on to the study of philosophy, received a doctorate in philosophy, and subsequently published a torrent of books, we are still left with something of a mystery: with the fundamental question,

---

[1] See M. Beigbeder, *L'homme Sartre*, Paris, 1947.

"What is this man seeking philosophically?" and the related question, "What has led him to undertake this search?" Let us take these two questions in order.

First, what is Sartre seeking? In the simplest terms, he is seeking to describe the being of man in reality, but to comprehend that being in a radical and irreducible manner. The object of existential inquiry is man's being in the world as such; and therefore it is concerned not with special aspects of the business, professional, or artistic world in which men live, but with the necessary and essential conditions for being in all realms, for all men. Before we are citizens or fathers or employees or Protestants or Kantians, we *are*: we find ourselves in the midst of things, we are beings in the world. To understand the full nature and significance of this being in the world is a central task for existential philosophy. Its importance is apparent only when we realize that all subsequent analyses in Sartre stem from the analysis of the ground phenomenon of being in the world. For Sartre, then, existential philosophy is the analysis of being, and proceeds through the study of man's being in the world. Such an analysis leads ultimately to the structures of the self, and the multiple aspects of the relationships between the self and other selves. The dialectic between self and other selves is the key to Sartre's concept of human freedom.

If Sartre's search is then the search for being, a search that will lead in its final consequences to man's freedom, we may now ask our second question: what has led Sartre to undertake this search? It is possible, of course, to answer this kind of question in a number of ways. We may try to develop a psychoanalytic interpretation of Sartre's behavior – which, by the way, has been done; [2] or, at the other extreme, we may attempt to analyze his problem purely on a philosophical plane. But more is involved: we are really faced with a basic problem, which is how to account for the multiple and divergent roots of existential philosophizing as they appear in the total cultural and historical heritage of man – for it should now be clear, even if it has not been explicitly stated, that existentialism as the search for man's being as such is an inseparable part of the organic nucleus of the human intellectual heritage.

As a distinctive attitude and cultural phenomenon, as a central nerve trunk in the corpus of world literature, and, finally, as an historical development, the content of existential thought may be summarily indicated by listing four of its predominant charac-

[2] See S. Naesgaard, "Le complexe de Sartre," *Psyché*, June 1948.

teristics. Existential thought is characterized, first, by a profound concern for the everlasting categories of man's being, his fear, dread, suffering, aloneness, anguish, and death; second, by the fact that it takes man as the object of its inquiry, but man as an "unhappy consciousness," as a fragmentary and fragmented creature who locates his existence in a cosmos that is at once overpowering, threatening, and demanding; third, by its internal un-neutrality toward God – the existentialist's dialogue takes place in an empty cathedral, and the protagonists debate the terminology of the mass and, more important, for whom the mass is to be said; and fourth, by a decisive concern with man's authenticity in existence, his gift of freedom which is his anguish, his total responsibility which is his dread.

If existential thought, both as an attitude and as a philosophy, is properly indicated by this characterization, it is now possible to understand the several roots for the development of existentialism in literature, history, and philosophy proper.

First, the literary background. When Ecclesiastes sought to transcend vanity in a sad and aching wisdom, when Job sought God's will from the embroiled margin of his distress, when Abraham wrestled with the paradox of faith and filial love, of God's will and man's obligation – in all of these instances the thread of existential distress and wonder began to be woven and defined.

It is impossible to read Dostoievski, Tolstoy, Kafka, without being faced with the existential problems of the human condition. "What if my whole life has really been wrong?" asks Tolstoy's Ivan Ilyich, who, in the illuminated immediacy of the realization that he is dying, is faced with the irrevocable mediocrity and banality of his lived life. One fine morning Kafka's Joseph K. is accused of an unknowable, transcendent guilt, is compelled to prepare a defense of his innocence before unreachable courts, and is ultimately destroyed in a moment of terrifying solitude by the bureaucratic agents of an incomprehensible power. Dostoievsky's Underground Man is hurled shivering and jangled into an alien and thwarting reality that blockades his soul and suffocates his sensibility; Raskolnikoff is spliced between Nietzsche and Kant, and the finality of every character Dostoievsky ever created is sounded by Ivan Karamazov, who cries, "I must have justice or I will destroy myself!"

In literature, then, the existential content is defined by the dualisms of man's existence: guilt and salvation, authenticity and self-deceit, necessity and freedom.

Now the historical background. Ages of crisis and upheaval have always produced characteristic literatures. An extended study might consider such literatures from Montaigne to the present day. We must restrict ourselves, however, to the historical background of Sartre's thought, and even more specifically to the notion of the "extreme situation." It should not be forgotten that the Paris school of existentialism is the product, historically, of two world wars. Sartre served in the French army, was captured by the Nazis, was incarcerated in a concentration camp, escaped, made his way back to France, and served with distinction in the French underground. The extreme situation is the sign of the underground movement: the lives of a large number of persons, known and unknown, depend upon the actions of a single person; capture and torture are an everyday affair; death is always a fellow traveler, likely to upset one's plans at any moment; the entire concept of time is transvalued and transformed.

Thus any analysis of Sartre's thought must take into serious account the general pattern of the historical situation: the phenomenon of the lost generation between the wars; the physical and cultural devastation of France during the occupation; the present conflict of parties wrangling desperately in the face of another and perhaps final wave of death.

And finally the philosophical background. Any serious consideration of Sartre's thought would have to go into extended analyses of the influence of Kant, Hegel, Kierkegaard, Nietzsche, Husserl, and Heidegger. Obviously this is not possible in a paragraph or two. I shall try, however, to do the impossible: to summarize in a sentence the basic influence that each of these philosophers had upon Sartre.

Kant: In the spirit of Kant's Copernican revolution, Sartre seeks to comprehend the nature of being via an analysis of man's being.

Hegel: Hegel's ideas of the "unhappy consciousness" and the dialectic between Master and Slave, in the *Phenomenology of Mind*, reappear in Sartre's main work and have central importance.

Kierkegaard: Kierkegaard's categories of man's fear, dread, trembling and anguish are transformed by Sartre so as to operate within an atheistic position.

Nietzsche: Sartre accepts Nietzsche's proclamation, "God is dead," and seeks to find the final expression of this dictum.

Husserl: Sartre, with Husserl, seeks to return to the "things themselves" of experience, and to describe those things phenomenologically, so that all analyses are essentially in terms of consciousness.

Heidegger: With Heidegger, and so too with Sartre, the starting point is man's being-in-the-world, the method is phenomenological, the result is a radical interpretation of self and authenticity.

These fragmentary statements of influences on Sartre have prepared the way for a statement of his general philosophical position, through which alone a real understanding of his philosophy of freedom is possible.

I shall first try to state the essence of Sartre's philosophic position in a few clear sentences. For Sartre, human being, as man's consciousness, is in a dialectical relationship with non-human being, the "stuff" of nature. The outstanding characteristic of this dialectic is the dynamic, changing, and flux-like status of human consciousness, which nowhere can find permanence, surety, or absolutes, but must continually define its condition and nature through the choices it makes in life. Thus for Sartre there are no eternal or a priori certitudes, there is no absolute basis for permanent relationships between persons. Man must make himself, that is, he must choose his ideals, his meanings, and his destiny. Freedom consists in such acts of choice and self-definition; but man is *forced* to define himself, since he has no permanent self upon which to rely. Man's state of perpetual redefinition and flux is what Sartre means by "nothingness," and to this nothingness man is condemned. We are, for Sartre, condemned to be free. The individual, reacting to this condition, can choose himself as authentic or inauthentic.

Some of these ideas may now be clarified in greater detail. Let us consider first the problem of being and its polarities. Being, for Sartre, is that which appears to us – phenomena, in the Aristotelian rather than the Kantian sense of the term. But there are two aspects of all being: the being of man, consciousness; and the being of objects, which is non-consciousness. The consciousness of man is in perpetual relationship with the things of reality. While consciousness is moving, shifting, altering constantly, non-consciousness is inert, non-reflective, a plenum.

Second, the self. If the human being is a consciousness in constant transition, then the essence of that transition, the very reason for that transition, is the nothingness of the self. Sartre conceives of the self as a kind of projectile, which implicitly lacks the ability to give itself a permanent foundation. All dimensions of the self share this impermanence: the past of the self, its past deeds, its memories, its recollections, are all subject to change in their meaning, as future events cause those happenings to be revaluated. The present of the self we have already characterized as the nothingness of a cardinal instability and projection. The future of the self is ambiguous, and to be chosen.

Third, other selves. Relations between selves are, for Sartre, essentially paradoxical and antagonistic. I first locate the Other epistemologically when he *looks* at me. The "look" of the Other causes a kind of hemorrhaging of my subjectivity: I feel like an object for the Other's subjectivity. Since I can never grasp the Other as subject for my subjectivity, the concrete human relationships of love, hate, sadism, masochism, and the like are all developed in the light of this subject-object dualism.

Fourth, the situation. Self and the Other, however, are not understood by Sartre in epistemological isolation. They are involved always in a situation. Sartre writes:

> For us, man is defined first of all as a being "in a situation." That means that he forms a synthetic whole with his situation – biological, economic, political, cultural, etc. He cannot be distinguished from his situation, for it forms him and decides his possibilities; but, inversely, it is he who gives it meaning by making his choices within it and by it. To be in a situation, as we see it, is *to choose oneself* in a situation, and men differ from one another in their situations and also in the choices they themselves make of themselves. What men have in common is not a "nature" but a condition, that is, an ensemble of limits and restrictions. The inevitability of death, the necessity of working for a living, of living in a world already inhabited by other men. Fundamentally this condition is nothing more than the basic human situation, or, if you prefer, the ensemble of abstract characteristics common to all situations.[3]

Fifth, choice and authenticity. Through choice the self constitutes itself, gives itself its unique content, and at the same time gives to its reality, to the world and other persons in the world, the special qualities and characteristics that make up the objective situation of the self. There are two fundamental modes of choice, which lead to authenticity or to inauthenticity. Either the self chooses self-consciously, wills its actions positively; or it seeks to flee from the grave responsibility of having to make choices. In the latter case the self is inauthentic. In his *Anti-Semite and Jew*, Sartre writes, "Authenticity ... consists in having a true and lucid consciousness of the situation, in assuming the responsibilities and risks that it involves, in accepting it in pride or humiliation, sometimes in horror and hate"[4]. The ground of existential freedom is thus, for Sartre, the self in a situation which it defines through choice. We are now in a position to examine this radical conception of freedom.

[3] Sartre, J.-P., *Anti-Semite and Jew*, New York, 1948, 59–60.
[4] *ibid.*, 90.

THE THEORY OF EXISTENTIAL FREEDOM

Sartre has given a brief definition of existentialism as the philosophy which holds that existence precedes essence. By this he means that there is no a priori, unavoidable, or instinctual "human nature" which makes men heroes or cowards, successes or failures. Rather, men define their peculiar natures through the actions, the deeds, that they perform. A coward is a man who has committed and who commits acts of cowardice. He may, however, alter his status as a "coward" by refusing to commit such acts again, by acting in a dignified manner. Moreover, the nature of a person is exhausted in the actions he has performed and does perform. Thus, for Sartre, it makes no sense to talk about the novels Thomas Wolfe might have written had he lived twenty years longer. Wolfe's genius was expressed in his written work; it *was* the expression of his work. Beyond that expression lies a void, as far as prediction or characterization is concerned, and it makes no sense to talk about possibilities that are in principle cut off from human action.

The notion that existence precedes essence means, then, that the self is the resultant of its choices, subject to change and alteration in principle. But there is a deeper philosophical issue involved. If the essence of the self is constituted by acts of existential choice, then the self *is* only in so far as it acts. We come here to an ego-less conception of the self that is characteristic of Sartre's ontology. The self is able to grasp its ego, its content, only *in* its acts. Thus the notion of choice is far-reaching, for only by choice, through acts, can I grasp myself: I live in my acts.

It is now time to examine, in greater detail, the specific relationships between the self and other selves. Let us analyze the relationships of sadism, masochism, hatred, and love.

Sadism. This is essentially the attempt to make the Other a complete object for my subjectivity. The sadist seeks to reduce his victim to the status of a "thing", to deprive him in this way of his freedom. We may here return to the earlier distinction between the polarities of being. Sartre's theory of sadism asserts that the sadist, as a consciousness, a self, attempts to reduce the Other to a non-conscious thing, to inner matter. It is to be noted that this kind of analysis of sadism is not concerned with the fact that there are different ways or modes of sadism. Sartre is attempting to describe the invariant, essential characteristics of sadism, and to show that these characteristics are the ground for all variant cases.

Masochism. In the case of masochism, the relationship between persons is one in which the masochist makes himself, desires himself to be made, an object for the Other's subjectivity. At the point that the masochist is reviled, stricken, and injured, he comes closest to achieving the status he yearns for: that of the complete object, freedomless and selfless.

Hatred. My hatred of the Other is really an attempt, at least a desire, to cause the Other's complete destruction, his death. The fulfilment of my hate would mean the total abolition of his consciousness, his freedom.

Love. In love I seek to possess the subjectivity of my beloved as a subjectivity, to possess the freedom of my beloved as a freedom. If it is recalled that for Sartre it is possible for the self to know the Other only as an object, it becomes clear that a paradoxical situation is involved in the relationship of love: the paradox is how we can ever possess the subjectivity of another and remain subjectivities ourselves. But this difficulty is really at the heart of all the relationships previously described.

For Sartre, the relationships of sadism, masochism, hatred, and love are all paradoxical and unstable relationships which end in frustration and defeat. In sadism, the sadist may be triumphant in the relationship almost to the point of completion and victory, but at the last moment an implicit and unavoidable defeat occurs: the sadist's victim *looks* at him and makes of *him* an object. The sadist is compelled to realize that it is not an object but a subjectivity that he has possessed and attempted to wound. A brilliant example of the failure of sadism through the *look* of the victim at his torturer is to be found at the end of William Faulkner's novel, *Light in August*. The scene is the mutilation of Joe Christmas, a Negro, by Grimm, a southern white man, whose sadism is the expression of an imponderable evil and guilt. Faulkner writes:

When the others reached the kitchen they saw the table flung aside now and Grimm stooping over the body. When they approached to see what he was about, they saw that the man was not dead yet, and when they saw what Grimm was doing one of the men gave a choked cry and stumbled back into the wall and began to vomit. Then Grimm too sprang back, flinging behind him the bloody butcher knife. "Now you'll let white women alone, even in hell," he said. But the man on the floor had not moved. He just lay there, with his eyes open and empty of everything save consciousness, and with something, a shadow, about his mouth. For a long moment he looked up at them with peaceful and unfathomable and unbearable eyes. Then his face, body, all, seemed to collapse, to fall in upon itself, and from out the slashed garments about his hips and loins the pent black blood seemed to rush like a released breath. It seemed to rush out of his pale body like the rush of sparks from a rising rocket; upon that black blast the man seemed to rise soaring into their memories forever and ever. They are not to lose it, in whatever peaceful valleys, beside whatever placid and reassuring streams of old age, in the mirroring faces of whatever children they will contemplate old disasters and newer hopes. It will be there, musing, quiet, steadfast, not fading and not particularly threatful, but of itself alone serene, of itself alone triumphant.[5]

The failure-in-principle of sadism is the failure also of masochism, hate, and even love. An epistemological and ontological gulf separates self from self, freedom from freedom, and each of us must choose himself within the closed circuit of his own solipsism.

If man's actions determine the content of the self that he is, and if his relations with others can be only further elements in that self, for what is the individual responsible in his freedom? In other words, how can his actions and status reflect outward to meet the objective conditions of the world and the needs and demands of other persons in the world?

The answer to this question involves a return to the notion of "situation." It will be recalled that for Sartre the self is always in a situation, but a situation that exists in virtue of the self's constitutive activities. As a self, it is I who give meaning, direction, and purpose to my associates, to physical location, to cultural heritage. In this sense I choose my situation and am responsible for it. To the extent that my choice involves other people, I choose for them also, in my decisions and actions. Whether I desire it or not, my choice of a situation involves others about me, and mankind in general.

It is here that we begin to realize the profound anguish that choice involves. There are two aspects of the problem. When I choose, I am constructing through my choices the person that I am and will be. I am responsible, then, for the image of myself that I construct. If man has no a priori nature, he chooses in total responsibility for himself. On the other hand, if in choosing myself I am choosing my situation and others in my situation, then I am responsible for them as well. The act of choice, for Sartre, is one of total responsibility and total anguish. Moreover, having chosen, I cannot, like a mason, rest with having constructed a permanent structure. My choices, my deeds, my existence are in flight, in flux, and I must reconstruct that existence as long as I live.

If the individual, in choosing, is responsible not only for himself but for mankind, it would seem that Sartre is really suggesting something akin to the Kantian categorical imperative. As a matter of fact, Sartre

[5] Faulkner, W., *Light in August*, New York, 1932, 439-40.

is suggesting such an imperative, but he has withdrawn the content of the imperative. In other words, the individual must act in such a way as to consider what is good for all men, but what it is, specifically, that is good he cannot determine in any form that would permit codification. Sartre suggests, "choose yourself in such a way as to be authentic, responsible, and thus existentially free in your self-awareness." But if we ask, "what is it that we must choose to achieve this?" the answer is, "define yourself, act, improvise." Beyond this, there is no answer.

In principle, Sartre cannot tell us what to do, or what we should take to be the good. We are in a world of ambiguity in which it is the essential nature of the self to be forced to decide for itself what is good and just and true and beautiful. The whole point, however, is that this determination is not arbitrary. Man must determine the content, but the form of the imperative is there: he chooses within the framework of responsibility, in self-acknowledgment of anguish, in the decisive clutch of requiredness. To be free, then, is not to choose one's freedom, but to be aware that one is free in any case – that one is condemned to be free – and from there to achieve authenticity, that is, self-conscious choice in the face of anguish, through acting in the world of contingent and modal realities.

As some of the existentialists have pointed out, this conception of total freedom and total responsibility is really a derivative of Dostoievsky's famous statement, "If God did not exist, everything would be permissible." Sartre has taken this seriously, and has attempted to find the final consequences of the assertion. His novel *Nausea* contains perhaps the most interesting description of this conception of freedom as the paradox of total responsibility and total contingency.

We have already seen that the fundamental ontological dualism of consciousness and non-conscious matter, of self and nature, is the ground for Sartre's theory of existential freedom. The self in situation is always, among other things, the self in its basic relationship to the external world of inert matter. Thus if the self is free, its freedom is, in part, a function of its relationship to nature. The real theme of Sartre's novel *Nausea* is the articulation of the self's experience of nature as absolute contingency, pure absurdity, an experience which is characterized by a root form of nausea of which physiological nausea is only one type.

The hero of the novel, Antoine Roquentin, is an individual involved passionately and reflectively in the problem of his own existence. Our brief considerations of the novel must center about the scene in which

Roquentin meets his own existence in an immediate experience of his own total contingency, his *being there*. The scene is a park. Roquentin has become absorbed in the existence, the very being, of his immediate surroundings. For a moment all reality external and secondary to the things about him has been put aside; he is faced with a brute givenness that clots his consciousness. Later, in his diary, Roquentin writes:

So I was in the park just now. The roots of the chestnut tree were sunk in the ground just under my bench. I couldn't remember it was a root any more. The words had vanished and with them the significance of things, their methods of use, and the feeble points of reference which men have traced on their surface. I was sitting, stooping forward, head bowed, alone in front of this black, knotty mass, entirely beastly, which frightened me. Then I had this vision.

It left me breathless. Never, until these last few days, had I understood the meaning of "existence." I was like the others, like the ones walking along the seashore, all dressed in their spring finery. I said, like them, "The ocean *is* green; that white speck up there *is* a seagull," but I didn't feel that it existed or that the seagull was an "existing seagull"; usually existence hides itself. It is there, around us, in us, it is *us*, you can't say two words without mentioning it, but you can never touch it. When I believed I was thinking about it, I must believe that I was thinking nothing, my head was empty, or there was just one word in my head, the word "to be."[6]

The crucial and qualitative transition, then, from existence as a concept, as a predicate, as a linguistic phenomenon, to existence as the experience of a radical contingency is the transition from the common-sense attitude to existential *pathos*. The original feeling that characterizes this transition is nausea. Sartre, in the same novel, attempts to describe the experience when Roquentin asks:

Had I dreamed of this enormous presence? It was there, in the garden, toppled down into the trees, all soft, sticky, soiling everything, all thick, a jelly. And I was inside, I with the garden. I was frightened, furious, I thought it was so stupid, so out of place, I hated this ignoble mess. Mounting up, mounting up as high as the sky, spilling over, filling everything with its gelatinous slither, and I could see depths upon depths of it reaching far beyond the limits of the garden, the houses, and Bouville, as far as the eye could reach. I was no longer in Bouville, I was nowhere, I was floating. I was not surprised, I knew it was the World, the naked World suddenly revealing itself, and I choked with rage at this gross, absurd being. You couldn't even wonder where all that sprang from, or how it was that a world came into existence, rather than nothingness. It didn't make sense, the World was everywhere, in front, behind. There had been nothing *before* it. Nothing. There had never been a moment in which it could not have existed. That was what worried me: of course there was no *reason* for this flowing larva to exist. *But it was impossible* for it not to exist. It was unthinkable: to imagine nothingness you had to be there already, in the midst of the World, eyes wide open and alive; nothingness was only an idea in my head, an existing idea floating in this immensity: this nothingness had not come *before* existence, it was an existence like any other and appeared after many others. I shouted "filth!

6 Sartre, J.-P., *Nausea*, London, 1949, 170-71.

what rotten filth!" and shook myself to get rid of this sticky filth, but it held fast and there was so much, tons and tons of existence, endless: I stifled at the depths of this immense weariness. And then suddenly the park emptied as through a great hole, the World disappeared as it had come, or else I woke up – in any case, I saw no more of it; nothing was left but the yellow earth around me out of which dead branches rose upward.[7]

Roquentin's experience of nausea is, for Sartre, the experience of what it means *to be*. The self as consciousness in a reality of total contingency is, in its nothingness, in flight from an instability it can never terminate to a synthesis it can never achieve. Were the self able to conquer its condition it could unite with the being of nature, but this, for Sartre, is precisely what the self cannot do. The union of self (consciousness) with non-reflective being (nature) would be the Absolute, God. Man is a being who seeks to be God, and is perpetually thrown back upon his finitude in decisive failure.

It is at this point that the core of Sartre's notion of existential freedom is to be grasped. Man, a failed God, is thrown back upon his own resources in a world in which the only directives and truths for him are those he himself creates. In one sense everything is lost – a permanent human nature, divine laws, certitude, salvation – and in virtue of this horrific loss, man is completely free: since he has lost everything, everything is possible to him. On a shattered and deserted stage, without script, director, prompter, or audience, the actor is free to improvise his own part.

THE THEORY'S CRITICAL RECEPTION

The reactions to this philosophy of freedom have been as lively and forceful and belligerent as the philosophy itself. The Marxists have called existentialism the "philosophy of the graveyard"; the work of Sartre is banned in the Soviet Union; it is on the Catholic Index; and, to stick our finger in a more logical pie, Sartre's existential philosophy has been called, by A. J. Ayer, the well known positivist, "a misuse of the verb 'to be.'" Thus the criticisms range from "danger" to "nonsense." The most that can be done here is to summarize the major criticisms of Sartre's conception of freedom. I shall do this by categorically listing seven major contentions made in these attacks on his position.

One, the self, far from being a "nothingness," is a stable, enduring structure which can achieve permanence and happiness in the world.

---

[7] *ibid.*, 180–81.

Two, the phenomenon of "choice" can be accounted for on purely psychological grounds, rather than making it an obscure metaphysical concept.

Three, even if Sartre has described an aspect of freedom, he has elevated this one aspect beyond all importance; there are many orders of human freedom – social, political, religious, and other – and each of these realms of freedom requires its own proper analysis.

Four, the dualism of self and nature in which freedom is grounded is an artificial one, which can be philosophically overcome or avoided by commencing analysis with society, and man within society, as the primal human situation.

Five, Sartre's descriptions have at best psychological and literary insight, and at worst they are simply meaningless in relation to any empirically meaningful criterion; this is not philosophy, but a poor mixture of sensationalistic literature and pseudo-psychology.

Six, freedom is not restricted to "extreme situations"; any analysis that forces such an artificial restriction ignores the multiple instances in the everyday world in which human beings are faced with problems of choice and self-determination – instances that are not in any way "extreme."

Seven, Sartre has given us not a philosophy of freedom but a pathology of freedom.

It is not possible here to expand upon these criticisms or to analyze their philosophical justification or lack of justification. Let us instead, for the sake of the argument, give Sartre the last word. In trying to formulate the answer he might give to these charges – or rather, to a thread common to most of them – let us try to look at reality through his eyes, try to grasp the whole thing as he has seen it.

The being of man is located primarily in his *being there*. You and I – apart from our special statuses, roles, or purposes at any moment, apart from the differences in our age, sex, personal history, religion, ideals, attitudes – apart from all this we are beings in reality. In an original and underivable manner we *are*, and the reality in which we *are* is philosophically prior to the content and methods of the special disciplines and the common-sense attitude – all of which take for granted, presuppose, our being.

This primal reality is an everlasting conflict, a dialectic in which man is in search of a synthesis, a peace and harmony, which he cannot, in principle, obtain. Within the bitter confines of this dialectic, man is condemned to act, to choose, to create what he is; but in the moment that he chooses, he feels the profound anguish of responsibility, for his choice involves all men. When the choice has been made, the dialectic continues, for choices are moments in the dialectic, never finalities. To be free is self-consciously to take upon oneself the burden of admitting and facing this condition, and acting within its confines. Condemned to the dialectic, we cannot choose it. But we can choose to acknowledge it, and to face its implications.

If the more than seven hundred closely printed pages of Sartre's *L'Être et le néant* could be reduced to a single sentence, that sentence would perhaps be this: the tragedy and the dignity of man lie in the dictum, to be is to be free.

PART TWO

AESTHETICS AND LITERATURE

7. *Toward a Phenomenology of the Aesthetic Object*

> "Art converts the natural attitude toward the experienced world into the transcendental attitude toward one's experience of the world."
>
> Fritz Kaufmann

What distinguishes phenomenological philosophizing from other avenues of approach is the central challenge it extends to the knower to hold himself back from, aside from, the "accepted" world of common sense: to hold in abeyance the judgments and decisions and attitudes that are characteristic of thought which begins with the "obvious" facts and existents of reality. If philosophy has a radical and unique core, it is that philosophizing at its finest is unwilling to go along with traditional presuppositions; it seeks the heart of the knowing of things. Philosophy is thus Kantian and Husserlian in so far as it examines the grounds of knowledge and distinguishes between the experienced world and our experience of the world. In the greatest sense philosophy brackets the natural attitude in order to penetrate to that order of knowledge in which distinctions between ground and object are possible. That consciousness, the ego, the *cogito* should then prove to be central to the entire inquiry is understandable and to be expected, for it is only through bringing our own awareness into the field of analysis that the pre-conditions of knowing can be explored.

The general tone of this order of procedure is set by Frédéric Amiel when he writes:

For myself, Philosophy is a manner of seizing things, a mode of perceiving reality. It does not create Nature, or Man, or God, but finds them and tries to understand them ... Philosophy is the ideal reconstruction of consciousness, it is consciousness understanding itself with all that it contains.[1]

Such a conception of phenomenology would seem to generalize its

---

[1] This translation is taken from "Phenomenology in France" by Jean Hering, contained in *Philosophic Thought in France and The United States* (edited by Marvin Farber), Buffalo, N.Y., 1950. The quotation is to be found also in *The Private Journal of Henri Frederic Amiel* (translated by Van Wyck Brooks and Charles Van Wyck Brooks), New York, 1935, 58.

purpose and structure beyond what Husserl intended as strict phenomenology; but it is along lines indicated by this generalization that I wish to discuss a phenomenological approach to certain aesthetic problems, in particular the notion of the "aesthetic object."

⟨I⟩

Aesthetic inquiry has a root level which transcends the history of aesthetics, theories of aesthetics, even semantical investigations of the meaning of crucial terms in the language of aesthetic theory. This root level considers such questions as What does it mean to speak of or refer to an "aesthetic *object*"? What determines the object-ness of the aesthetic work? What determines the stability and enduring unity of the aesthetic object? The aesthetician as philosopher is distinguished from the art critic, the literary analyst, the art appreciator, etc., because he is the only one to question the meaning and attempt to analyze the nature of the fundamental and ultimate art unity: the object in art. That the object *is*, that we may begin analysis of the art work since it *is* – such attitudes are commonly shared by the literary critic and art appreciator. The art critic proceeds to question the value and meaning of the art work, he may suggest criteria for such judgment, he may conclude that a specific art work fails, i.e., that it is not adequate in terms of some set of standards, but nowhere does he raise the question What does it mean to say that this is an "aesthetic object"? Nowhere does the critic ask How is the work of art constituted as an aesthetic object, i.e., as a unitary and stable structure presented to consciousness as a type of *thing*? What we may then call the natural attitude in art consists in the failure to recognize that there is an epistemological level of analysis in aesthetics and that this level is naively pre-supposed by the art critic.

A distinctive role for philosophical analysis in aesthetics is the exploration of the epistemological grounding of the aesthetic object both in the consciousness of the artist and the consciousness of the art appreciator. Such an exploration, however, is no more possible if we assume the nature of the art object than an epistemological analysis is possible if we remain naive realists. In short, both investigations become possible in principle with the bracketing of the natural attitude. The question is: What type of reduction is required here? In essence, a bracketing that will serve to isolate or restrict a part of the Given in experience, but not (and here we depart from Husserl) to claim "purity" for that which is isolated. Our thesis is that such "bracketing" does, as a matter of fact, take place in art creation and that an analogue of this reduction occurs in the appreciation of an art work, and further that such dual reduction is a phenomenological pre-condition for the possibility of an "aesthetic object." [2]

⟨ II ⟩

Art-creation may be understood as a revolt against the ordinary modes of cognizing reality. The artist is extraordinary in so far as he takes a magical [3] view of the content of experience. The very production of a work of art is possible only through concentrating upon a section of the screen of ordinary perception. The act of framing, of literally surrounding a canvas with sides of wood or metal, is the astonishing sorcery of the art apprentice. To frame a picture is to separate a part of experience from its context. This is the first meaning of reduction. To create, then, is to separate, to exclude, to deny a whole by intending a fraction of that whole. The daring and inventiveness of the artist lie in the risk he takes in rejecting both the traditional picture of experience and the

---

[2] To avoid confusing the notion of the "reduction" we are expounding here with Husserl's *epoché*, we will term what we are describing "reflexive" analysis; hence, reflexive reduction. The choice of the word "reflexive" is not arbitrary; it is suggested by the sort of philosophizing Sartre does in *L'Être et le néant*. As Hering points out (*op. cit.*, 73), much of Sartre's analysis poses the "problem of perception, representation, memory, and of numerous analogous problems, *in terms of consciousness*." (*ibid.*). This is primarily what we mean in speaking of "reflexive" analysis. (I believe that Gilbert Varet was the first to suggest this terminology in regard to Sartre's work (*L'Ontologie de Sartre*, Paris, 1948)). However, Hering says that much of Sartre's analyses "belong to genuine phenomenology" (*op. cit.*, 73). It is at this point that serious difficulties arise in attempting to differentiate between reflexive phenomenology and Husserlian phenomenology. I think it is true that Sartre is making use of a *kind* of phenomenology, but the important thing is to understand what order of phenomenology is involved and what one means by a "genuine phenomenology." The failure to differentiate between Husserl's *epoché* and Sartre's "reflexive" reduction leads Helmut Kuhn to classify Sartre as a Husserlian phenomenologist. Kuhn writes: "Sartre, less original than Heidegger, is to a still higher degree a typical phenomenologist of the Husserl tradition. His descriptive analyses of the nature of sense perception, of the body which the individual not only 'has' but 'is,' and of the individual's relationship to 'the other' belong among the finest specimens of phenomenological research." (*Encounter With Nothingness*, Hinsdale, Ill., 1959, 132). I have presented my reasons for opposing this interpretation in *A Critique of Jean-Paul Sartre's Ontology*, University of Nebraska Studies, New Series No. 6, March 1951.

[3] Sartre writes: "the categories of 'suspicious,' of 'alarming,' designate the magical insofar as it is lived by consciousness, insofar as it urges consciousness to live it. The abrupt passage from a rational apprehension of the world to a perception of the same world as magical, if it is motivated by the object itself and if it is accompanied by a disagreeable element, is horror; if it is accompanied by an agreeable element it will be wonder." (*The Emotions: Outline of A Theory*, New York, 1948, 85). "In emotion, consciousness is degraded and abruptly transforms the determined world in which we live into a magical world." (*ibid.*, 83). The traditional "emotionalism" of the artist is the foundation, then, of his "magical" existence.

traditional way of comprehending that experience. In this view the art object becomes the resultant ultimately of an act or acts of segregation and placement. But an example may be of aid here.

Taking the drama as an art-object, we have a group of scenes ordered into acts which are in turn integrated into a whole that can be observed as a unity by the audience. If the drama be *Hamlet*, we have a set of incidents associated together in such a way as to form a story that describes those events and, in describing them, sets forth the meanings and significances they contain. But the telling of Hamlet's story, the enactment of the drama, forces us to focus our attention upon a set of happenings and meanings that prevail apart from the rest of our experience. When *Hamlet* was written, the playwright constructed his play by selecting from the mass of possibilities just those aspects which he wished to set apart. The very act of setting apart, here, is the artistic venture. The non-artist is he who fails not only to effect a reduction from the whole of experience but also to recognize the meaning of such a reduction. The setting apart is not haphazard: it is self-conscious, figured, and permanent in the sense that what is set apart or reduced is given form and endurance.

Not only does the artist have to bracket the natural world to secure his "yield" of the art-object, but the very fact that the art-object was originally made possible only by the reduction carries with it the associated quality which perpetuates its "reduced" nature; not only the artist but the art appreciator as well must bracket the rest of experience. Thus, the audience at a showing of *Hamlet* (to continue our example) must recognize that a play is being produced. In traditional theatre, the stage is the frame and the audience is expected to recognize the stage not merely as separating the players and play from the audience but as being a tacit agreement between speakers and listeners that one group may communicate with the other group only through form, i.e., only through the play itself. The failure to recognize this agreement – the failure to reduce – is observed frequently in children attending the theatre: they cry out and must be hushed, they see the action as an adult might see a street scene. The child must be forewarned about his conduct not because he will annoy others but because the curtain must be respected; the play is in the form and the form demands reduction. But the adult may also fracture the bond of reduction, and when he does, we say that he was "carried away," that he "forgot himself." The viewer of *Hamlet* may thus be so involved in the drama that he forgets that it is "only a play" and cries out toward the end: "Don't drink it! It's poisoned!" But his breech of accepted behavior lies not in trying to alter the actions of Hamlet when it is understood that those actions are pre-determined by the course of the play itself, but rather in the failure to realize that what we seek in art can be given to us only if we permit and enact the reduction which makes art possible.[4]

⟨ III ⟩

If reflexive reduction is the pre-condition of an art work, reflexive reconstruction is no less necessary for the being of the aesthetic object. Reflexive reconstruction will be taken to mean in its widest sense the intentional act of synthesis by which the aesthetic object achieves unity and life. What is synthesized is a complexus of meanings: the artist intends the meaning of his work. Such intention may be highly self-conscious and critical, or it may have a minimum of cognitive direction. The act of synthesis, however, unifies both the meanings intended and the content of the work in the artist's primary decision to constitute his work as a synthetic unity. But the reduced elements of the art work must be re-constituted as a part of reality, albeit a special part, an independent unity. To understand the need for reconstruction we must realize that in itself the art-object is only a mass of possibilities: a potential for the viewer. It is only when we observe the work as a formed whole that we are experiencing an art work. Apart from the intention, then, the art work is *nothing*. The nothingness of the art work is recognized in many ways: in the multiple and variant interpretations of it by various critics and ages, in the problem of what the art work is apart from its audience and what it can be if in principle there should be no audience possible. Is the art work a unity in its utter solitude, in the confines of the museum without guests, the room that permits no entrance? Do we mean by the art work this complexus of

[4] Perhaps the physical location of the art work inspires part of the reduction. It is interesting to note that many of Sartre's scenes, both in his literary and philosophical works, are associated with parks and are replete with benches and chestnut trees. The park is the point of separation from the rest of the world; in it we are reduced from the business world, the academic world, the realm of other worries. We go to the park for greenery and release, for a soothing contemplation, and for love; yet for Sartre the bracketing out of other worlds in the park produces a perverse effect: it is in the park that the Other *looks* at us, that we are made an object for the Other's subjectivity. It is in the park, seated on the bench, that existence, being itself, overwhelms us. But even in nausea the brackets of the park make possible what is akin to artistic awareness: a reflexive consciousness that momentarily isolates the park from the huge givenness of reality and permits the artist to achieve a fresh mode of cognition.

canvas, wood, smears of color, and areas of shade and light? Without initial intention by the artist these elements are only scattered and empty qualities; with the intending of the work arises the being of the aesthetic object as unified: the canvas and smears of oil become qualities *of an object*. However, the meanings which the artist intends in the art work achieve only temporary unity, for continual reconstruction is necessary. The art work is the idea of the artist, and the meanings comprising that idea must be given new life: the art work must be perpetuated in intention if it is not to lapse into nothingness. Just as reduction had a dual aspect: the reduction of artist and art appreciator, so reconstruction has two sides. The intended unity which the artist constitutes originally in his art work is taken up by the audience: they, too, must reconstruct for themselves the meaning-complex at hand, the art-object. Thus, art commences with the act of intention on the part of the artist and depends for its existence upon the audience which experiences it.[5]

It is at this point that the entire problem of understanding the art work arises, for if the reader must himself reconstruct the meanings of the novelist, how can he be certain that his reconstruction is correct: that he has, in fact, reconstructed what the author intended? But this uncertainty is the necessary separation of the artist from society, from his audience. The artist has no guarantee that he will be understood; more frequently he knows or suspects before creation that he will probably be misunderstood. Yet the tie between the artist and his audience is absolute and binding, for it is only in virtue of the reconstruction by the audience that the art work has a chance of survival. The artist has created something that cannot stand by itself, for in

---

[5] Sartre writes: "The creative act is only an incomplete and abstract moment in the production of a work. If the author existed alone he would be able to write as much as he liked; the work as *object* would never see the light of day and he would either have to put down his pen or despair. But the operation of writing implies that of reading as its dialectical correlative and these two connected acts necessitate two distinct agents. It is the conjoint effort of author and reader which brings upon the scene that concrete and imaginary object which is the work of the mind. There is no art except for and by others.

"Reading seems, in fact, to be the synthesis of perception and creation (Sartre adds in a footnote here: "The same is true in different degrees regarding the spectator's attitude before other works of art (paintings, symphonies, statues, etc.)"). It supposes the essentiality of both the subject and the object. The object is essential because it is strictly transcendent, because it imposes its own structures, and because one must wait for it and observe it; but the subject is also essential because it is required not only to disclose the object (that is, to make *there be* an object) but also so that this object might *be* (that is, to produce it). In a word, the reader is conscious of disclosing in creating, of creating by disclosing." (*What is Literature?*, New York, 1949, 42–43). The constructive role of the art appreciator is thus clear: "the imagination of the spectator has not only a regulating function, but a constitutive one .... it is called upon to recompose the beautiful object beyond the traces left by the artist." (*ibid.*, 47).

addition to the original ordering of his intention, the art work requires the sympathetic re-ordering of the audience. Each art work is, then, a set of meanings for which an infinite number of reconstructions are possible. In itself, i.e., apart from the reconstructor, the art work is dead. The unread novel, the forgotten novel, the ignored novel – all are diseased with a kind of catatonic suspension. The novel stands waiting for the mind of the reader. The books on the stall are there dead-for-a-time, and the power of the reader is the power of revival, almost of resurrection.

〈IV〉

There is a special aspect of reflexive reconstruction which requires separate attention, an aspect which might be termed "intentional perception." In ordinary perception – simply looking at – I passively see what is in the field of my vision: that chair, that person, this book. But it is possible so to direct my active attention that, via a reduction of this book on this table, from the ordinary seeing of the book on the table I am able to frame a "scene," a freshly observed relationship which can best be understood by imagining the content of the field of vision to be a still life: Book on Table. Such intentional perception – the framing of otherwise passive aspects of what we experience – takes place quite naturally on many occasions: "Look at that sunset!" we are told, and we look not simply at what is before us, but at what is before us as it has been ordered into *a scene*, an object for scrutiny, an area of beauty to be examined as area. We have fancifully framed the sunset we were told to witness, and we have elevated it from part of the Given to a special fragment of the Given: however momentarily, obscurely, and inadequately, we have created what approximates an art-object.

Intentional perception is possible as a mode of general perception. We are surrounded by potential scenes if only we can snare them between our brackets and give them intentional unity. The reduction and reconstruction which are the grounds for such unity may be understood as aspects of a generalized phenomenology of consciousness in which are located the roots of art-creation, art-appreciation, and the fundamental relationship of the artist to his product.

8. Phenomenology and the Theory of Literature

I should like to begin with a declaration not of principles but of contents, a declaration that is not a manifesto but a manifest of conceptual cargo. The theme of this paper is the relationship between philosophy and literature; its thesis is that the microcosm given to us in a literary work is founded on and in turn illuminates the transcendental structure of common-sense experience. I wish to explore this foundation of daily life by way of phenomenological philosophy. The outcome is a recommendation for a philosophically grounded theory of literature. I shall do my best, however, to get through customs an undeclared commitment to reality, an insistence on the primordial, "originary" givenness of our world. In this sense, the task of both literature and philosophy is the reconstruction of mundane existence.

Apart from the warfare between philosophy and literature and the skirmishes between philosophy and criticism, there is a tension between these disciplines which is the result of a confusion concerning their relevance for each other. The field of philosophy of literature is ill-defined; the study of philosophy in literature is at best rather dimly focused. In the last, for example, it is sometimes held that the study of so-called "philosophical literature" offers a non-technical kind of introduction to philosophy to the student whose primary concern is literature or fine arts. In such a course, presumably, the student is able to locate the great issues of philosophy without having to be overly bothered with matters of formal logic, epistemology, ontology, or axiology. The professional philosopher sometimes treats such a course as a diluted substitute for the "real thing"; accordingly, he may tend to patronize such efforts. Since the relationship between literature and philosophy is vague to begin with, suspicions proliferate. And whatever good will may be realized within the band of teachers of philosophy is sometimes threatened by the resentments of those outside. Academic banking restrictions are brought into play: credit toward a major may be given or withheld for a course taken in another department. In the midst of these scandals we must search for order. What relevance does philosophy have for literature, and what gift does literature hold for philosophy?

Let me begin with a distinction between philosophy of literature and philosophy in literature. Very simply, "of" leads to problems in formal aesthetics, "in" marks a dimension of literature which informs us philosophically. "Of" raises questions about the categories of literature and their relationship to the mode of being of an art work. "In" *presents* the realized work and summons us to an appreciation of its implicit philosophical achievement. Although these titles are often interchanged as synonymous, I propose to hold to this difference of purpose and level between philosophy of and philosophy in literature. An immediate advantage of the distinction is that it permits a reassessment of the relationship between literature and philosophy. Although there are many novels that qualify by most criteria as philosophical literature, they are philosophical to the extent that they present a fundamental critique of reality, a concern with the totality of what there is. Philosophy arises in literature when the question raised is that of Being. Another way of saying this is that philosophy in literature has an ontological placement; the author is not asking about aspects of reality but about the ground of reality. The study of philosophy in literature is an effort to make explicit what is implicitly sedimented in the art work. Philosophy of literature may concern itself with the concept of reality as dealt with in literary works, but the discipline of philosophy in literature turns to the very experience given in art and attempts its reconstruction. Far from being a dilution of "real" philosophy, it is its living extension.

Ultimately, the "of" and "in" distinction ends, as all such relationships must, in a root junction. The problems of an aesthetic proper to literature merge with those encountered in a study of philosophy in literature. But keeping these domains separate for at least part of our way may enhance the journey. It may help us to understand what it is that certain literary works have which leads us to call them philosophical. For surely, literature is not philosophical merely because it discusses ethical choice, cosmic destiny, or the meaning of temporality and death; it is philosophical when it returns us to the phenomena of our being. It is not a matter of grandiose themes but of concern for what is given in our experience of reality as such in its fundamental modalities. The philosophy of literature may tend to obscure this concern; it leads away, at the beginning at least, from the phenomena, and this means necessarily that it is tempted to abandon the literary work in favor of theory. An *a fortiori* argument of a sort could be made out for the relationship between philosophy and criticism. What is at issue is precisely the old antagonism between philosophy and literature. Just as philosophy of literature may be accused of sacrificing the novel or the poem for ulterior passions, so a philosophically grounded or oriented theory of literature or approach to criticism may be rejected as barren, for all its presumption. Thus Allen Tate speaks of the "fenced-in apriorism of the merely philosophical approach" and says, "Its conclusions are impressive and are usually stated at length, but I have never seen one of them that increased my understanding of the XXVIIIth Canto of the *Paradiso,* or even of "Locksley Hall." [1] If this reaction is justified for the style of philosophical analysis involved in philosophy of literature, it does not follow that it holds for what may be done in studying philosophy in literature. Mr. Tate's own philosophical sophistication is reason enough to distrust his distrust; but nothing can be gained by pushing this point. Instead, I propose to illustrate the relevance of philosophy for literature – even philosophy at its a prioristic worst – by investigating a concrete problem of philosophy in literature. The problem is that of the literary microcosm. I shall restrict myself to the novel form.

⟨ I ⟩

It is a commonplace to speak of a novel presenting a microcosm; but the meaning of this commonplace is far from clear, precisely because the meaning of "microcosm" is far from clear. A novel presents us with a little world which is said to be a reflection in some sense of the big world of real life. "Reflect," "mirror," "represent," are all variants for a central term of nexus between two domains held to be isomorphic in certain respects. Indeed, this relationship of microcosm to life is sometimes taken as a necessary part of the definition of all art. Erich Kahler, for example, defines art as a "human activity which explores, and hereby creates, new reality in a suprarational, visional manner

---

[1] Tate, A., "The Hovering Fly," in *The Man of Letters in the Modern World: Selected Essays, 1928–1955,* New York, 1955, 151.

and presents it symbolically ... as a microcosmic whole signifying a macrocosmic whole." [2] Despite the general reliance on "microcosm" as a central term of discourse in aesthetics and in criticism as well, I insist on a further, more careful delineation of its scope and signification. In what sense, then, does a literary work give us a world?

A typology of elements comprising even the minimal features of a world would exceed the limits of my powers and your patience. I propose to restrict myself for the moment to one nuclear feature of any possible world, its *horizonal* character. Things, events, states of affairs are said to be "in" the world. The epistemologist's dearest possessions, his desk and his chair, are said to be in his room, and we know that his room is in his house, his house in the town, and that all of this leads eventually to the world, which contains them all. The movement from chair to all the rest is horizonal. Taking the world as an outer limit, its horizon is the condition for bounding what can be experienced. For something to be "in" the world means that we can grasp it through the primal horizon of its being. Everything experienced in this world is more or less familiar, more or less strange to us; but the familiar and the strange are not more or less "in" the world. Instead we should say that familiarity and strangeness are themselves comprehensible only through the horizon of their being. My world includes zones or regions of intimacy, familiarity, and strangeness. I move conceptually and conatively from those persons I call my father and my mother, my wife and my children, my friends and my acquaintances, to others known about but not known. And there are those I shall never come to know as well as those I shall never even know about. Yet all of them are comprehensible in terms of the world which includes them as actualities or possibilities. This world I grasp only as that matrix within whose horizon persons and events appear and transpire. It is not the world that gives itself to me, but its horizon.

A thing or event, then, is horizonal at the outset. For something to be or to transpire is for it to have regional or zonal character. Meeting my friend is an event which has whatever temporal and spatial features it possesses because time and space are of the world. Saddened or pleased by his conversation, I confront my friend within a context of what may please or sadden, and that context is placed within the horizon, ultimately, of our friendship in a life which is a fragment of all that there is. His news, his ideas, his projects are aspects of my friend's

[2] Kahler, E., "What is Art?" in *Problems in Aesthetics* (ed. by Morris Weitz), New York, 1959, 171.

existence because that existence is in movement toward whatever fulfillment his life is to have. Fulfillment is in its very texture horizonal. It does not follow, however, that experiencing something within the horizon of the world involves a self-conscious awareness of horizon. In everyday life the horizon of the world is taken for granted, and this very taken-for-grantedness is itself a crucial part of our experience of the world. I hope to develop this theme later; the immediate issue is horizon as a root clue to the kind of world given to us in the literary work of art.

It is certainly common to speak of the world of Thomas Mann or William Faulkner, and it is sensible to refer to the world of *The Magic Mountain* or *Light in August*. Perhaps it is not as obvious that these usages are different. The world of Thomas Mann as a literary figure can be comprehended only through his writings, and then we mean ordinarily that his novels and stories presuppose a certain outlook. And we mean that while Mann was alive, we expected certain things of him, we expected him to enrich his concerns, fulfill his promises, and develop his manifold talents through that outlook. To know the world of Thomas Mann, in this sense, means to understand his concern with problems of representation, mediation, and historicity. Any discerning reader of Mann knows that his works deal with the artist's relationship to spirit and nature, that temporality and death are leading themes, just as he knows that leitmotifs and patterns of stylistic recurrence enrich his creations. The world of Mann here is synonymous with the mind of Mann. But the world of *The Magic Mountain* is something else. And here we encounter directly the problem of the literary microcosm. In what sense does such a work as *The Magic Mountain* present us with a world?

Earlier we dodged the problem of establishing a typology of elements essential to the concept of world. A little more responsibility is necessary now. But I intend to be as evasive as possible, which means as superficial as possible. The world of *The Magic Mountain* contains a host of constants: the characters and action are temporally and spatially bounded, their affairs constitute a history supported by the narrative, the characters grow older and, in some instances, die; in the time that we follow their lives they suffer and exult, they explore a great range of emotional and conceptual reality, and finally, they are enmeshed in the symbolic forms of existence and transcendence. So far these elements are also true of our own world. The differentia, superficially at least, are not hard to find. The world of *The Magic Mountain* is a fictional, not a real world, and this means that the constants we have located have at best "As-If" status. The history told is not an account of events that ever "really" happened, the characters that inhabit this imaginary world are not people who ever actually lived, and so the whole thing is a remarkable fabrication, a studied deceit, in short, a fiction. The trouble with this account of the literary microcosm is simply that it will not do.

An acceptable account of the concept of world must include some distinction between "real" and "imaginary," between "fictive" and "actual." To say that the difference between the world of a novel and the world of daily life is that the one is synthetic, the other historical, is to presuppose the very problem at issue. But above all, what is taken for granted in this account is "world" itself. To do better here means to confront these presuppositions and disentangle their roots. As a start, I submit the following characteristics of a literary microcosm which I think are essential features: first, a temporal-spatial matrix of some order is necessary for the characters and action. Second, the story presenting the action presupposes that this matrix has functional limits which set off what occurred prior to the story told as well as what might occur after the story ends. Third, the action involved is action *for* the characters. Their world is interpreted by them. Its meanings are disclosed originally through their action. Fourth, that there is and that there continues to be a coherent reality for the characters throughout the narrative, a reality that is intersubjective, that embraces their lives, is a necessary condition for the possibility of their world. And fifth, underlying every possible element of the literary work is the horizon which defines and limits the world created.

These *a prioris* of the literary microcosm present the image of a world interpreted from the outset by the characters within it. Our analysis of their actions is therefore necessarily a second order translation. We interpret their interpretations; we encounter their encounters; we subscribe to or deny their faith. The world of the literary microcosm, then, is a *pre-interpreted* one, to follow the terminology of Alfred Schutz. And to see how this is the case, we must consider the structure of human action. Unfortunately (to my mind at least), the paradigmatic image of action for our time is external, physical movement. An act is taken usually as an event which gears into the external world, something seen or felt or heard, something that moves something else, or something that causes a change. The blow struck, the ball thrown, the shout voiced, the order announced – these are clearly acts, and

their positive ring is unmistakable. The soldier, the athlete, the states-
man, the entrepreneur, the adventurer are all typically men of action.
The poet, the philosopher, the artist, the dreamer remain spectators.
They are contemplatives. An act, in these terms, is primarily something
done whose effect can be marked in the world around us, a public
affair. The trick now is not to say that poets are also men of action,
but to reconsider the very meaning of action presupposed in the criterion taken for granted in common-sense life. I accept Max Weber's
definition. "In 'action,'" he writes, "is included all human behaviour
when and in so far as the acting individual attaches a subjective
meaning to it. Action in this sense may be either overt or purely
inward or subjective; it may consist of positive intervention or passively acquiescing in the situation. Action is social in so far as, by virtue of
the subjective meaning attached to it by the acting individual (or
individuals), it takes account of the behaviour of others and is thereby
oriented in its course." [3] For Weber, "subjective meaning" refers to the
interpretive understanding by the actor of the meaning of his own act;
it has absolutely nothing to do with personal or psychological attitudes.[4] In this sense, the action which characterizes the literary microcosm is subjectively defined by the characters. And as we take up their
story we enter a world pre-interpreted by its fictive inhabitants.

  If action is disclosed through interpretation, interpretation in turn
points back to its horizonal ground. The meaning an actor bestows
upon his act is defined by his intent. And his intent is guided and
circumscribed by the horizon of value and purpose toward which he
moves. But values are located as worldly, as part of the framework of
our lives. Whether they are held to be transcendent or immanent is
irrelevant here. Valuing takes place within a pre-established horizon
of the world. Intent, then, is intent *toward* some aspect of the real. And
this holds for every dimension of awareness: thinking, remembering,
imagining, dreaming, and feeling. The holiness of Father Zossima, the
lust and buffoonery of Feodor Karamazov, and the divergent styles of
being of his sons are comprehensible only as they unfold within the
horizon of the world they project. That world has its antecedent
history of which we know relatively little, and it has a future which is
equally obscure. But past and future are related to each other by the
common reality they bound. Zossima's past and Alyosha's future are
perspectives of a single horizon interior to the novel. That we as readers

[3] Weber, M., *The Theory of Social and Economic Organization*, New York, 1947, 88.
[4] See chapter 13.

comprehend these temporal dimensions is a crucial yet secondary fact, for we are witnesses to a world born of its own generative power and sustained by its own scaffolding.

Yet the remarkable thing is that we *do* grasp the literary microcosm as a world, understand immediately that the story it tells is *worldly*, and through a decisive act of intuitive extrapolation come to share its axial horizon. When we say that a literary work illuminates our own lives, we trustingly presuppose that our intuitive sense of world is warranted. And even if we cannot account fully for the nature of the literary microcosm, the assumption is that we certainly know what we mean by our own world. This assumption must now be placed in serious question. Our description of some of the essential features of the microcosm must be matched by an examination of the fundamental structure of the world of daily life. Out of this confrontation between literature and life our conclusions and recommendations will arise.

⟨ II ⟩

Each of us in one dimension of his being is a common-sense man living in the daily world. As Kierkegaard puts it, each of us has "an interest in this big enterprise they call reality." [5] Yet we need no teacher to inform us that there is a world, that there is daily life, and that we are part of this affair. We receive instruction regarding its elements, its component parts, its cunning machinery; never are we taught that there *is* reality. This strange omission in our education is more than instructive, for it provides a clue to the horizon of our being. Whatever questions are raised about the world are raised within it. We may doubt some part of our experience, however great, but our doubt leaves standing the undoubted framework in terms of which a solution can be recognized and accepted. Behind, beyond, over and against even the potentially doubtful is the unquestionable ground in contrast to which the dubious is dubious. The central thrust of our lives is believingly toward reality; and that our belief in this reality is warranted is never, fundamentally, an object for inspection. The horizon through which the world is given to us is our natural, unselfconscious believing in daily life. This believing-in is the taken-for-grantedness I mentioned earlier. A quick inventory may prove helpful.[6]

[5] Kierkegaard, S., *Repetition*, Princeton, 1941, 114.
[6] In what follows we are indebted to the work of Alfred Schutz. See his "On Multiple Realities," *Philosophy and Phenomenological Research*, V, June 1945, 533–576; "Choosing Among Projects of Action," *ibid.*, XII, December 1951, 161–184; "Common-Sense and Scientific Interpretation of Human Action," *ibid.*, XIV, September 1953, 1–38.

As a common-sense man in daily life, I take it for granted that the world of which I am part is real, essentially trustworthy, reasonably disclosed by the normal senses, and continuously coherent. Furthermore, I take it for granted that this world is perceived in much the same way by all other normal men. I take it for granted that this world has a past as well as a future; that my fellow men, like myself, are born and will die; that just as there are those who occupied this world before I did and just as there are those with whom I share this world now, so there will be those who will follow after me. The startling aspect of this incomplete list is not the set of statements included; it is rather that the taken-for-grantedness of these truths is itself taken for granted. Here we come to a kind of bed-rock of belief.

Whether we call it "animal faith" or simple horse sense, there is not the slightest doubt that belief in reality is overpoweringly universal and indelibly a part of daily life. Often, the student in an introductory course in philosophy smirks at Cartesian doubt and privately unseats Bishop Berkeley. The high point of the course comes for him when he learns that several philosophers died insane. The teasing possibility that perhaps after all, despite everything, reality might be problematic at its very root – that possibility cannot withstand the triumph of common sense. In the end, the idea that a philosopher might be telling the truth about reality is as incongruous as the image of Wanda Landowska playing rock and roll.

It is at least certain that the common-sense world has constants of its own, including this utter faith in itself. Again following Alfred Schutz, we may designate these universal features of daily life "metaphysical constants" for human existence. Being born into the world, being born of mothers unique to us, being born into a world already inhabited as well as interpreted by others, having to grow older in this world and having to die in it are all inescapable realities; and it is just as true to say that as metaphysical constants they have absolutely nothing to do with obstetricians, gereatricians, census takers, or undertakers. Instead, they illuminate and are in turn illuminated by the cardinal horizon of our being in the world. They refer not to public affairs of state but to an ontological state of affairs. They have to do with our being as such, and they form the anatomy of our world.

The metaphysical constants underlying common-sense life are relevant to our theme in two ways. First, it is characteristic of daily life that in it these constants are taken for granted; their philosophical significance lies sedimented in our experience. Second, the interpretation of these constants requires a distinction between two aspects of human existence: the directly given world each of us possesses is radically different from the derivative world we gain from natural science, history, and sociology. Following the second point will lead us back to the first. A study of Helmholtz's *Physiological Optics* tells me nothing about the visual experience I have in its qualitative immediacy. Nor will a more recent treatise help. There is a decisive gap between my color experience and a scientific account of its causal structure. My color world is first of all *mine*; it is not mediated by expert knowledge of its conditions, nor is the theory of vision in any way relevant to its presentational validity. It is only in a derivative sense that the case of my color experience falls under the general scientific category of visual perception. In one sense, then, my color world is a privileged one: the total scope and content given in it possess an experiential depth that is independent of subsequent theoretical explanation. What holds for vision holds for my entire world. The particulars of my existence are not decided on by some conceptual apparatus of the discipline of history or sociology or psychology; they are primordially given states of affairs uniquely and irrevocably *mine*. To say that they are mine means first of all that they are given to me through a certain vantage point, a certain location. My body, in fact, is the point of reference in terms of which perceptual phenomena achieve location and placement. And once again, my body is an immediately intuited reality, not the product of a sophisticated knowledge of physiology. To say that I possess a qualitatively given, privileged domain of immediate experience is to suggest that this primordial given has precedence of a certain order over the derivative world of science. That precedence must be clarified.

Just as action has been taken in our time as external, physical efficacy, so the quality of immediately given experience has been subsumed under the causal categories of natural scientific explanation. What is often referred to as the "real" explanation of a state of affairs involves a reduction of something given to an appraisal of its antecedent conditions and relations. My sorrow is explained when an account is given for what is said to have produced it; my anguish is understood when earlier events in my life are located and classified; my emotional reality is illuminated through a schematism of stimulus-response mechanisms. However subtle these accounts may be, they have in common a refusal to consider phenomena as given, as integral presentations of consciousness which have sovereign status. A vast genetic fallacy informs much of contemporary psychology, and it is in reaction against that total style of analysis that we speak of the primacy of immediate experience. The frantic search for origins, conditions, causal grounds, and neurological antecedents goes on at the expense of ignoring the richness and complexity of concrete awareness. Just as action in Weber's language includes the full intentional life of the subject, so awareness itself has an architectonic built of meaning. It is within the horizon of my world that all scientific and historical determinations are ultimately grasped, translated, and acted upon. Causal-genetic analyses themselves come to be understood in my world. Of course, this understanding may be severely limited, but then it is this stricture which colors my projection of the world. The attainment of all disciplines is destined to be brought back to the sphere of immediate existence. In this sense daily life maintains precedence over all the rest. Within its limits are the conditions for the validity of our lives.

The metaphysical constants, then, apply to the immediately given reality of daily life, not to the derivative world of natural science. And at the same time their application is to a forceful, "thick" experience, the world of our errors and our confusions as well as of our victories and insights. If science gives us a "clean" reality, the world *we* begin with is fringed with torment. And part of the complexity of daily life is that the constants of birth and death and the rest are elements of a taken-for-granted existence. The horizonal features of these constants are sedimented in immediate experience. This means that being born into the world and dying in it are thematic to our lives in a completely *a priori* sense. We cannot be taught what birth or death mean because any teaching presupposes that we already know. At best our experience occasions this learning. We teach ourselves to be able to say what we know but cannot utter. In Platonic terms, the metaphysical constants are themes for recollection.

We have before us now at least some of the essential features of two worlds, that of daily life and the literary microcosm. Their convergence is the clue to their disjunction. Together they present the world of immediately given experience; separately they bring into relief the conditions *a priori* which make common-sense life possible. Both worlds are horizonal, both presuppose a taken-for-granted set of elements, both are defined axially by metaphysical constants. What, then, distinguishes the fictive from the real world? I shall answer this indirectly by exploring a certain relationship between the reader of a novel and the world he encounters in his reading. To enter the world of *The Brothers Karamazov* requires a peculiar decision to suspend our ordinary believing in our own world. "Suspend" is an unhappy term here, but a further account of what is involved may overcome the difficulties. My decision to enter the world of Dostoievski's novel is essentially a resolve to set aside the ordinary flow of daily life, by attending only to the horizon given to me in the literary work. The real world, of course, continues to exist. Suspending my belief in it does not in any way involve denying it. Rather, in shifting the focus of my attending to another world, I bring into view the continuing awareness of my thinking, my anticipating, my remembering, my wondering. It is now the very structure of these activities of consciousness which becomes the object of my concern. I am not suggesting that reading a novel means becoming introspective about that reading. Just the opposite. There is an extrospective character to our attending to *The Brothers*. But in that complex awareness we call reading, there is presented directly the continuing consciousness of the world we encounter. Our own world has not been negated or cancelled; it persists. But it continues as methodically out of play in order to make possible at each moment the literary microcosm.

My decision to suspend my believing in common-sense reality is the key to the creation of the fictive world. The world of the novel is not imaginary but real in its way, a way that is made possible by the activity of fictive consciousness. Consciousness does not discover a fictive being in *The Brothers*; rather, it fictively thinks that being.[7] In this sense, to enter the world Dostoievski created is to participate in a suspension of one attitude and the bringing into focus of another. This transposition marks the difference between fiction and life. There are no criteria which enable us to differentiate the literary microcosm from the human world; there is an *experience* of transposition in our modes of attending to what there is. And in this fundamental change in awareness the illumination of common-sense existence is rendered possible in a radical manner. The achievement of fictive consciousness is the revealing of the transcendental structure of daily life. And this was the thesis I set out to present. That transcendental structure consists of the horizon of daily life and the *a prioris* which attend it: the metaphysical constants of our being. What we ordinarily take for granted in daily life is rendered explicit by the constructive activity of fictive consciousness. Far from the literary microcosm reflecting the world, it reveals to us the experiential foundation of our world. In a moment

[7] In speaking of "fictive consciousness" I am adapting the terminology of Dorion Cairns.

I shall turn to a final illustration of this thesis, but now a methodological interlude is necessary.

Sooner or later all titles must be justified. Curiously enough, the title for this paper is "Phenomenology and the Theory of Literature." Those of you who are acquainted with the writings of Edmund Husserl, the founder of the phenomenological movement, must be wondering when I will come to a discussion of his views in the exotic language that is his hallmark. And those who are unacquainted with phenomenology must have wondered all along when I was going to explain what it means. The apology I owe both plaintiffs is lost in a private euphoria, for I consider it a triumph to have fulfilled a promise I made to myself, to present phenomenology without phenomenological jargon. Apart from this sentence, my paper contains no mention of intentionality, phenomenological reduction, epoché, noesis, noema, and the rest of the phenomenologist's stock in trade. Instead of talking about phenomenology, I have tried, within very modest limits, to give some example of its style and direction.

But with regard to the last part of my title, I find myself thinking of a course in mathematical logic taught by a famous philosopher. Toward the end of a semester devoted completely to technical considerations, a student suddenly asked, "But Professor Whitehead, what has all of this to do with death?" To pick up that magic thread which will lead us to the theory of literature, we must return to an earlier distinction. This procedure is in perfect keeping with the established dictum that whenever a philosopher cannot answer a question, he draws a distinction. In this case, the distinction is between philosophy in literature and philosophy of literature. Our discussion of the literary microcosm and the world of daily life concerned problems of philosophy in literature. The *a prioris* underlying the very concept of world were given in and through the literary work. Now, if we were to explore the aesthetic issues relevant to the world of the novel, we would then confront the questions of a philosophy of literature. The ontological status of the microcosm, the sense in which literature gives us knowledge, the truth of the art work – these are typical problems for a philosophy of literature. The central contribution of phenomenology to this domain would be a clarification of the essential terms, concepts, and meanings involved in aesthetic experience through a tracing back of their epistemic genesis in the activity of consciousness. The dominant concern would be a description and understanding of the constitution of the aesthetic object. The *a prioris* located in the novel would find their rationale in a phenomenological philosophy of literature.

At the same time, such a discipline would be able to provide a grounding for a conceptual framework valid for the whole range of literary art. Such a framework would be what I understand by a theory of literature. And here, if I interpret these authors correctly, I find myself in agreement with Wellek and Warren. A theory of literature for them is a "rationale for the study of literature." [8] Although they do not utilize a phenomenological approach to their problems, and despite their distinct, though appreciative criticism of the work of the Polish phenomenologist Roman Ingarden, who has written on *The Literary Artwork*, I still think that Wellek and Warren have made an important advance toward the ideal of a philosophically grounded theory of literature. Rather than attempt the overwhelming task of expounding a full typology of the problems involved in such a theory, or outlining the procedures of a phenomenological philosophy of literature, I have followed a more modest course. In turning to a concrete problem of philosophy in literature, I have sought to illustrate the relevance of philosophy for literature. And it is with a final extension of that illustration that I wish to conclude.

The last scene in *The Brothers Karamazov* is a triumph over bathos. Every element of that ending conspires against the author; yet his genius transcends them all. The death of an innocent, the gathering of the band of boys who first taunted him and later befriended him, the memory of that child's humiliation in the humiliation of his father, the farewell of Alyosha and his speech to the children – all these closing moments of the novel are fused in a strength and a truth that are undeniable. The power of that scene is not pedagogic. Alyosha's message is merely a fragment of gospel transformed in the passion of Dostoievski's art. Yet the message of love that Aloysha brings to the children is fresh and mysterious because the horizon in which it is given is recognized as valid for our world. The point in the story when the children meet at the stone for Ilusha's grave is not merely the end of the tale, it is the focus for a movement outward toward life. Their being there is identified by the death of a child, by the memory of his torment, and by the horizonal image of a destruction that implicitly awaits them all. When Alyosha speaks to the boys, he is prophesying their encounter with evil and imploring their goodness. He is predicting the becoming of their lives and pleading for the preservation of innocence. Of course, the instructions he gives the children are hopelessly inadequate,

[8] Wellek, R. and Warren, A., *Theory of Literature*, New York, 1956, 26.

incredibly naive; and that is their overriding strength. The world of *The Brothers* meets our own in a moment of epiphany. Taken by surprise, our shrewdness down, our arguments asleep, our orthodoxies suspended, we with Alyosha are asked by Dostoievski's child, "Karamazov ... can it be true what's taught us in religion, that we shall all rise again from the dead and shall live and see each other again, all, Ilusha too?" [9]

[9] Dostoievski, F., *The Brothers Karamazov*, New York, 940.

9. *Existentialism and the Theory of Literature*

Philosophical change, if not progress, may be measured by the nature and frequency of its embarrassments. An earlier age in Anglo-American thought was dominated by a passion for the Absolute. Questions concerning the nature of Man, the Cosmos, Life, and Death were familiar and valid. Even those, like William James, who thumbed their noses with pluralistic fingers were at home with big issues. Today the scene has changed. Anyone who went about the smoker of the American Philosophical Association asking members what their philosophy was would be considered a crank, a fool, or at best, someone who wasn't interested in a job. If some extraordinarily considerate philosopher were to venture an answer, it would probably be something of this sort: "If you mean by 'my philosophy' some grand metaphysical system, I'm afraid I don't have one. But I can tell you something about the way in which I approach what I take to be the issues of philosophy." And what would follow would be an inquiry into the rather strange question posed in asking about "your philosophy." It would not be surprising if the questioner were told that his question was a misformulated one, or even a meaningless one.

I'm not sure that our questioner would fare any better on the Continent, but I believe he would feel more at home in his disgrace. In any event, the kinds of questions raised by some contemporary European thinkers might well appear to him closer to the spirit of his question. He might be confused by the language of phenomenology and existentialism, but he would sense in that language a concern for major themes. Whatever the achievements of contemporary French and German philosophy, they have at least led to new embarrassments. Explanations for the new mode of philosophizing are abundant.

Existentialism, for example, is often treated as a side-effect of the second World War, as a philosophical equivalent of Dada or Futurism, as, in the words of Louella Parsons, the product of the failure of the French to read their Bible, or simply as a disease. Fortunately, existential philosophy in its technical achievement is sufficiently known today to make further comment on these animadversions unnecessary. It is to the more serious reactions to existential philosophy that we must turn. And here the difference between Anglo-American thought and the philosophy of the Continent is striking in its disparity. A distinguished British pilosopher told me not long ago of a conference he had joined in France devoted to phenomenological problems and attended chiefly by European phenomenologists. "They are very sweet people," he said, "but quite hopeless philosophically." Soon after I had a report from the other side. "He's a very nice man," it was said of the Englishman, "but philosophically naive." The score sheet for such a misencounter could only read "scratched."

Whatever other reasons may account for the astronomic distance between the parties involved here, there is, I think, one very basic difference between them which is worth attending to: the qualitative difference in their very sense of reality. In reading Heidegger, Sartre, and Marcel, I am presented with a world that is essentially dramatic, a world in which people suffer and dream, in which they triumph and die. Whatever is given is fringed with the ambiguities of a life involved in radical choice, tormented commitment, despairing allegiance. Vanity, pride, deceit, despair, creation and faith are endemic features. Reality is forceful in its impositions and disguises. Above all, the quality of existence is alchemic; its substance is magic. A much tidier reality seems to be given to Anglo-American philosophers. Reading Ayer, Austin, and Ryle and then their Continental opponents is like going from a matinee of *The Importance of Being Earnest* to an evening performance of *The Lower Depths*. The point is made neatly by Iris Murdoch when she says of a book by Gilbert Ryle, "The 'world' of *The Concept of Mind* is the world in which people play cricket, cook cakes, make simple decisions, remember their childhood and go to the circus; not the world in which they commit sins, fall in love, say prayers or join the Communist Party." [1]

My problem now is to probe the sense of reality which existential philosophy articulates. But before I begin, I must pause for a breath of explanation. This paper will have as its central concern the implications

[1] Murdoch, I., *Sartre: Romantic Rationalist*, New Haven, 1953, 35.

of Jean-Paul Sartre's contributions to aesthetic theory. In particular, I wish to explore his ideas on the nature of literature. The more generalized theme involved here is the relevance of a phenomenologically grounded existential philosophy for the theory of literature, understood as a fundamental rationale for literary art. Although I am deeply indebted to a remarkably conceived and brilliantly executed essay on "Phenomenology and the Theory of Literature" by an earlier investigator, the present paper is intended as an independent contribution.

If we turn to literature for an expression of the sense of reality, the distance between alternative philosophical attitudes is apparent, indeed unavoidable. But even within an existentially oriented literature the differences are striking. The work of Camus possesses a Mediterranean horizon, a presence of the sea, an indication of lands split off by air which gives his art an openness into which corruption can empty without limit. His is essentially a Milesian world. Celine, whose existential relevance is dubious but nevertheless interesting to consider, hammers out an Eleatic plenum replete with the evilly condensed bitterness of a world of malintention, small-time greed, pent or exhausted virulence: the full measure of our insolence, gossip, antagonism, and being toward craft and guile. Whatever interstices might be caught in this world are plugged instantaneously with a gummy venom that saturates the whole. The sense of reality here is unredeemed by even the hope of love or the memory of friendship. If the absurd can be transcended for Camus, it can only be endured for Celine as the inwoven fabric of our being. As his titles tell us, existence is a journey to the end of night and life is death on the installment plan.

These considerations provide a focus, perhaps, for our theme of the sense of reality, but they hardly constitute an inroad into the philosophical issues. It is the sense of reality itself which must be existentially interpreted. Perhaps the best place to begin is where I am. I shall speak for myself. The world I inhabit is from the outset an intersubjective one. The language I possess was taught to me by others; the manners I have I did not invent; whatever abilities, techniques, or talents I can claim were nourished by a social inheritance; even my dreams are rooted in a world I never created and can never completely possess. The texture of this social reality is familiar to me; it seems to have always been close to me, a necessary companion. I cannot recapture in its original quality the familiarity of the world which I experienced as a child; but *that* I experienced it is so. The forbidding problem that arises here is when and how the familiarity of the world became thematized for me as an explicit object of reflection and concern. Here autobiography can give way to a phenomenology of discovery. However philosophy began, a philosopher begins in that privileged moment when the experienced world achieves explicit thematization in his consciousness, when he for the first time self-consciously experiences his own being in the world.

Becoming aware of the texture of existence as possessing the underlying, implicit quality of being given in a certain way to consciousness is at least part of the meaning of wonder. And to say that philosophy begins with wonder may be transposed into the claim that the philosopher begins as philosopher when his own being becomes a distinct theme for self-examination. Why there is philosophy at all is a curiously disturbing question. The attitude of daily life is almost antiphilosophical in its general tenor. The man who says at a moment of crisis or despair, "We must take things philosophically" is really saying that the ordinary run of daily life need not be taken philosophically, that it is only the atypical which requires profound explanation. The underlying style of daily life, then, involves an unconscious suspension of doubt.[2] But more than this, common sense projects a world that is reassuring in its typicality. The very objects of that world are seen in the horizon of the familiar. An illustration from the realm of painting may help.

As I write this, I am looking at a set of reproductions entitled "A Norman Rockwell Album." The Editor of *The Saturday Evening Post* introduces the sketches with these words: "It is no exaggeration to say that Norman Rockwell is the most popular, the most loved, of all contemporary artists." I am sure he is, and looking over these examples of his art tells me why. The legends under each painting are cross sections of mundane existence typically apprehended. "Thanksgiving, 1951" depicts a woman and child seated in a cheap restaurant, sur-

---

[2] We are indebted here to Alfred Schutz. In his article "On Multiple Realities" in *Philosophy and Phenomenological Research*, V, June 1945, on pp. 550–551 he writes: "Phenomenology has taught us the concept of phenomenological *epoché*, the suspension of our belief in the reality of the world as a device to overcome the natural attitude by radicalizing the Cartesian method of philosophical doubt. The suggestion may be ventured that man with the natural attitude also uses a specific *epoché*, of course quite another one than the phenomenologist. He does not suspend belief in the outer world and its object but on the contrary: he suspends doubt in its existence. What he puts in brackets is the doubt that the world and its objects might be otherwise than it appears to him. We propose to call this *epoché* the *epoché of the natural attitude*."

rounded by truck drivers and working people who stare at them as they pause, their hands locked together, saying a silent prayer of thanksgiving. "The Inexperienced Traveler" presents us with a little boy seated alone in the diner of a railroad train, ordering for the first time probably, while the colored waiter stands by with a loving smile. "The Satisfied Swimmer" tells us the story of the salesman who has stopped his car by a stream one hot August day and has taken a dip, just as he must have done at the old swimming hole of childhood. The other titles tell their own stories: "Off to College," "The Facts of Life," "The Sick Dolly," and a weary so on. Each item depicted is as clear as Mr. Rockwell's signature on the painting. His technical skill returns us to the fat blackness of the physician's medical bag, the creases in the leather of his old-fashioned high shoes. Nor is there any chance for misunderstanding. We know that he is a physician because the signs of his profession are directly given: his stethoscope, his diploma, his medical books. Similarly, we are able to identify the "satisfied swimmer." His car shows the emblem of the company he represents, his bow tie and eyeglasses and cigar are clearly in view. And if everything else failed to place him, that grin of his would recall the sunny face of every salesman we ever met. Mr. Rockwell's talent gives us the world we look at but never see. The simplest element of that world, the slightest detail is seen for us, not by us. These faces are the nonchalant equivalent of figures from a wax museum nobody would ever knowingly enter, for there are no stinkers in Mr. Rockwell's world.

If the realm of anonymity will not do, how then *is* the reality of our lives given? Philosophy and art, in some of their forms at least, have suggested an answer. The challenge is to be shrewdly naive, to learn to stop looking and to begin seeing. We must, in the language of phenomenology, return to "the things themselves" of our experience. Whatever else Husserl means by this advice, he is suggesting that the given in experience cannot be gotten at second hand, through the lens of the family camera or through borrowed binoculars. It is necessary to rediscover the given for yourself in its immediate quality, *as* given, as presented directly in the focus of awareness. Consciousness as a movement toward, as a directionality, is the root concept of phenomenology, and it provides as well the key to Sartre's form of existential philosophy. The sense of reality, the rediscovery of what is given in experience, is made explicit in Sartre's description of consciousness. That description will lead us ultimately to the formulation of his aesthetic.

In his essay on "The Transcendence of the Ego," Sartre presents what has been termed a "non-egological" conception of consciousness. Stripped of phenomenological jargon, his argument amounts to this: there is no self behind the activity of consciousness. The ego is located as out there, in the world, and my ego is encountered in the same way that I encounter the ego of another. Consciousness is directional in its very nature because it hurls from its vortex the meanings, attitudes, interpretations, and qualities we then claim to be "ours." I discover myself in my acts, and if I try to knock on my own door with the expectation of being greeted by an interior resident, I am destined to disappointment. "When I run after a streetcar," Sartre writes, "when I look at the time, when I am absorbed in contemplating a portrait, there is no I. There is consciousness *of the streetcar-having-to-be-overtaken*. ... In fact, I am then plunged into the world of objects; it is they which constitute the unity of my consciousness; it is they which present themselves with values, with attractive and repellant qualities – but *me*, I have disappeared; I have annihilated myself. There is no place for *me* on this level. And this is not a matter of chance, due to a momentary lapse of attention, but happens because of the very structure of consciousness." [3] The I or ego arises only through a reflexive act, as the result of reflecting on the original directional activity of consciousness. It is as though I unexpectedly encountered my face in a wall mirror and said, "Oh, there you are!" Prior to the ego, then, is an original activity of consciousness which is the condition for the possibility of reflection and the peculiar quality of our being in the world.

The lucidity of consciousness, however, is fundamentally betrayed not only by the typifications of common sense but by an epistemic disjunction: the break-up of awareness into a subject-object dualism. As soon as a here-there sort of attitude filters into a philosophic perspective, everything is organized into a self as subject and the thing known as object. And when this happens, a fatal gap divides awareness into a double camp. For Sartre, the directionality of consciousness means above all that this dualism is not only dispensable but false. The object is not at distance from me, it does not subsist over there. These threats I hear announced are not apart from me, the thousand living movements of the world, its scandals and treasures are not messengers from the outside; they are all known, observed, comprehended, entertained as an integral part of my awareness. They are *mine* precisely

[3] Sartre, J.-P., *The Transcendence of the Ego*, 48–49.

because they manifest themselves as moments of consciousness, as *meant* unities in the flow of my temporal being. In a word, Sartre has erased the distance between consciousness and the world. Henceforth, solipsism and realism are coparts of a single untruth; existentialism transcends them both.

Reality, then, is given by way of consciousness. There is no need to attend to the relative contributions of mind and matter because the fused world Sartre presents antedates both categories. It makes possible, for the first time perhaps, a full realization of the existential sense of reality. Returning to "the things themselves" means attending to the given in experience precisely *as* it is given, neither altering for the sake of appearances nor forgetting for the sake of propriety. The task is to see even the barest fragment of our lives in utter nakedness, to see it "in person." Such seeing is the beginning of art. The astonishments of van Gogh and Cezanne, of Dostoievski and Kafka are phenomenologies of the world unbetrayed by sensibility or understanding. They move tropistically toward the given. This movement toward reality, this insistence on attending to the sheer quality of the achievement of consciousness is the victory of a phenomenologically grounded existential philosophy, but it has been sensed by a variety of writers. I hope that both Husserl and Sartre would recognize their deepest motives in the rhetoric of James Agee. "For in the immediate world," he writes, "everything is to be discerned, for him who can discern it, and centrally and simply, without either dissection into science, or digestion into art, but with the whole of consciousness, seeking to perceive it as it stands: so that the aspect of a street in sunlight can roar in the heart of itself as a symphony, perhaps as no symphony can: and all of consciousness is shifted from the imagined, the revisive, to the effort to perceive simply the cruel radiance of what is." [4]

The phenomenological sense of reality arises in existential literature in several ways. First, we are presented with reality as the magical product of consciousness situated in the world; second, there is a kind of metalinguistic reflection or commentary on the affairs of consciousness. The given is both presented and reflexively considered. The contrapuntal effect attained in this way leads to an internal questioning of the literary work. This self-interrogation finds its stylistic form in the confession, the diary, the embattled monologue. *Notes from Underground* is the clearest expression of this mode of self-exami-

[4] Agee, J. and Evans, W., *Let Us Now Praise Famous Men*, Boston, 1941, 11.

nation. What is at issue here is not the paradoxalist, but the trembling status of every particular he encounters. Once the horizon of typicality has been abandoned or transcended, each fragment of experience takes on multiple possibilities for interpretation. Signs of the world proliferate and darken; their very being wavers and the given turns problematic. But rather than an endless manufacture of particulars, it is their underlying essences which become manifest. To put the matter phenomenologically, the "irrealization" of the particular is the condition for the possibility of seeing the universal.

The logician's distinction between token and type may serve as an illustration of what is meant by irrealization. Your copy and my copy of the same edition of Euclid's *Elements* have, we say, the same geometrical figures on the same pages. The triangle that appears on the upper right hand portion of page 89 is the same triangle that appears on the corresponding part of the page in your copy. Obviously, there are two triangles being compared, yet we commonly say that they are the same triangle. They are tokens of the same type. Just as we must not confuse the token with its type, so we must not confound the printed illustration of the type with the ideal object it represents. We cannot, strictly speaking, draw triangles at all. The visual aids we use are merely graphic conveniences. Yet we do not, or at least should not see the tokens as tokens when we do geometry. As an eidetic scientist, the geometrician sees through the token to the type. He manipulates tokens in order to comprehend the relations of types. We may say that he irrealizes the token in apprehending the type.

Is there an analogue of this procedure in existential literature? I am suggesting that self-interrogation, the reflexive concern of the existential hero is a comparable activity. The paradoxalist strikes the particular from its pedestal of typicality and confronts the ruins of his act. Seeing through the multiple facets of the given he creates, the interior questioner exposes their essential features. But even more than this, he irrealizes the world and constitutes the realm of the imaginary. Again, existential literature both presents this remarkable action and provides a commentary on it. The commentary will lead us back to the act. But first of all, what do we mean by the "imaginary"?

Sartre, in the tradition of phenomenology, distinguishes three related but quite different structures: memory, anticipation, and imagination. Something remembered, something anticipated, and something imagined are not three variations on the same perceptual theme; they are radically different modes of awareness. When I remember, I recapture a state of affairs that is real in the mode of the past: what I remember happened, and it is that happening, now past, which I search for in memory. The past event is not an unreality but a reality whose mode of being is its being past. "The handshake of Peter of last evening in leaving me," Sartre writes, "did not turn into an unreality as it became a thing of the past: it simply *went into retirement;* it is always real but past. It exists *past*, which is one mode of real existence among others."[5] But if I anticipate shaking hands with Peter tomorrow, the anticipated handshake is not there waiting for me to join up with it; rather, it is *not* there. To anticipate that handshake means to posit it as though it were here, to treat it as here in a fugitive sense. This subjunctive presentation is close, in some of its forms, to the constitution of nothingness. Anticipation involves the detachment of the future from the present to which it is bound and presenting it to myself.[6] In imagination, however, I posit nothingness, I posit Peter as an unreality. It is only by a fundamental negation of the real that I imagine shaking hands with him. Imagination is an act of wrenching oneself from the reality of the world; it is a disengagement from my being-in-the-world made possible through a simultaneous affirmation of that world. "In order to imagine," Sartre writes, "consciousness must be free from all specific reality and this freedom must be able to define itself by a 'being-in-the-world' which is at once the constitution and the negation of the world; the concrete situation of the consciousness in the world must at each moment serve as the singular motivation for the constitution of the unreal." [7]

It is this simultaneous affirmation and negation of being-in-the-world which so much existential literature illustrates and explores. The particulars given in a situation are exploded by consciousness into a kind of shrapnel. Each character not only interprets the fragments of his experience but causes them to be. By irrealizing their ordinary mundane signification, the existential hero brings into being their essential qualities. These qualities arise against the background of the world, but that world is negated in the moment in which it is affirmed and is affirmed in the moment of its negation. The characters of the novel cause their world to be. In positing the unreality of their acts, they secrete the imaginary. It would seem from these remarks

[5] Sartre, J.-P., *The Psychology of Imagination*, New York, 1948, 263.
[6] *ibid.*, 264–265.
[7] *ibid.*, 269–270.

that a kind of literary solipsism is being advanced, that novels write themselves and read themselves and then put themselves away. To be misled here would mean that the imaginary has been treated apart from the imagining consciousness of the author and reader. This is not the case. What has been said so far about the imaginary is a shorthand for a full account of the relationship of the reader to the literary work. Without that relationship, in fact, the microcosm of literature would collapse. The being of the characters in the novel has all along been our being; their world is our responsibility. "The literary object," Sartre writes, "has no other substance than the reader's subjectivity; Raskolnikov's waiting is *my* waiting which I lend him. Without this impatience of the reader he would remain only a collection of signs. His hatred of the police magistrate who questions him is my hatred which has been solicited and wheedled out of me by signs, and the police magistrate himself would not exist without the hatred I have for him via Raskolnikov. That is what animates him, it is his very flesh." [8]

The reader, too, is limited in his creativity. If the microcosm of *The Trial* depends on his participating consciousness, it is no less the case that participation must be along restricted lines. Everything will not do. Sartre tells us that the degree of realism and truth of Kafka's mythology is never given. "The reader must invent them ... in a continual exceeding of the written thing." [9] But "to be sure," he adds, "the author guides him." [10] Thus Kafka demands that we become responsible for his world, but that world remains *his*. The text of *The Trial* may be understood as a necessary but not a sufficient condition for the constitution of the art work. In order to see how we are at once free yet restricted by the novel, we must attend to its status as an aesthetic object. All of our considerations so far have led to this problem. In approaching Sartre's aesthetic we are at the same time exploring a possible line of connection between philosophy and literature. Or to put the matter in a different way, we shall be interested in the relevance of aesthetics for the theory of literature.

Suppose we get a rough summary statement of Sartre's aesthetic before us. It is something like this. The novel is an aesthetic object in so far as the reader moves from the descriptions given in the book to the imaginary microcosm toward which they point. The story by itself is not enough to reach the fictive world it promises. The characters,

---

[8] Sartre, J.-P., *What is Literature?*, New York, 1949, 45.
[9] *ibid.*
[10] *ibid.*

events, general action are all *analogues*, in Sartre's language, which may lead us to the aesthetic object. It is always possible to read fiction as a report of real events, or to read an historical account as fiction. The pronouncements, questions, and wonderings of Joseph K. are merely clues or guides to the microcosm of *The Trial*. If I take the descriptions of the life of Joseph K. as a report of true happenings or if I simply note what is said in the way in which adults at breakfast may read the messages to children on the backs of cereal boxes, then an imaginative consciousness is not functioning. The movement toward the aesthetic object is short-circuited. I find myself merely with a book in my hands.

The necessary condition for the constitution of the aesthetic object is that an imaginative consciousness posit it as unreal.[11] "It is self-evident," Sartre writes, "that the novelist, the poet and the dramatist construct an unreal object by means of verbal analogues; it is also self-evident that the actor who plays Hamlet makes use of himself, of his whole body, as an analogue of the imaginary person. ... The actor does not actually consider himself to be Hamlet. But this does not mean that he does not 'mobilize' all his powers to make Hamlet real. He uses all his feelings, all his strength, all his gestures as analogues of the feelings and conduct of Hamlet. But by this very fact he takes the reality away from them. *He lives completely in an unreal way*. And it matters little that he is *actually* weeping in enacting the role. These tears ... he himself experiences – and so does the audience – as the tears of Hamlet, that is as the analogue of unreal tears ... The actor is completely caught up, inspired, by the unreal. It is not the character who becomes real in the actor, it is the actor who *becomes unreal* in his character." [12] Such, in outline, is Sartre's account of the constitution of the aesthetic object. It is, of course, unfair to refer simply to his "aesthetic"; he offers no aesthetic, merely some nuclear hints which, if developed, would lead to a systematic theory. But these hints are enough, if taken in the context of his total position, to warrant serious consideration. How much of lasting value does Sartre offer here?

The central achievement, it seems to me, is the phenomenological uncovering of the imaginary as the informing structure of the literary microcosm. The imaginary is not found but constituted by consciousness. And the essential character of imagination consists in its negation

---

[11] *The Psychology of Imagination*, 277.
[12] *ibid.*, 277–278.

of mundane existence. My being-in-the-world carries with it all along the possibility of its nihilation. In different terms, the imaginary is the implicit margin surrounding the horizon of the real. Just as the child is destined to discover his gift for dreaming, so the adult lives in a world whose limits will be announced by his imagination. But the condition for the imaginary is the paramount reality of worldly existence. It is because the imaginary is unreal that it can be deciphered. The decoding presupposes the natural language from which it was translated and transposed. Without the real the unreal is unthinkable, indeed unimaginable. Art, the province of the imaginary, returns us to reality and to the theme with which we began, the sense of reality. It is time to close the accordion.

The sense of reality, being-in-reality, the irrealization of the particular, the return to "the things themselves" are all problematic aspects of an aesthetic whose dominant concern is the constitution of the aesthetic object. If, as reader, I cause there to be the imaginary by disengaging mundane existence, then I assume an epistemic responsibility for the art work. "You are perfectly free to leave that book on the table," Sartre writes, "but if you open it, you assume responsibility for it." [13] The true meaning of responsibility here, however, is founded on the directional activity of consciousness. Causing there to be the imaginary means that I move from the world to the horizon of its unreality; I discover the limits of the mundane, and in transcending those limits I affirm the very reality I have outdistanced. It is consciousness which holds the clue to reality; consciousness is the secret of ontology. Again Sartre's debt to phenomenology is great. His conception of consciousness can be understood only if we return once again to Husserl.

The non-egological theory of consciousness which Sartre advances denies Husserl's doctrine of a transcendental ego supporting or directing the acts of awareness. All knowledge is still knowledge *of* something, all memory is memory *of* something, all anticipation is anticipation *of* something, and all imagining is imagining *of* something. But the full weight is given over to the act within whose structure the meant object is located. The object of the act of consciousness is regarded neutrally; I neither affirm nor deny its real being, its objective status, its causal relations. In concerning myself phenomenologically with the act of awareness, I make a decision to attend only to what is presented, *as* it is presented. My ordinary believing in the world, my knowledge of its

[13] *What is Literature?*, 48.

historical past, its scientific explanation, are all set aside for present purposes. In virtue of this reflexive attention I decide to pay to the stream of my own awareness, I uncover a pure field of essential relations. The objects given in that field comprise my phenomenological data. What Sartre has done with this Husserlian doctrine is to reject its transcendental condition in affirming its sovereign status. The data of consciousness are intrinsic aspects of the directionality of consciousness. My responsibility for the given is absolute. It arises and is sustained through my epistemic fiat. And since, according to Sartre, the "I" or ego is found in and through the acts of consciousness as a product of reflection, in the same way in which a fellow man is located, I am thrown out of the vortex of consciousness into the being of the world. Sartre quotes Rimbaud with approval: "I is *an other*." [14]

The total result, then, of Sartre's version of a phenomenology of consciousness is to rid mind of a transcendental agent and make the acts of awareness the sole domain of our being-in-the-world. Consciousness is worldly to begin with, and its activity is thrown outward in the midst of the human condition. It is the doctrine of the directionality of consciousness which alone can account for the existentialist's sense of reality. Sartre has removed us from our place in the endless waiting line of the Hegelian Absolute, stamped our ticket, and put us on the train. With him we are *en route*. Far from phenomenology leading to a philosophical idealism, an avoidance of the brute features of existence, Sartre maintains that the victory of phenomenology is in a completely different direction. "The phenomenologists," he writes, "have plunged man back into the world; they have given full measure to man's agonies and sufferings, and also to his rebellions." [15]

It might seem that phenomenology and existentialism offer a very long way around to their final point. Is it really necessary to provide a theory of consciousness in order to read novels and plays and poems with full sensitivity? Even in the literature of the existential writers, is it necessary to study *Being and Nothingness* as an endless footnote to *Nausea*? Must there always be categories? This complaint has a cousin who asks similar questions: Is a theory of literature really necessary? Why can't we read a poem as a poem, and let it go at that? A just answer to these criticisms would require first that we have a solid formulation of the problems of the theory of literature. We don't. The only defense possible here must proceed along other lines. It seems to

[14] *The Transcendence of the Ego*, 97.
[15] *ibid.*, 105.

me that what must be defended is the relevance of philosophy for literature. And the only way of doing this is to explain the nature and necessity of theory.

When a blunt, robust, and fair-minded critic waves away abstractions and urges us to attend to the concrete work of art, how are we to follow his advice? Is the poem the printed token that appears on my copy or his? Should I recite the lines or listen to somebody else read them? Will diligent study locate a normative structure of some sort which we will agree is the poem as the author meant it, or as it might be understood, or as it must be interpreted? Can we wave these cautions aside as abstractions, too? With all the good will and fairness of mind I can muster, I must confess that the critic's directions confuse me. But worse, I cannot discuss these confusions in his presence; he will not hear of them. The critic who does attend to my worries attends to my theorizing, and the discipline which tries to formulate, clarify, and resolve these torments is the theory of literature. Abandoned by the man who will not hear of categories, I find some intellectual solace in reading Wellek and Warren. Perhaps, as Marcel remarks of Jaspers, "I can only proceed in this kind of country by calling out to other travellers." [16]

Unfortunately, the situation in contemporary philosophy is equally unsettling. The philosophical problem of communication, the problem of intersubjectivity, has given way to the conversational silence held between analytically oriented philosophers and those sympathetic to phenomenology and existentialism. We are back to that conference of phenomenologists which the English philosopher attended. It is curious that most attempts to explain the gap between the opposed camps rely on psychology. Differences in temperament are noted; some even turn to psychoanalysis for guidance. But the psychology of philosophers, however interesting and fruitful it might prove to be, cannot satisfy us. Splits in philosophy are themselves philosophical problems. If I cannot account for the division today between so much of Anglo-American and Continental philosophy, I can at least describe a few of its features.

Much analytic philosophy attends very seriously to the formulation of philosophical assertions. Language has become a leading concern, and the ordinary language of everyday discourse has been analyzed in remarkable detail. Whatever the results of this analysis, it can at

[16] Marcel, G., *The Philosophy of Existence*, London, 1949, 29.

least be said that it is guided by certain suspicions. The great treatises of Bradley and Bosanquet have given way to more modest, less Germanic ventures; the style is crisp, the sentences clearly structured, the movement of the argument distinctly articulated. Although literary styles vary among analytic philosophers, some of them seem to strive for an almost schoolboy effect: titles are quite short, illustrations are often bits of casual dialogue, the manner is tart. We cannot ask, What manner of men write these works?, but we must pose another question: What sense of reality informs these writings? Instead of generalizing, I prefer to restrict myself to one analytic philosopher of great distinction who has said something about his way of regarding the world. I can think of no better way of pointing to everything phenomenology and existentialism are not than to quote G. E. Moore when he writes: "I do not think that the world ... would ever have suggested to me any philosophical problems. What has suggested philosophical problems to me is things which other philosophers have said about the world ..." [17] This is not intended as an admission but as an affirmation. It must surely be considered one of the remarkable embarrassments of our age.

---

[17] *The Philosophy of G. E. Moore* (ed. by Paul Arthur Schilpp), The Library of Living Philosophers, IV, Evanston and Chicago, 1942, 14. I note that this quotation, cited more fully, and the one from Iris Murdoch referred to above appear also in Walter Kaufmann's *Critique of Religion and Philosophy*, New York, 1958.

10. Existential Categories In Contemporary Literature

Presenting a paper on existentialism is somewhat like escorting a lady of rather dubious reputation to a party: the half-smiles and half-concealed glances are matched by an absorbing interest in the new-comer, and there is a nervousness in the discussion. Among philosophers the term "existentialism" is unique in this respect: no other term can make philosophers smile. What they are smiling about remains a mystery; *that* they smile, however, is no less mysterious. Again, there is a nervousness which teases about the subject, and which, in the end, is often all that ever emerges from the discussion. But even where existential philosophy is given a more serious hearing, the sense of mystery never quite vanishes; it transposes itself instead into an almost eschatological expectancy, the awaiting of a resolute answer to the jocular yet desperate question, "Well, what exactly *is* existentialism?" Unfortunately, most goodwilled and competent efforts to answer this question are blocked at the outset by misunderstandings, mistaken pre-conceptions on the part of the questioner. Moreover, the questioner too often falls into one of several patterns. Perhaps the best way of intro-ducing my conception of existential philosophy is by indicating, briefly, some of the typical objections raised against it and then proceeding to a positive statement of what I take to be the "real thing."

From among the many typical challenges extended to existentialism, I'd like to select four examples: First, the objection is made that existentialism is the product of post-war despair, the nihilism of a shattered Europe, or, to cite a variation of this theme, the distorted, violent world of the resistance movement, the underground. The point intended here is that this is not philosophy but at best an unhappy feature of a passing despair generated out of the cruelty of war. A second objection is argued in a very different way. It is agreed that there are some serious philosophical themes explored by existentialists but that all the shouting, the publicity, the stir is undeserved, since whatever is valuable here is not new but old. It was all said before by Socrates, by Augustine, by Montaigne, by Pascal or at the very least by Hegel, who said everything. Existentialism is then merely a new version of very old ideas. Still another pattern of objection stresses the ambivalence of existential ideas, their unhealthy mixture of philosophical and literary categories, their academic duplicity. The existentialist woos the student of literature with philosophy and the philosopher with literature. This is scandalous. Finally, it is objected that existentialism is neither philosophy nor literature but what can only be termed a mystique. Here the emphasis is on existentialism as a movement which attracts a variety of marginal figures: intellectual drifters, bohemians, politicos, faith seekers, and assorted magicians and wizards from the arts. This too is scandalous.

The fundamental inadequacy of most of these charges is clear in at least an historical sense, for it is surely the case that there is no philosophical position which is "existentialism"; instead there are a number of existentialist philosophers who represent existentialism in very different ways. It is obvious, first of all, that existential philosophy, whatever its ancient or classical roots, is at least as old as its modern father, Søren Kierkegaard, who lived during the first half of the 19th century. Kierkegaard can hardly be accused of being generated out of post-second world war nihilism. Further, it is no secret that there are both theistic and atheistic varieties of existential philosophy, the former having Protestant, Catholic, and Jewish subvarieties. Finally, a Kierkegaardian-inspired existentialism is quite different from Sartrean and Heideggerian philosophy, at least in some of its major motives and themes. An understanding of Socrates and Hegel would help greatly in appreciating Kierkegaard, whereas a thorough knowledge of the phenomenology of Edmund Husserl is necessary to read Sartre and Heidegger with understanding. If we turn from the historical to the systematic dimension of problems, it is still the case that there is nothing that can be called "existentialism" without serious qualifications. Such existential themes as man's aloneness are matched by an emphasis on community, as in the thought of Martin Buber. Concern with anguish in Heidegger and Sartre is matched by the examination of hope in the writings of Gabriel Marcel. The search for essential themes and attitudes becomes more complex the more carefully one reads the history of existential philosophy. One point, I think, is evident: the charges against existentialism just discussed are, in a very real sense, issued against a phantom. No one has ever seen "existentialism," only existentialists, and they derive from a rather complex history which must be delineated carefully before very much can be said about existentialism that is meaningful. These remarks, however, have not faced one of the four patterns, the charge of old wine in new bottles. The best way of meeting this point, I think, is to turn to a positive statement of what existential philosophy is, and to see then whether anything distinctively new is suggested. Once we get a coherent notion of the meaning of existential philosophy we then have won our right to proceed to an exploration of certain problems in contemporary literature.

What I take to be central and decisive for all existentialist philosophy is a concern for what I wish to call man's being in reality. I am trying, first of all, to describe a phenomenon given to consciousness, an experiential structure for all human beings, not some mystical awareness granted to a chosen few. The phenomenon I am dealing with is open, public, available, and evident, but the description of it depends first upon ridding ourselves of a certain deeply rooted attitude, suffusing consciousness, which renders being in reality obscure to the point of hopelessness for the philosopher committed to its articulation. Suppose I proceed by a general statement of what I understand by the idea of being in reality and follow then with an illustrative explanation.

Being in reality is the location of the self as *there* in any moment of the flow of temporal consciousness. Being "there" is an underived and irreducible datum given directly to consciousness. The placement "there" refers to an awareness of the self in reality as such, in reality as the total reference, the complete remainder when I subtract myself from all that there is. The clarification of being in reality requires a preliminary inquiry into the component words "being," "in," and "reality." By "being" I mean here the activity of consciousness; I understand consciousness as directive, in movement, intentional in the broadest sense of that term. Furthermore, "being" is always *my* being, *my* consciousness, *my* openness and presence to the world. I am *in* reality in the sense of involvement rather than spatial placement. The "in" is not "*in*side," not "with*in*"; rather I am *in* the world of my activity and awareness as the agency of choice and action, as the support, finally, for the object of my consciousness. The last term, "reality," is the broadest frame I can express for what there is, the total, the inclusive all for my consciousness. It is no part of "world" or "universe" but all that my horizon of awareness leads me toward. Now let me try to say this again in a different way.

Being in a concrete situation of any type, being involved in specific, limited action of any order, presupposes my being involved. To be involved, then, is itself a structure of experience which demands its own explanation. But to be involved, quite apart from what I am involved in, to be involved as such, presupposes my presence in the world and my being in reality. Before I become interested in this or that, concerned with such and such a problem, involved in one thing or another, I am in a reality in which all these specifics manifest themselves. My point is that there is a ground, a fundamental structure which is the necessary condition for there being specificities in experience; that ground is what I have termed being in reality. And being in reality is not merely a logical requirement or conceptual device in explaining the meaning of my experience, it is, above all, a datum given to me in immediate awareness, given as *sui generis*.

Let me try it a third time. We know, in common-sense fashion, what being here or there means, and we know what it means to be in typical situations: the classroom, the market, the shop, the library, the town square. Physical presence and psychological presence in these sorts of places are indicated through the "yes" or "no" answer to the question, Were you there? or Are you here? Thus I am in a room, in an argument, in a quandary, and in a situation in essentially the same sense, whatever the obvious differences are. In each case the description of the structure of *being in* is dominated by certain kinds of questions which reveal the level involved. Did you answer "present" when the roll was called? Did you get the better of him? Did you decide what to do? Did you succeed? In each case these questions are defined by their limits, by their being understood as having limits, as encompassing only a sector of our world and a segment of our experience. When I speak of being in reality, however, everything is at once different. My being in reality cannot be circumscribed by specific questions; my being in reality does not take a particular stratum or sector of experience, and my being in reality cannot be articulated through lines of analysis which presuppose the very object at issue, reality in the sense of all that there is. Being in reality is a fundamental givenness in my experience which occupies the unique position of being basic to all concrete events and to all particular situations. It is the cardinal presupposition of there being experience at all.

Now some explanation may help. Let each one of us try to locate, through active experiment, what I claim is a possible datum for experience. In what way may I locate my being in reality? First of all, it is necessary to be clear about the way in which we are going to pursue being in reality. I am not suggesting that we are to enter upon a metaphysical treasure hunt. What is at issue is a concrete datum; the problem is to overcome certain root-attitudes which obscure this datum and render it unavailable. Thus it is not a question of sharpening some special sense, of looking in some extraordinary corner of the mind, or of locating the philosopher's stone. What is called for, above all, is that each one of us examine his style of being in the world at the level of ordinary, common-sense life, so that the philosophical character of that level of experience be clarified. If that can be done, I maintain that at least a necessary condition for possession of the datum is fulfilled and that we are close to the goal. What, then, is it that the character of common-sense life is going to reveal which will make being in reality understandable? The direct answer is curious: the mark of common-sense life, the very essence of its style of being, is its failure to make itself an object for its own inspection. Common-sense life does not reflect upon common-sense life; at best it makes some particular event within the stream of daily life a topic for analysis and reflective scrutiny. That common-sense life has a style, has an essential structure, is an insight that necessarily transcends the understanding of common-sense men. We may at various times see ourselves as we are engaged in an activity – the barber for a moment aware of himself *as* barber, the waiter self-consciously grasping his act of moving to the left of the person he is about to serve, the concert goer fleetingly aware of himself as a concert goer – but we never place the whole of our common-sense attitude itself in question. Yet it is exactly that absolute awareness of the style of our being in common-sense life which must be made an object for inspection if the datum of being in reality is to be gotten. And this is the most difficult of all tasks, largely because grasping what it is that is required of us is exactly the problem. There is a built-in mechanism of protection in the stream of daily life which guards against this awareness; philosophy is an effort to crack this barrier. Existential philosophy is a force directed against this most subtle of all barricades.

The initial step then in coming to an understanding of our being in reality is the absolute, the overpowering obstacle; it is to place in radical question the very meaning of our way of living in day to day existence. And here difficulties proliferate. Not only is the sense of daily life, what I have called its style, cunningly elusive, but the typical ways in which we in daily life try to explain ourselves and our lives are charged with prejudices of a distinctive sort – philosophical commitments we are unaware of, emblems of our time. The typical analysis to which I refer might be given the block title of the psychologistic or scientistic attitude, i.e., a basic way of explaining phenomena by tracing out their genetic origins. Something is "explained" in this sense when *how* it came to be, *how* it arose, has been made evident. The qualitative character, the *what* of the phenomenon is said to be appreciated when the how and the why of its coming into being are accounted for systematically. If we proceed in this way, the problem of being in reality is transposed into something utterly different, the psychological question of what accounts for our having such an experience. The methodological character of such a transposition is evidenced in its causal mode of analysis. To account for the phenomenon psychologistically is first of all to look to its genetic history in causal terms. When the causal series is thoroughly clarified, the phenomenon is said to be explained. In all of this, the qualitative *what* being described is gone, for it vanished at the outset, or better, was eliminated.

In order to gain access to the phenomenon of being in reality then, I insist that we must, for purposes of our analysis, set aside the whole of the causal-genetic mode of analysis characteristic of natural science and its methods. We must return to the phenomenon in its givenness; we must make a radical effort to, quite literally, *see* what gives itself directly to consciousness. The prime step in getting at the datum we seek is a purposeful bracketing of what we know about ourselves and our world from the sources of science, history, psychology, and all other systems of explanation. We must seek the purely given features of consciousness, what directly presents itself. That this is difficult to do, I grant; that it is strange, I admit; that it is impossible or purposeless, I deny. If we can, right now, at least get a notion of what is at issue, I think the effort of our experimenting will be rewarded.

I begin, then, and so must you in experimental spirit, by trying to focus upon the general character of my – your – style of being in daily life, not on this or that event or problem, but on the total range of existence. At the outset I purposely set aside my commitments to particular ways of interpreting the world and I decide not to permit myself the wicked luxury of invoking causal-genetic categories of explanation. I am trying to look at my world as it directly gives itself to consciousness. What I have left behind, what I have bracketed, what I am doing without now interests me, for I find myself confronting reality in a completely fresh, original way. The world in this sense can no longer be explained by giving its history, the scientific laws which describe its behaviour, or by tracing out the why and how of its development; and I have no discipline or system or person to count on for my understanding. I am now directly confronted with reality and I find myself in this world with its complex horizons; I find myself as a being in reality.

This is as far as I can go within the limits of this paper. But if what I have struggled to explain is suggestive to you at all of the problem involved and if you get some sense of the philosophical roots of the issue, then what follows will be meaningful in a particular way: something of the relationship between philosophy and literature will have been illuminated. If we have at least pointed to the datum of being in reality, if we are at worst in the suburbs of its locale, we have a feeling for what we have abandoned or set by the wayside. At this moment we must grasp ourselves as being in reality. This means that apart from our historical and cultural heritage, apart from our personal histories, apart from all scientific categories of explanation, we simply *are*, we locate ourselves in reality. The original theme of our common-sense lives has been rendered an object for inspection. And we are now in a position to ask what existential philosophy *does* with the datum it has located and to decide whether all this effort will bring forth something splendid.

My thesis has been that existential philosophy is properly defined as having as its crucial concern man's being in reality. Those who want to get the meaning of this without going through the exasperation of its philosophical signification are asking for trouble. I prefer to think that there are among us no men of resentment. Having made an effort to explain something of the philosophical problems at issue, I want now to turn to some of the implications of my thesis, and in particular to the categories which are intimately related to man's being in reality.

The broadest publicity given to existentialism emphasizes its dramatic categories: fear, dread, anguish, suffering, aloneness, choice, authenticity, and death. I suggest that what is distinctively existential about these categories is their grounding in the matrix of man's being in reality and that these categories are generated out of the awareness of that foundational reality. By a category, first of all, I understand a concept of the widest generality. One thinks of Kant's categories: quantity, quality, relation, and modality. When I utilize the term "category" I do so in a traditional sense, despite the fact that the existential categories are not those of traditional philosophy. The meaning of category remains constant in my discussion; which terms are selected as categories is the innovation of existentialism. It is not the case, however, that traditional philosophy has nothing to say about such problems as choice, authenticity, and death; it is rather that these are treated as themes for classical philosophy and not as distinctive categories. A theme is, most simply, a problem for inquiry; a category is an instrument for inquiring into a problem. As I interpret them, then, the existential categories operate specifically as philosophical instruments for exploring human experience. To suggest, as I have, that these categories are generated out of the awareness of man's being in reality is to claim that what is new and commanding in existentialism is its very procedure in exploring man's being *through* categories which are independent of common-sense experience and scientific method and which take as their object not particular features of human existence but existence itself.

At this point it becomes necessary to justify the title of my paper. Rather than analyze the existential categories as philosophical instrumentalities and see in a technical way how they relate to the ground of being in reality, I wish to examine the categories as they are decisively present in literature, especially contemporary literature. Proceeding with my thesis means that I wish to show how being in reality may be encountered as a literary theme and how, then, the existential categories spring into meaning when their literary manifestation is given in this encounter. All this presupposes that these structures *are* involved in literature, that they are there to be encountered. This assumption in turn involves a certain way of looking at the relationship between philosophy and literature which is my subordinate theme. A quick statement will have to do. I maintain that philosophy is sometimes encountered in literary works. I believe that authentic instances of such philosophy in literature are neither popularizations of philosophy nor substitutes for philosophy. Obviously, the differences between technical philosophizing and philosophy in literature are enormous; it is their underlying continuity which interests me. And it is this continuity which I shall consider, however indirectly, in what follows. The appropriate subtitle for this paper is: "A study in the relationship between philosophy and literature."

Of the existential categories I shall select two for close consideration: aloneness and anguish. What I shall say about them holds, I believe, *a fortiori* for the others. Each category will be taken up with regard to a particular author: aloneness in Kafka, anguish in Dostoievski. In each case the problem will be to see the relationship between the category and the general ground of being in reality as revealed in literature.

Whether apocryphal or not, the story is told that a friend lent Albert Einstein a copy of *The Trial* and was surprised when Einstein returned the volume before very long only half read, with the apology, "The human mind is not complicated enough." The paradox in reading Kafka is the density of the apparently simple. Complexity here is not a matter of deciphering a symbolism but of holding on to a microcosm in which the self slips from all control, past all stability, into the imbalance of a universal quest: the demanding, unswervable search for resolution. The story of *The Trial* is desperately simple: Joseph K. is "arrested one fine morning," under a charge which is never revealed to him, which he seeks to defend himself against in endlessly complicated court procedures, and for which he is finally executed. His innocence is protested, and that is the measure of his guilt. In the cathedral scene the priest says to Joseph K.:

"You are held to be guilty. Your case will perhaps never get beyond a lower court. Your guilt is supposed, for the present, at least, to have been proved." "But I am not guilty," said K.; "it's a misunderstanding. And, if it comes to that how can any man be called guilty? We are all simply men here, one as much as the other." "That is true," said the priest, "but that's how all guilty men talk."[1]

The efforts of K. to vindicate himself prove pointless. But the pointlessness of his action, pointlessness, one might say, *in* action, is expressed through the web of connections K. establishes with the human elements of his world. The hopelessness, the uselessness of his defense is exactly his aloneness in a world he can never join. The litigant K. proceeds to establish the lines of his defense. He secures the services of an advocate, but his advocate, he learns, has many other cases pending. K. is not his only client. K.'s troubles are not his sole concern. Still he represents K. to those others somehow knowledgeable about the courts, those with access to the higher ups. The lines of the web become more tenuous still. K., finally, is in the absurd position of trying to take independent action in his case. Not only is independent action impossible, but all action must be sifted through the mesh of representation. And deliberation is endless. Intermediaries, messengers, representatives bear the weight of social action. K.'s aloneness is absolute. He is surrounded by a world he can never reach, a world whose texture can never be touched but only guessed at. It is a world in which

[1] Kafka, F., *The Trial*, New York, 1945, 265–266.

verification is necessary and unattainable, an impossible possibility.

In what sense are we faced here with an existential category of aloneness? In what way does it relate to the ground of being in reality? To speak of aloneness as a category means first of all in Kafka's context that the concept of category is dictated by a thematic experience, by a substantive experience and not a theoretical need. The category is made possible by the experience and then the category makes possible the interpretation of the experience. This order is essential, for aloneness is not an idea but an encountered experience which makes the idea possible. The structure of the experience has already been outlined. "One fine morning" K.'s world, the common-sense everyday business world of a bank employee faithful in his duties, is placed beyond him, in the instantaneous moment of the charge. Access to his world is transposed, for although he continues more or less at liberty in his activities he finds that the routine of his life slips from his grasp and he becomes increasingly involved in the problems of his case. Accusation is the moment in which aloneness is realized, in which the theme of daily life suddenly comes into question. And here it is possible to see the way in which the category of aloneness arises out of an awareness of being in reality. K.'s trial is a movement into the horizons of the world, from the fragmentary to the absolute. At the time of the original charge, that fine morning, K. tries to convince his warders that a mistake has been made:

"Here are my identification papers." "What are your papers to us?" cried the tall warder. "You're behaving worse than a child."[2]

The common-sense world has hitherto, for K., been assuring in its recognition of his existence: witness his identification papers. Now the fragment, the surface fragment of recognition gives way and the warders are the first indication that a horizon of meaning is opening up for K. in which everything that he has been, the identification papers for every level of his being will prove worthless, irrelevant, subject to the mockery of hirelings, subordinates, and wretches. The first awareness of his being lost in the world that has hitherto been his home is directed already to the final scene of his execution. There we find the clearest expression of the horizon which I have called being in reality. The place of execution is a deserted stone quarry at the edge of the town, close enough to have in the near distance what Kafka calls "a still completely urban house." Here K.'s executors come to a standstill, Kafka writes, "whether because this place had been their goal from the very

2 *ibid.*, 9.

beginning or because they were too exhausted to go farther." And here the execution occurs. K. turns his head while waiting for the knife to be driven into him and, at the last moment, Kafka writes,

His glance fell on the top storey of the house adjoining the quarry. With a flicker as of a light going up, the casements of a window there suddenly flew open; a human figure, faint and insubstantial at that distance and that height, leaned abruptly far forward and stretched both arms still farther. Who was it? A friend? A good man? Someone who sympathized? Someone who wanted to help? Was it one person only? Or were they all there? Were there some arguments in his favour that had been overlooked? Of course there must be. Logic is doubtless unshakable, but it cannot withstand a man who wants to go on living. Where was the Judge whom he had never seen? Where was the High Court, to which he had never penetrated?[3]

This final awareness of K. is the datum of his being in reality. The total horizon of his world opens up at that last moment and the possibilities of the world reach toward him in darkness and confusion. His aloneness is his complete severance from a world which contains hope and love and goodness as impossible possibilities. The existential corollary of such aloneness is anguish, and this takes us from Kafka to Dostoievski.

It might appear that in moving from the world of Kafka to that of Dostoievski we are abandoning the referential standpoint of common sense. Is it not true that the world of daily life is the thematic background against which Kafka's hero emerges, whereas Dostoievski's world is marked precisely by an almost complete absence of the normal stream of day to day existence? It is out of the uninspected, taken for granted realm of the wide awake man, typified by the business world, that Kafka's hero is catapulted instantaneously. In Kafka's *Metamorphosis* Gregor Samsa awakes one morning to find himself "changed in his bed to some monstrous kind of vermin."[4] And his transformation is over and against the literal samples of his occupation. His bedroom contains a collection of cloth swatches; Gregor is a commercial traveller. His first thoughts are reflections on his business life: "God!," he thought, "What a job I've chosen. Traveling day in, day out."[5] And with this Gregor goes on to prepare himself for meeting his obligations. Metamorphosed into the horrific, aware of the utter impossibility of carrying on his job, Gregor nevertheless says to himself, "I must get up, for my train goes at five."[6]

Seemingly in contrast, the world of Dostoievski's heroes is seldom, if

[3] *ibid.*, 287–288.
[4] Kafka, F., *Metamorphosis*, New York, 1946, 12.
[5] *ibid.*, 13.
[6] *ibid.*, 14.

ever, the workaday world. In fact, these heroes are notoriously unemployed and unemployable: they are the marginal figures of the social world: criminals, neurotics, gamblers, drunkards, epileptics, and saints. The normal world seems to have disappeared or never to have been at all. If there is a thematic quality to this style of life it is complete, pure, yet bearable desperation. It would appear that rather than locating being in reality with regard to the character of common-sense life, we have moved to a literary scene which is defined by the very lack of such a structure. The explanation of the paradox provides an approach to Dostoievski.

By desperation I understand a fundamental removal of the self from concrete possibilities of resolving a problem. I am desperate about this or that, I need something or somebody desperately, and these situations are solvable and so resolvable. But desperation as such, not my being desperate about this or that, but my desperation as a mode of being, a permanent possibility of human existence, is unaffected by events or persons. Events and persons, to the contrary, are seen and treated as fearful, awesome, lovable, or hateful, in virtue of the self's desperation. The desperate man is not one who is desperate about this or that. Each one of us lives through moments or times of desperation, but we are not because of that desperate men, nor are we desperate men at the time of being desperate about a concrete, over-powering problem. The desperate man has a style of being; his world is structured in terms of his way of being in the world. And that way of being, I now want to suggest, is crucially related to both the problem of common-sense life and being in reality. Essentially, the desperate man builds his existence on an inversion of common-sense life; he operates on the terrain of nothingness which is the immediate character of being in reality. The desperate man is above all the prime example of one whose being in reality is the starting point for his life's odyssey and the continual image in which he encounters the world.

Dostoievskian desperation is one mode of existential anguish. To be anguished is to define one's life as perpetually lived in confrontation with the datum of being there. Anguish as a category is discovered through the immanence of existence. The substantive experience of anguish, perpetual confrontation with one's being in reality, locates the conceptual meaning of the experience, and the conceptual structure then realized is itself utilized as a way of grasping the meaning of experience. In this way, the existential category of anguish fulfills a double service: it derives from an experience it helps to define. In the case of anguish this double character of the existential category is an aspect of the self-reflective Dostoievskian hero. The anguished man is not only aware of his anguish, he is critically concerned with its nature, with the full signification it bears. In *Notes From Underground* the paradoxalist analyzes his own motives in presenting his confession. "Hadn't I better end my 'Notes' here,?" he asks, after revealing himself to us.

I believe I made a mistake in beginning to write them, anyway I have felt ashamed all the time I've been writing this story; so it's hardly literature so much as corrective punishment. Why, to tell long stories, showing how I have spoiled my life through morally rotting in my corner, through lack of fitting environment, through divorce from real life, and rankling spite in my underground world, would certainly not be interesting; a novel needs a hero, and all the traits for an anti-hero are *expressly* gathered together here, and what matters most, it all produces an unpleasant impression, for we are all divorced from life, we are all cripples, every one of us, more or less.[7]

The self-reflection of the anguished man renders him an anti-hero. He is forever at issue with himself, an issue for himself: his world is suspended on the moment in which his being in reality gives itself to him and holds him possessed.

Essentially the same analysis is true for the positive hero, rather than the anti-hero, in Dostoievski's world. The arguments of Ivan Karamazov are dialogues with himself in which his passion for conviction meets his absolute demand for truth. The theme that tortures him is the problem of theodicy: man's anguish is located in that single, overpowering issue. And the placement of the issue, I would hold, is at the level of man's being in the world, seen as a moral search for resolution. Anguish here is the awareness of a root mode of being: the inescapable and radical reality of evil. The difficulty in defining evil is an indication of its foundational character. Evil cannot be defined operationally; for it is not defined but encountered in reality. Again, it is not a matter of concrete acts which are evil but the quality in life which marks an act as evil. Evil is disclosed as a feature of the horizon which is man's being in reality. The sense of moral requiredness is built upon the confrontation with the evil we must face and live against. The terms of discourse here are universals transcendent to anthropology or history, relative only to the human condition they define. "With my pitiful, earthly, Euclidian understanding," Ivan says, "all I know is that there is suffering and that there are none guilty." To give a rationale for this condition, to resolve its demands on moral intellection is the force

[7] Dostoievski, F., *Notes From Underground*, New York, 1943.

of Ivan's life. "I must have justice," he cries, "or I will destroy my-self."[8] And this cry is the voice of existential anguish calling into judgment its own desperation.

In both aloneness and anguish existential literature has discovered and invoked substantive experiences as fundamental categories for the interpretation of experience. The genius of Kafka and Dostoievski is in their literary creations, but their philosophic insight is no less extra-ordinary. One expression of that insight is given in the way in which aloneness and anguish are shown, implicitly, as deriving their unique force from the very style of man's being, the condition of his existence, his being in reality. One moves into the worlds of these creators through a metaphysical trap door. Fallen suddenly into the atmosphere of existential concern, the participating reader encounters himself without pretence, his social roles cast aside, his public masks undone, his naive original wonder about the meaning of human existence regained. These authors return us to ourselves.

Perhaps the peculiar quality of existential literature is the demand it makes on the reader that he possess a metaphysical dimension. This is at once the admission price and the barrier. For many it is their devotion to the naively given world, their rootedness in the common-sense attitude, that rebels against categories which are felt to be morbid and at best partial truths. The existential underground seems distant from the warmth and brightness of reason and the com-forts of a trust in the advance of science. Dostoievski's underground man is entitled to his reply. He asks:

Does not man revel in destruction and confusion because he instinctively dreads that he may attain his end and crown the work he has begun? And perhaps — who knows — the end of mankind on earth may consist in this uninterrupted striving after something ahead, that is, in life itself, rather than in some real end which obviously must be a static formula of the same kind as '2 and 2 make 4.' For 2 and 2 make 4 is not a part of life but the beginning of death ... And why are you so firmly and solemnly convinced that only that which is normal and posi-tive, in a word, his well-being, is good for man? It is possible that, as well as loving his own welfare, man is fond of suffering, even passionately fond of it ... I am sure that man will never renounce the genuine suffering that comes of ruin and chaos. Why, suffering is the one and only source of knowledge.[9]

Aloneness and anguish, together with fear, dread, suffering and death are the central concern of those who bear a metaphysical dimension; and irrationalism here is not so much an attack against the traditional

---

[8] Dostoievski, F., *The Brothers Karamazov*, New York, 1945, 289.
[9] Dostoievski, F., *Notes From Underground*.

categories of reason as an abandonment of the natural attitude of daily life in favour of the magical and the mysterious.

I fear that these last words will probably wreck everything I have been trying to construct in this paper, but I would be avoiding my goal if I failed to include them here. To see the world as magical is to have a feeling for the extremity of man's fundamental condition, his being confronted with the task of answering the most tortured of all questions, What does it mean to be an existent in reality? Magic is an effort to transform ourselves, not the world. The magician is a fraud; he knows he cannot change objective nature, and so his art consists instead in changing us, in deceiving us into believing what is false. To view the world as magical is to transform our experience of the world through the alchemy of the existential categories. Above all, to treat the world as magical is to discover it as ultimately mysterious. Magic leads to mystery.

By mystery and the mysterious I do not mean the occult or that which is beyond explanation. Rather I use the term in Gabriel Marcel's sense, i.e., as a problem which for certain reasons has no univocal solution possible. Marcel distinguishes between a problem and a mystery. A problem may be overpoweringly complex, but in principle there is a way of approaching it which will lead to a solution. The data of problems are always exterior to us, they are never inwoven in the human fabric of the investigator himself. A mystery, on the contrary, has interiority as the mark of its data; it is the inquirer himself who is at issue in his inquiry. "A mystery," Marcel writes, "is a problem which encroaches upon its own data, invading them, as it were, and thereby transcending itself as a simple problem."[10] The metaphysical dimension can be defined in these terms. To treat the world as mysterious, to take the existential categories as mysteries, to concern ourselves with ourselves as more than problematic, is to stand in a radical relationship to reality. And paradoxically, it is the most ordinary, common-sense structures of human experience which magic transposes into mysteries. Being born into this world, existing in it, and dying in it become themes which no psychology can even approach. It is rather in philosophy and in literature that we find such mysteries expressed and explored. Magic and mystery return us to our metaphysical origin, to the moment when we are shot like rockets into midnight, and we are born.

[10] Marcel, G., *The Philosophy of Existence*, London, 1948, 8.

11. *The Privileged Moment:*
a Study in the Rhetoric of Thomas Wolfe

> "Every language is the whole of a world, a space in
> which our souls live and move. Each word breathes
> the air of the whole. Each is open toward an unbound-
> ed horizon. A language is not an aggregate of words
> and rules. It is a potential world, an infinity of past
> and future worlds, merely a frame within which we
> speak and can create our world, actualizing ourselves
> and our language."
>
> *Kurt Riezler*

⟨I⟩

The rhetoric of Thomas Wolfe is part of his legend.[1] Building a fury of
signs, he elevated words and sounds to an intensity which is qualitatively their own and unique to his style; protean and boundless, he
urged language into a wildness and power that signalized his transcendent view of the world as a labyrinth of the lonely and the alone.
Wolfe's style, then, is as striking as his great figure must have been;
and there is no critic of his work who has failed to remark its reach and
also its problematics.[2] But as with so many other features of the Wolfe
legend, there has been more mention of his rhetoric than there has been
serious analysis of it.[3] Somehow it has been taken for granted for the
very reason of its immediacy. That much has been lost in this way I
hope to show; but the present essay cannot claim to be a study of
Wolfe's style or an anatomy of his language. Rather, I am here concerned with his rhetoric as a single, though crucial, facet of a
phenomenology of language, a facet which will, however, lead to
nuclear issues in rhetorical theory.

[1] See Herbert J. Muller, *Thomas Wolfe*, Norfolk, Conn., 1947, Chapter 1.

[2] For a sympathetic treatment of Wolfe's style, see Pamela Hansford Johnson, *Thomas
Wolfe: A Critical Study*, London and Toronto, 1947, 17–33; the case against Wolfe is presented by Alfred Kazin, *On Native Grounds*, New York, 1942, Chapter 15. Kazin writes (p.
480): "Wolfe was the Tarzan of rhetoric, the noble lover, the antagonist of cities, the spear
of fate, the Wolfe whose rhetoric, swollen with archaisms out of the English classics, can be as
painful to read as a child's scrawlings. His rhetoric, pilfered recklessly from the Jacobeans
and Sir Thomas Browne, James Joyce and Swinburne, Gilbert Murray and the worst tradi-
tions of Southern oratory, was a gluttonous English instructor's accumulation. He became
enraptured with the altitudinous, ceremonial prose of the seventeenth century, with the
vague splendors of a dozen assorted romanticisms, and united them at the pitch of his father's
mountain oratory."

[3] There is no title on Wolfe's rhetoric contained in the bibliography of the secondary literature which appears in Thomas Clark Pollock and Oscar Cargill, *Thomas Wolfe at Washing-
ton Square*, New York, 1954, nor is there any article specifically concerned with Wolfe's style
included in *The Enigma of Thomas Wolfe* (ed. by Richard Walser), Cambridge, Mass., 1953.

Although it is not within the scope of this essay to consider the problems of a phenomenology of language or the more general philosophical issues involved in clarifying the relationship of language to reality, I do wish to indicate the immediate sense in which I am using the term "rhetoric" in the present discussion. Negatively stated, I am not interested here in anything that can be called traditional rhetoric, i.e., the history of rhetoric in Greek and Roman thought, nor am I concerned with recent discussions of the status of theory of rhetoric.[4] Furthermore, I am not talking about anything which has been discussed under the rubric of rhetorical criticism or poetic. Although the style of my problem may be closest to the spirit of the "New Rhetoric," I have developed my ideas from distinctively philosophical considerations and from a particular philosophical tradition that are not proper parts of the "New Rhetoric." Positively stated, I have used "rhetoric" as an inroad to the philosophical problem of how language both fixes and realizes the complex "moments" of meaning which announce reality. Rhetoric here is developed, however, within and through the context of Wolfe's writings rather than in philosophical terms. I have started with the naive sense of rhetoric which has been used to characterize a distinctive aspect of Wolfe's style, but my point is that this sense of rhetoric as high-flown, charged, and rhapsodic usage is a clue to a profound dimension of language which has been obscured or ignored – the power of language to epiphanize transcendent meanings through its own instrumentality. The rationale of such a concept of rhetoric, the analysis of its structure, is the task of a phenomenology of language which would account for and describe the logical genesis and foundation of meaning in subjectivity. The philosophical achievement of Edmund Husserl has given us the groundwork for such an investigation. Alfred Schutz' "Symbol, Reality, and Society"[5] is a decisive contribution to recent discussion of these problems. But such phenomenological investigations of language and reality are beyond the limits of my remarks on Wolfe. Here I wish to restrict the problem to exactly what I have attempted: interpreting the rhetoric of Thomas Wolfe as the articulation of reality through privileged moments.

---

[4] E.g.: My article, "The Limits of Rhetoric," *Quarterly Journal of Speech*, XLI, April 1955, is completely unrelated to the present essay, apart from the identity of philosophical standpoint underlying both papers.

[5] In *Symbols and Society: Fourteenth Symposium of the Conference on Science, Philosophy and Religion* (ed. by Lyman Bryson, Louis Finkelstein, Hudson Hoagland, R. M. MacIver), New York, 1955.

Our first problem is one of definition. Traditionally, by the rhetoric of Thomas Wolfe has been meant his charged language, those extensive passages throughout his works which are stylistically reminiscent of Whitman and Melville and which bear the fiery and solemn cadences of the Old Testament.[6]

Who has seen fury riding in the mountains? [Wolfe writes]. Who has known fury striding in the storm? Who has been mad with fury in his youth, given no rest or peace or certitude by fury, driven on across the earth by fury, until the great vine of the heart was broke, the sinews wrenched, the little tenement of bone, marrow, brain, and feeling in which great fury raged, was twisted, wrung, worn out, and exhausted by the fury which it could not lose or put away? Who has known fury, how it came? [7]

Such passages appear in at least two ways in the novels: they are interspersed, usually following scenes or vignettes, and serve as a kind of chorus for the works; also they are binding and bridging structures which function as motifs at the beginning of each novel, as connective tissue between sections, and as poetic finales.

As a chorus, Wolfe's chanting voice takes up again and again the central themes of his work: the self in its solitude and lostness in reality, the self in the image of Telemachus, the self's rootedness in earth, history, and the prime memories of family and home, and, finally, the voyage of the self in search of itself through the mysteries of time and the haunting domain of death. Suffusing these passages is a sense of root loss, an *a priori* of something sought for and somewhere missed, as though what structures human experience into the relatedness of men were itself flawed -- not failure here but the impossibility of fulfillment:

Which of us has known his brother? Which of us has looked into his father's heart? Which of us has not remained forever prison-pent? Which of us is not forever a stranger and alone? [8]

As binding and bridging forces, such expressive passages are distillations of things done, places seen, persons encountered, and experiences suffered and reveled in. The connections are both immediate and indirect: they lead from one set of affairs to another in the novelist's story and they also thrust back and forth in the substance of events.

---

[6] Two collections of rhetorical-poetic passages from the writings of Wolfe have appeared: John Hall Wheelock, *The Face of a Nation*, New York, 1939 and John S. Barnes, *A Stone, A Leaf, A Door*, New York, 1945.

[7] *Of Time and the River*, New York, 1944, 27–28.

[8] *Look Homeward, Angel*, New York, 1929, motif, facing p. 3.

Throughout *Of Time and the River*, for example, the image and theme of death is taken up in manifold ways – the deaths of the hero's father and brother are the points of central reference – and returned to through the instrument of rhetorical passages. Immediately after a comic interlude in the novel, Wolfe turns to the theme of his brother's death and resurrects his image:

> And then he would hear again the voice of his dead brother, and remember with a sense of black horror, dream-like disbelief, that Ben was dead, and yet could not believe that Ben had ever died, or that he had had a brother, lost a friend. Ben would come back to him in these moments with a blazing and intolerable reality, until he heard his quiet living voice again, saw his fierce scowling eyes of bitter gray, his scornful, proud and lively face, and always when Ben came back to him it was like this: he saw his brother in a single image, in some brief forgotten moment of the past, remembered him by a word, a gesture, a forgotten act: and certainly all that could ever be known of Ben's life was collected in that blazing image of lost time and the forgotten moment. And suddenly he would be there in a strange land, staring upward from his bed in darkness, hearing his brother's voice again, and living in the far and bitter miracle of time.[9]

After this section devoted to Ben, there is an immediate return to the earlier scene. This kind of placement can only be understood as connective ordering which illuminates the themes of a novel by rhetorical emphasis. The connection is direct to the extent that it instantly binds together parts of a single sequence; it is indirect, however, in its very persuasion, for it calls the reader back to fragmented moments of the theme's expression at the same time that it promises a re-sounding and rearticulation in pages to come.

But defining rhetoric in this context as charged language, dominated by poetic image, and having the several stylistic functions just discussed, is far from arriving at an acceptable analysis of the problem. It is my thesis that there is much more involved in the rhetoric of Thomas Wolfe; that we must go beyond the character of rich, compressed, and pulsating language to the interior and essential meaning born and expressed by the order of prose-poetry commonly associated with Wolfe. I wish to suggest that that meaning lies in a certain attitude toward language itself, a certain appraisal of the limits of language, and a certain refusal to accept those limits – at least not without raging. To put the entire matter in a different way: Wolfe's rhetoric involves a conception of language, its inherent powers and possibilities, and, I would add, its relationship to the reality it describes and engages, and to its votaries, like Wolfe, whom it demonizes.

---

[9] *Of Time and the River*, 200–201.

⟨ II ⟩

For many and divergent reasons, ours may be called the century of language: whether we consider the contributions of philosophers, psychologists, or novelists, the central impression that a new "key" (to use Susanne Langer's term) has been struck in the whole range of knowledge and art is unavoidable and undeniable. In philosophy the work of such variant thinkers as Peirce, Husserl, Cassirer, Heidegger, and Wittgenstein has created a rich literature concerned with the problems of symbol, concept, and form: in psychology (broadly taken) the work of Freud, George H. Mead, the Gestalt school, and Kurt Goldstein has opened up a new terrain of relevances for language in its relationship to mind and action; and in literature, the revolutionary contributions of Proust and Joyce have liberated and made explicit a generative force in art.[10] Even if we restrict ourselves to literary influences, the impact of the century's discovery on the consciousness of Wolfe was enormous. Joyce's influence on Wolfe may serve as an approach to the problem of rhetoric.[11]

Only obliquely in *Ulysses* and *A Portrait of the Artist as a Young Man*, but explicitly in *Stephen Hero*, Joyce formulates his theory of *epiphany*.

By an epiphany he meant a sudden spiritual manifestation, whether in the vulgarity of speech or of gesture or in a memorable phrase of the mind itself. He believed that it was for the man of letters to record these epiphanies with extreme care, seeing that they themselves are the most delicate and evanescent of moments.[12]

An epiphany is a momentous and instantaneous manifestation of reality; it is a sudden breaking into experience with arterial force, revealing "that which is" with utter truth and candor. The greatness of an artist may be measured by the epiphanies he gives us, those revelations that turn on vast lights in our consciousness, which in

[10] T. S. Eliot writes of *Ulysses:* "I hold this book to be the most important expression which the present age has found; it is a book to which we are all indebted, and from which none of us can escape." ("Ulysses, Order, and Myth," in *James Joyce: Two Decades of Criticism* (ed. by Seon Givens), New York, 1948, 198).

[11] See Thomas Wolfe, *The Story of a Novel* in *The Portable Thomas Wolfe* (ed. by Maxwell Geismar), New York, 1946, 566 and also cf. Nathan L. Rothman, "Thomas Wolfe and James Joyce: A Study in Literary Influence," in *The Enigma of Thomas Wolfe.*

[12] Joyce, J., *Stephen Hero* (A Part of the First Draft of *A Portrait of the Artist as a Young Man*), (ed. by Theodore Spencer, New York), 1944, 211; see Spencer's Introduction, *ibid.*, 16–17 and cf. Irene Hendry, "Joyce's Epiphanies," in *James Joyce: Two Decades of Criticism* and Harry Levin, *James Joyce: A Critical Introduction*, Norfolk, Conn., 1941, 28–31 and *passim.*

searching out their hidden objects, their shadowed forms, search out in us the gift of understanding. Joyce presents his theory in quasi-satiric scholastic terms:

First we recognize that the object is *one* integral thing, then we recognize that it is an organized composite structure, a *thing* in fact: finally, when the relation of the parts is exquisite, when the parts are adjusted to the special point, we recognize that it is *that* thing which it is. Its soul, its whatness, leaps to us from the vestment of its appearance. The soul of the commonest object, the structure of which is so adjusted, seems to us radiant. The object achieves its epiphany.[13]

An epiphany may be generated out of compounded objects and experiences, however, and the moment of insight and expression goes beyond the Thomistic trinity of "wholeness, harmony, and radiance" which Joyce discusses.[14] An epiphany in the compounded sense, generalized into the total world of experience, is the discovery of a thematic meaning which has been lost in its "sedimentations" (to borrow a term from the language of phenomenology), which has encysted in its complexity within experience, but below the threshold of explicit awareness. It is this distillation of meanings which is tapped by creative genius and brought to expression in epiphany. And, I would suggest, it is precisely the stylistic methodology of Joyce that recommends itself to Wolfe, for he too is haunted by epiphanies potential to creation, awaiting the season of their unfolding.

If the epiphanies of Joyce are revelations of Man, they are for Wolfe outpourings of the person, the self alone; yet the starting point, stylistically, is historical for both. Just as *Ulysses* is the exploration of consciousness through the single day of Leopold Bloom, a moment in time, so, it may be remarked, the novels of Wolfe begin with a dating of the action or a statement of the historicity of the theme.[15] The beginning of *Look Homeward, Angel* is the clearest announcement of Wolfe's intentions: the prologue of the first chapter presents a colon to which the totality of the rest of the novel is a restricted, implicit remainder:

Each of us [Wolfe writes] is all the sums he has not counted: subtract us into nakedness and night again, and you shall see begin in Crete four thousand years ago the love that ended yesterday in Texas.

---

[13] *Stephen Hero*, 213.

[14] *ibid.*, 212–213 and *A Portrait of the Artist as a Young Man* in *The Portable James Joyce* (ed. by Harry Levin), New York, 1947, 478 ff.

[15] The opening sentences of *Of Time and the River* and *You Can't Go Home Again* date the action of the novel in terms of the hero; the opening sentence of *The Web and the Rock* and the third paragraph of the opening page of *Look Homeward, Angel* date the action in terms of the hero's ancestors.

The seed of our destruction will blossom in the desert, the alexin of our cure grows by a mountain rock, and our lives are haunted by a Georgia slattern, because a London cutpurse went unhung. Each moment is the fruit of forty thousand years. The minute-winning days, like flies, buzz home to death, and every moment is a window on all time.

This is a moment: [16]

Each person, each event, each history of affairs is a compressed cipher for which Wolfe's art is hermeneutic. The world of each man is a microcosm in which is pressured the totality of all that ever was, implied in an almost Hegelian trail of connections that return the moment to Time, the event to Process, the individual to the Absolute. Wolfe's world is a world of moments, highly structured and individuated, yet caught up in the themes of a mutual destiny, a single attraction that gives them valence and defines their signification.

The placement of meaning and insight in the moment is inescapable to any reader of the novels: the stranger seen in the street, on the train, from afar, glimpsed for that instant of recognition and then forever vanished back into the web of anonymity, the face at the window, the brief look of the bank teller, the sight of the salesman, the suddenly-caught movement of the laborer, the craftsman, the stitch of the tailor, the trucker shifting heavy gears, the frosty face of the trainsman signalling in an early hour of winter, the soft cry of a child – all these are familiar moments in the pages of the novels, and Wolfe is unimaginable without them. But these moments are usually described as "far and lost," as instantly gone, as "forever lost." They are instantaneous irruptions in consciousness which fill the hero with sadness and longing and despair and wonder; they are always sudden, always intense, and always remembered. It is in these moments that Wolfe's epiphanies manifest themselves.

But it is necessary to examine these moments most rigorously if we are to go beyond the simple marking of them: what content do they inform us of, what indeed do they epiphanize? In answer to this question one commentator has suggested that the passion of the moment is in its givenness and that the meaning of the moment invariably escapes both novelist and reader.

Everything for Wolfe is in the moment [writes John Peale Bishop], he can so try to impress us with the immensity of the moment that it will take on some sort of transcendental meaning. But what that meaning is, escapes him, as it does us. And once it has passed from his mind, he can do nothing but recall

---

[16] *Look Homeward, Angel*, 3.

another moment, which as it descends into his memory seems always about to deliver itself, by a miracle, of some tremendous import.[17]

But Bishop views these moments in an almost moral context: they represent efforts on the part of the novelist to embrace his characters and their truth as well; and since Wolfe, according to this critic, was ultimately incapable of love, those moments fail to achieve resolution: they are mounting crescendos in a symphony that moves, quickens, and elevates without ever coming to climax.

The most striking passages in Wolfe's novels [Bishop says] always represent these moments of comprehension. For a moment, but a moment only, there is a sudden release of compassion, when some aspect of suffering and bewildered humanity is seized, when the other's emotion is in a timeless completion known. Then the moment passes, and compassion fails.[18]

But I think Wolfe's moments may be viewed apart from Bishop's moral framework, that they do reveal an interior signification, and that though they lapse in the temporal movement of the novel, they remain constant in the articulation of Wolfe's vision. It is as instrumentalities of rhetoric that their import may be grasped and their positive quality seized.

⟨ III ⟩

Someone has remarked that all Wolfe's novels are about a novelist writing a novel. Whatever truth there may be in this, in addition to surface observation, it may tend to obscure a deeper truth about Wolfe's work: that much of it is self-critical in the sense of being meta-linguistic. There are sections of the novels, in addition to *The Story of a Novel*, which are directly concerned with the problems of language and language users, though those sections often take the form of meditations on language and art rather than academic or philosophical critiques. In an epiphanous moment Wolfe presents the bond and power that bind the writer to his art:

At that instant he saw, in one blaze of light, an image of unutterable conviction, the reason why the artist works and lives and has his being – the reward he seeks – the only reward he really cares about, without which there is nothing. It is to snare the spirits of mankind in nets of magic, to make his life prevail through his creation, to wreak the vision of his life, the rude and painful substance

---

[17] Bishop, J. P., "The Sorrows of Thomas Wolfe," *Kenyon Review*, I, 1939, 10–11.
[18] *ibid.*, 14–15.

of his own experience, into the congruence of blazing and enchanted images that are themselves the core of life, the essential pattern whence all other things proceed, the kernel of eternity.[19]

The epiphany Wolfe gives us is the revelation of language itself: the artist in words is more than storyteller or technician; he is in possession of the quintessence of existence if only it can be tamed into expression, worked into "the congruence of blazing and enchanted images." Language, for Wolfe, is both battering ram and castle, it is weapon and wound, for the moment's meaning is that language *is* reality, bound to it in the way of its being and in the form of its substance. Wolfe's quest for linguistic dominion is the effort to wrench from language its capacity to penetrate reality, to gain an inroad into being, to achieve the miracle of epiphany in which language reveals itself as reality and reality reveals itself through image, form, and the magical terms of language. "Could I," Wolfe cries, "weave into immortal denseness some small brede of words, pluck out of sunken depths the roots of living, some hundred thousand magic words that were as great as all my hunger, and hurl the sum of all my living out upon three hundred pages!"[20] And this cry, itself a moment, is the confession that language is superior to any of its concretizations, that it remains, like earth and the seasons, a quest for the wanderer and a home for the lost.

The moment, then, is revealed in language because its very character is constituted of language: the image of the real *is* the real or as much of it as man can grasp, and language draws us into the vortex of full expression. The points in language when such perfection of meaning and image, of word and reality, is achieved are epiphanies; they are, we may say, *privileged moments* of consciousness. And now the full relationship of rhetoric and language may be seen, for rhetoric, as we choose to interpret it in our present framework, is the complete expression which embodies an epiphany, and makes of it a privileged moment. It is not a question of poetic expression or high-flown language; rather it is the victory of language over its object when form fixes content with purity and high purpose. The fixation intended here is the expression of consciousness divorcing from its interest, momentarily, the irrelevancies which bind us to the meanings sedimented in reality. In this sense, rhetoric liberates consciousness from a burden of connections and opens it up and out into a world of unlimited truth. It re-teaches us how to *see* what is given us in experience; by its very power and elevation

---

[19] *Of Time and the River*, 550.
[20] *The Web and the Rock*, New York, 1937, motif on page preceding p. 3.

it draws us up to face what hitherto in seeing we have always ignored: rhetoric gives to the privileged moment a privileged status. Though his essay is concerned with different problems from those we have been dealing with here, a passage from Camus' *The Myth of Sisyphus* gives a penetrating statement of what we may call the rhetoric of privilege:

> Thinking is learning all over again how to see, directing one's consciousness, making of every image a privileged place ... From the evening breeze to this hand on my shoulder, everything has its truth. Consciousness illuminates it by paying attention to it. Consciousness does not form the object of its understanding, it merely focuses, it is the act of attention, and, to borrow a Bergsonian image, it resembles the projector that suddenly focuses on an image. The difference is that there is no scenario, but a successive and incoherent illustration. In that magic lantern all the pictures are privileged. Consciousness suspends in experience the objects of its attention. Through its miracle it isolates them.[21]

Consciousness attains to the privileged moment through its capacity to fix it in symbols, to announce its coherence through the coherence of language itself. In this sense, rhetoric as "fixative" is a special moment, a privileged moment, in linguistic expression, and in the purest form it can attain, it transcends itself into poetry.

If we have presented rhetoric in a rather unusual light, it is no less the case that we have turned to perhaps curious features of language and consciousness itself. The world examined in these terms is hardly the world as it is ordinarily regarded. Our excuse, if one is necessary, is that the world as it truly presents itself to human experience is elusive and that the privilege of epiphany commends itself in making substantive to consciousness what otherwise remains tormentingly adjectival. Rhetoric seems, from a theoretical standpoint, to be all things to all men, and we offer here only a little suggestion regarding one possibility of interpretation which we think has been overlooked. However, if what we say about Wolfe's rhetoric is true, we can no longer talk about "mere" rhetoric again. Even at its shallowest, most hollow worst, rhetoric is an instrument capable of a magnificence: as we use it, it may be, but rhetoric itself is never "mere." At its finest, as in the writings of Thomas Wolfe, rhetoric reveals the privileged moment in which human consciousness discovers its passion and power, its capacity to bind up the wound reality inflicts upon those who discover it, and in discovering it, transcend it.

[21] Camus, A., *The Myth of Sisyphus and Other Essays*, New York, 1955, 43. Note that we are taking this statement out of its context in the essay, considering its meaning for our present discussion quite apart from Camus' interpretation of Edmund Husserl's phenomenology – an interpretation we cannot follow.

12. Albert Camus: Death At The Meridian

⟨ I ⟩

"The great question as to a poet or novelist is," Henry James once said, "How does he feel about life? What, in the last analysis, is his philosophy? When vigorous writers have reached maturity, we are at liberty to gather from their works some expression of a total view of the world they have been so actively observing. This is the most interesting thing their works offer us. Details are interesting in proportion as they contribute to make it clear."[1] In the case of philosophical writers, of poets and novelists whose work is centrally directed toward metaphysical questions, the relevance of James' remark is intensified in several ways, and also rendered strikingly complex. The philosophical novelist is not only concerned with issues generated out of the essential terms of our existence, he is self-consciously committed to creating a work of art whose very character expresses the urgency of his quest. A philosophical novel, let us say, is about itself; it is a meta-literary performance which reveals the triple bond that compels author, characters, and reader to come to terms with themselves and each other. That bond is an existential commitment to self-justification, to engaging impossible questions and to the despair of an enterprise that is destined to perpetual renewal. Philosophy becomes the conscience of art.

Too often the interior dialogue between the author and his story is translated into the problem of "autobiography." In these terms, the commitment of the philosophical novelist to his work is interpreted as revelatory of the dialectic of his own life, as manifesting the history of his personal struggles and aspirations. One then looks in the novel for a chapter in the life of the author, and one interprets the hero of the

---

[1] quoted by Eliseo Vivas in *Creation and Discovery*, New York, 1955.

story as the instrument of his confession. Such a translation both obscures the meaning of autobiography in literature and limits its possible range. What is important is not whether an event in a story had a counterpart in the actual life of the author but, instead, whether the life of the novel is informed by the mind of the novelist. The question is, Can you locate in the literary work the hypothetical alternatives the artist ponders in his creative task? Are you drawn into dialogue with his possibilities? Or are you left searching for the strands of his life? If the commitment of the philosophical novelist is to the urgency of fictive possibilities, the search of the creative reader must be for an author's questions, not his conclusions. And not merely those questions which are announced in the novel, but especially those which antedate the written page and which return us to the torment of making a start.

The philosophical novelist, then, is a writer in dialogue with himself, his work, his readers, and, in a sense that is ordinarily missed in the use of a phrase which should tell us much, with his time. It is here that a more profound notion of "autobiography" comes in. A writer's time is his age perceived in the metaphysical perspective of his insertion in a temporal world. And to say that a writer expresses the problems or paradoxes of his time or that a writer symbolizes the essential anxiety of his time is to imply that his act of creative representation provokes and is provoked by the infoldment of experience in the magic circle of his own awareness. To represent an age is, in this sense, to re-present its cardinal content, to bring once again into unity, into the unity of a single consciousness, the elements that comprise its anger, its pride, and its secret shame. All of the metaphysical novelists have been privileged witnesses to the infoldment of consciousness. In different ways such writers as Dostoievski, Kafka, and Melville contribute a literature of dialogic commitment; it is *they* who are at issue in their work, and it is *they* we meet in reading their books. In our own day, Albert Camus has come to stand for the same kind of involvement. His books and his life appear to fuse in the image of philosophic concern, artistic strength, and human integrity. He has become for many almost the imago of a contemporary hero, the metaphysical man within whose life our own autobiographies achieve illumination. The recent death of Camus, death in a senseless automobile accident, death in his forties, death in the midst of his creative involvement, is the lonely occasion for an inquiry into the philosophic dimension of his art.

⟨ II ⟩

Camus seems destined for a period of misunderstanding before his themes and positions achieve some security in the minds of his readers, especially his readers in this country. And this is not just a matter of the immediacy of his work, his proximity to the disorder of these times. No waiting period will help to set straight the peculiar misreadings his books seem to attract and his life seems to encourage. Paradoxes have in their turn generated cross-purposes. Camus is thought of as a French writer, as a Frenchman; not only was he born in Algeria, he remained throughout his life emphatically sensitive to the world of Algeria, to its climate, its horizon. Camus is known in the United States primarily as a novelist and essayist; in France he was as much thought of as a man of the theater, not only a playwright but a director, once an actor. But there are more important impasses and confusions: it is commonplace to speak of Camus as a poet of the absurd; that he transformed this position in many ways in the later part of his life is not so much forgotten as unrecognized. Finally, Camus is thought of most often as an existentialist. His own repudiation of much of existential philosophy or his declaration of his ignorance of some of it have not caught up with the fancies of his public. Many of his readers prefer him to be an existentialist. That they cannot explain very much of what they mean by such a classification only adds to its charm. The worst of it is that Camus' split with Sartre has been interpreted by some people as the repudiation by an honorable man of a dishonorable Left. Unfortunately, Camus' rebellion in this incident does not even make sense in what we call political terms; we, Camus' American audience, are unexperienced in the apparatus of metaphysical defection. Immersed in what schoolboys call "current events," we find it difficult to attend to history. Dialogue with Camus is possible only if we bracket what we have heard about him and listen to what we may hear from him.

At the center of Camus' thought is a struggle to locate the limits of a radical humanism which at once frees man of his bondage to God and permits him to realize a moral life. The struggle has a dozen roots and manifold reasons; it arises out of a concrete historical experience that commenced with the collapse of the Crystal Palace, the dream of a lost humanism, and it may be traced through two World Wars and the spectacle of disaster familiar to everyone who has lived through the years of war. But the concrete events are merely touchstones for a more generalized collapse of values which has been felt, as a tremor of the earth is felt, by men everywhere who ask themselves how it is possible to be decent in a fallen world. In other terms, the struggle for a new humanism is one consequence of an epistemic disjunction between self and world which has always haunted the philosophic mind. How is it possible to claim objective validity for moral concepts that appear to be subjectively rooted? How is it possible to ground moral truths in a certitude that goes beyond mere attitude or opinion unless such a ground lies outside and beyond man? And if the truth does transcend man, is it possible to live with what one has, with an untruth achieved under the duress of absolute commitment? Camus' search is born of a rejection of tradition and an abhorrence of anarchy. The truth, for him, is neither in the middle nor at the extremes of theism or atheism; the truth has no position, no placement in terms of spatial metaphors. It is instead that tension, that intellectual passion, and that conative thrust which men can realize in their lives in the very act of moral commitment in a world defined by men. And beyond this there lies a peace and joy which are purely human possibilities, a release from exasperation into love. The way into that jubilation of consciousness is by passage into the absurd. The first category of a radical humanism is the problematic concept of the absurd. It is the threshold to the art of Camus.

As with every term fundamental to a fairly rich schema, the absurd operates at different levels and with varying meanings in Camus' thought. Its common denominator may not be the best way of expressing what is of major importance here. Instead, a definition that proliferates, that moves in several directions at once, that hesitates as much as it affirms – this perhaps is the proper procedure. The absurd, for Camus, is the location of the world in the perspective of human reality. World and self, being and consciousness, can never find a principle of reconciliation. For man the world arises to be known, to be judged, to be embraced; but knowledge, judgment, and love remain fugitive structures. Man is the being who yearns for justification. "I said that the world is absurd," Camus writes, "but I was too hasty. This world in itself is not reasonable, that is all that can be said. But what is absurd is the confrontation of this irrational and the wild longing for clarity whose call echoes in the human heart. The absurd depends as much on man as on the world. For the moment it is all that links them together. It binds them one to the other as only hatred can weld two creatures together. This is all I can discern clearly in this measureless universe where my adventure takes place."[2] The absurd,

_____
[2] Camus, A., *The Myth of Sisyphus and Other Essays*, New York, 1955, 21.

then, is measure and measured; it is both a condition and the agency of revolt. But there are other ways of presenting the absurd.

Imagine several situations. First, you have quarreled with someone. Harsh words were exchanged. Voices were distorted in anger. A verbal mesh of fury enveloped the scene. Now imagine that the argument was secretly recorded and that you are made to listen, months after the affair, to all that was said. You hear yourself, you listen to your angry noises, you avoid looking at anybody for fear of smiling. Is it not absurd? Second, in the act of performing your daily job you suddenly become aware of yourself as performing that job. So, for instance, you become aware of yourself as being the person who is asking a customer to please wait a moment. When you turn to the customer a little later, you recognize yourself as a person part of whose task it is to ask people to wait. Isn't that absurd? Third, you are asked to join an organization for the achievement of world peace. You don't think that world peace can be attained by such organizations, but you are not sure how else you can help. You decide to think the matter over, but other problems come up and you forget about it. Months later you remember that you were to decide, and feeling a bit guilty over your long silence, you mail in your dues. Meanwhile the organization has collapsed. You send several letters in trying to get your money back. Now, a final encounter with the absurd reported in Eugen Kogon's book on Nazi concentration camps, *The Theory and Practice of Hell*:

All prisoners in the concentration camps had to wear prescribed markings sewn to their clothing – a serial number and colored triangles, affixed to the left breast and the right trouser leg. At Auschwitz the serial number was tattooed on the left forearm of the prisoners. Red was the color denoting political prisoners. Second offenders, so-called recidivists, wore a stripe of the same color above the upper edge of the triangle. Criminals wore a green triangle, with a surprinted S for the SV category. Jehovah's Witnesses wore purple; 'shiftless elements,' black; homosexuals, pink. During certain periods, the Gypsies and the shiftless picked up in certain special campaigns wore a brown triangle.

Jews, in addition to the markings listed above, wore a yellow triangle under the classification triangle. The yellow triangle pointed up, the other down, forming the six-pointed Star of David. Jews and non-Jews who had violated the Nuremberg racial laws – so-called 'race defilers' – wore a black border around or athwart the green or yellow triangle. Foreigners had a letter surprinted on their triangles – F for France, N for Netherlands, etc. Special political prisoners picked up at the outbreak of the war, for supposed unreliability, wore their serial number across the triangle, the others about an inch below the bottom point. Starting with the war, certain prisoners were admitted who had a K printed on their triangles. These were 'war criminals' (*Kriegsverbrecher*) and they were always permanently assigned to penal companies. Their offenses were often trifling. Occasionally a prisoner long in camp was likewise assigned to this K company. Only a very few of them survived. 'Labor Disciplinary Prisoners' wore a white A on their black triangles, from the German word for labor, *Arbeit*. Most of them were in camp for only a few weeks. Members of the penal companies showed a black dot, the size of a silver dollar, between the point of the triangle and the serial number.

Prisoners suspected of plans for escaping had a red-and-white target sewn or painted on chest and back. The SS even devised a special marking for the feeble-minded – an armband with the German word *Blöd*. Sometimes these unfortunates also had to wear a sign around their necks: 'I am a Moron!' This procedure was particularly provocative when the prisoner in question also wore the red triangle reserved for avowed opponents of the Nazi regime. The feeble-minded enjoyed the freedom of the camp and were the butt of the cruelest jokes. Eventually they all perished or were killed by injection.

The camps were a veritable circus, as far as colors, markings, and special designations are concerned. Occasionally prisoners were decked out in nearly all colors of the rainbow.[3]

As Sartre, as well as many other commentators, has pointed out, the absurd, for Camus, "is both a state of fact and the lucid awareness which certain people acquire of this state of fact. The 'absurd' man is the man who does not hesitate to draw the inevitable conclusions from a fundamental absurdity." The distance between self and world, consciousness and nature, not only exists, it is recognized. The absurd is not only a quality of man's reality, it is encountered. Beyond the limitations of the petty and the overpowering, the distant garble coming out of the recording machine and the inventory of concentration camp symbols, there is the texture of the absurd felt, handled, immediately given in an overarching design: it is precisely the world which is encountered as absurd. And to speak of the world here, not of its fragments, is to make a claim about "our time" – that its foundation is built of an evil that can never be rectified, that its spirit has no ulterior support, and that the possibilities of transcendence are only toward that lucidity of consciousness which Camus discovers, ultimately, in the simple joys of this earth. The recognition of evil, the rejection of divine transcendence, and the oblique yet purposeful movement toward joy are moments (in the Hegelian sense) in a triple progression. They constitute the matrix of the absurd.

Discussions of the problem of evil in professional philosophy and theology seem to be at a standstill today. Theodicy is, if anything, a contemporary embarrassment. Yet in literature the issue is very much alive, and in the writings of Camus theodicy is again put at the center of our worldly concern. The question, far from exhausted, is given renewed urgency: How is it possible to justify the existence of radical evil? How is it possible to understand the suffering of the innocent?

[3] Kogon, E., *The Theory and Practice of Hell*, New York (Berkley Book ed.), 41–42.

And how is it possible for men in daily life who strive for a moral order of existence to build their lives on the unhappiness of others? Camus is beginning not where Dostoievski left off but where Dostoievski began. Camus' question is Ivan's appeal to Alyosha in The Brothers Karamazov:

Tell me yourself, I challenge you – answer. Imagine that you are creating a fabric of human destiny with the object of making men happy in the end, giving them peace and rest at last, but that it was essential and inevitable to torture to death only one tiny creature – that baby beating its breast with its fist, for instance – and to found that edifice on its unavenged tears, would you consent to be the architect on those conditions? Tell me, and tell the truth.[4]

Camus is compelled to say "no" with Alyosha, but unlike Alyosha his is a "no" without recourse to Christ, a "no" that in its finality can only hope for man's achievement of lucidity within an irrevocably faulted world. And just as Ivan builds his case on the irrefutable data of the suffering of the children whose cases he cites, so Camus stocks his ammunition dump with the unavoidable terror given in the death of a child. He writes in The Plague:

They had already seen children die – for many months now death had shown no favoritism – but they had never yet watched a child's agony minute by minute, as they had now been doing since daybreak. Needless to say, the pain inflicted on these innocent victims had always seemed to them to be what in fact it was: an abominable thing. But hitherto they had felt its abomination in, so to speak, an abstract way; they had never had to witness over so long a period the death-throes of an innocent child.
     And just then the boy had a sudden spasm, as if something had bitten him in the stomach, and uttered a long, shrill wail. For moments that seemed endless he stayed in a queer, contorted position, his body racked by convulsive tremors; it was as if his frail frame were bending before the fierce breath of the plague, breaking under the reiterated gusts of fever. Then the storm-wind passed, there came a lull, and he relaxed a little; the fever seemed to recede, leaving him gasping for breath on a dank, pestilential shore, lost in a languor that already looked like death. When for the third time the fiery wave broke on him, lifting him a little, the child curled himself up and shrank away to the edge of the bed, as if in terror of the flames advancing on him, licking his limbs. A moment later, after tossing his head wildly to and fro, he flung off the blanket. From between the inflamed eyelids big tears welled up and trickled down the sunken, leaden-hued cheeks. When the spasm had passed, utterly exhausted, tensing his thin legs and arms, on which, within forty-eight hours, the flesh had wasted to the bone, the child lay flat, racked on the tumbled bed, in a grotesque parody of crucifixion.[5]

Our world is founded on the death of that child, and our hopes are nourished with the bounty of his suffering. There is, for Camus, no

[4] Dostoievski, F., The Brothers Karamazov, 291.
[5] Camus, A., The Plague, New York, 1948, 192–93.

escape from this moral datum. At the heart of man's being in the social world is the infection which shadows his plans, a residue of pus that can never be squeezed dry. That it is absurd that this is the case can only mean that God can never justify his creation and that man is left with the responsibility of accounting for himself in a life made possible by death. There is, however, a strange alternative.

In some of its forms Gnosticism suggests a distinction between the Demiurge as creator of this world and the Divine Being who is truly God. The evil of the world is the work not of the ultimate God but of an intermediary. There then exists not only evil but a structure of evil. In Camus' terms the absurd might be understood as the creation of the Demiurge, but a creation set adrift from the Divine Being. Man's yearning to return to his source, his divine source, is a thematic element of all of Camus' books. His early and serious interest in the philosophy of Plotinus makes itself manifest here. But against Plotinus and Christian doctrine as well, man is fallen in a world abandoned by its creator. If God cannot be reached, the question is whether the world is contrived in the mold of an inescapable evil. One of Faulkner's characters says, "Perhaps it is upon the instant that we realize, admit, that there is a logical pattern to evil, that we die." Camus' answer to this is given in the context of his religious rejection of God.

In a way, Camus' conception of God and man is the reverse of that of Ivan Karamazov. Ivan accepts God but rejects His world; Camus, we might say, rejects God but accepts His world. And in fact it is notorious that Camus has been received most enthusiastically by the church, especially those within it who sense in his work the existence of an authentic religious dialogue. Parodoxically for our time, the rejection of religious transcendence has become a way of formulating, for those who would be believers, the very problem of transcendence. The question for Camus as well as for his audience is, Can humanism be revitalized? Is a radical humanism possible which can adequately pose the issues that confront men today? Can we live religiously without God? Camus gives us the question, not an answer. How is this to be understood?

Philosophical questioning, whether in philosophy proper or in literature, comes alive only when the questioner is at issue in his question, when he commits himself, opens himself to the possibility of change and upset. This is why questioning is a hazardous affair. On the dust jacket of the American edition of *The Myth of Sisyphus* is the phrase: "a lucid invitation to live and to create." This appears on the cover, not in the blurb. It happens to be the truth. Camus is well aware of the ironies possible between author and audience. In the face of these dangers – the dangers of patronization and phony devices – he extends to us, to each of us, an invitation to consider the dialectic of his theme. On opening his book we are struck with the personal quality of his thought. He is not speaking for us but to us. His thoughts require that we involve ourselves in the struggle to articulate, in true form, the questions that are implicit within us. Camus, then, is a dialectician following an ancient tradition. But the tradition is French as well as Greek; it is French and Danish too. The being of the questioner is the theme of Socrates as well as Pascal and Kierkegaard.

We are given a question, then, not an answer. But this does not mean that in being called to self-examination we are left without suggestions. Rather, we are left with an image of the absurd that is rendered possible by a dialectical consideration of a Godless world. The image is that of daily routine: "Rising, streetcar, four hours in the office or the factory, meal, streetcar, four hours of work, meal, sleep, and Monday Tuesday Wednesday Thursday Friday and Saturday according to the same rhythm."[6] But in the very activity of routine the absurd is encountered: "one day the 'why' arises and everything begins in that weariness tinged with amazement."[7] The "why" is not a transforming agency; it merely slips into the work of the day and sticks there as a disturbance. The logic of inquiry here leads, Camus says, either to suicide or recovery. In fact, the whole of Camus' encounter with the absurd comes into focus at this point. The committed questioner who asks with Camus whether he can live with what he knows is really asking whether it is possible to transcend the appeal of suicide as a completely valid refusal to bear the human condition. Camus does not make that refusal. He accepts instead a world in which men define themselves authentically in persisting in an unbright search for honor and decency. The Hegelian moments of theodicy and the rejection of divine transcendence lead, finally, to the prize of the venture, the recovery of joy as the victory of and over the absurd.

Earlier we said that Camus is as much Algerian in spirit as French. This should now be qualified. If anything, he is more Algerian than French. But it is not a matter of political or cultural loyalties. Camus' France faces Africa; his Africa opens out into a Mediterranean horizon. The beach and the sea beyond are more than facts of nature; they are

---

[6] Camus, A., *The Myth of Sisyphus and Other Essays*, 12–13.
[7] *ibid.*, 13.

guide lines to a serenity, a way of being, a style of life that Camus knew
and to which he remained true. "In Algiers," he writes, "no one says 'go
for a swim,' but rather 'indulge in a swim.' " Bathing in the sea is an
almost ritual reliving of a natural drama. Like fishermen of the flesh,
Camus' young men go out by boat to swim in the sea that brings them
its treasures of vitality and quickness. Their return is almost mythic:
"At the hour when the sun overflows from every corner of the sky at
once, the orange canoe loaded with brown bodies brings us home in a
mad race. And when, having suddenly interrupted the cadenced beat
of the double paddle's bright-colored wings, we glide slowly in the
calm water of the inner harbor, how can I fail to feel that I am piloting
through the smooth waters a savage cargo of gods in whom I recognize
my brothers?" [8]

The simple joys that Camus returns to or, better, that he rediscovers
in himself, are misleadingly formulated, for the vocabulary of simpli-
city is disarming. Swimming together, talking together, joking together,
playing together, making love together – these are wonders that we
recapture after the agonies of the absurd: they are the fruits deliciously
hidden in the absurd. But before a return to them is possible, we still
confront the daily world of insolence, deceit, yearning, and reprisal.
Toward what we must now call the end of his life, Camus felt that he
had broken through the walls that make of our world a labyrinth, that
he had rediscovered a vein of joy that lay concealed in his flesh. In an
essay recording his return to the North African city of his youth, he
remembers himself:

I discovered once more at Tipasa that one must keep intact in oneself a freshness, a
cool wellspring of joy, love the day that escapes injustice, and return to combat
having won that light. Here I recaptured the former beauty, a young sky, and I
measured my luck, realizing at last that in the worst years of our madness the
memory of that sky had never left me. This was what in the end had kept me
from despairing ... In the middle of winter I at last discovered that there was in
me an invincible summer. [9]

Evil cannot be justified, God cannot be, but the absurdity of existence
can be suffered with a heart that guards its interior freedom, a freedom
that can transform terror into a triumph of consciousness. It is here that
Camus' style becomes the banner of his cause. His central terms are
charged simplicities: joy, lucidity, summer, and the sea. The language
of the absurd returns us to that infoldment of consciousness which

---

[8] *ibid.*, 143.
[9] *ibid.*, 201–202.

marks the mind of its author. Joy is the dialectical transformation of man's being into that lucidity in which the absurd is at last shackled. It is as close to transcendence as man can come.

⟨III⟩

Final sections seem destined to raise questions such as, What is the place of Camus in the total literary scene? How much is there in his work which will last? Is Camus a truly great artist? In a way, what difference is there if one answers such questions with thumbs up or thumbs down? And who are we to be executioners or saviors? I prefer to turn to other problems. We have considered Camus as a philosophical novelist. Is he then to be taken as a philosopher? It would be a mistake to answer yes or no to this question without first asking whether the function of philosophical literature is clearly delineated. I think it is not; in fact, the entire region is obscure. We are able to point to philosophical novelists and poets, but we find it extremely difficult to explain what it is we are pointing to. It is necessary to go beyond the statement by Henry James with which we began. A philosophical novelist not only raises metaphysical questions, he explores their nature in the framework of human action. He develops philosophical concepts as well as utilizes them. But there is always a hazard: the writer is most often not a professional philosopher; is it quite fair for him to employ categories and themes which are deeply rooted in the soil of philosophy and then to claim literary immunity if he is critized at a technical level? Is Camus, then, destined to be called a good philosopher by the writers and a good writer by the philosophers? Such dodges can never be fair to anyone. Still, they form the first rank in a series of criticisms and charges the philosophical novelist must face. Everything depends here on the placement of the problem. We are interested in the writer as a philosophical artist.

To be sure, Camus' themes are not new. His art is heavily indebted to an existential tradition in both philosophy and literature. Yet it is not enough to say that he has given new life to old ideas. Camus' originality lies in a confrontation with the absurd which ends, as we have seen, neither in capitulation to transcendence nor the chaos of death. The tension that flows through his work is the power of revolt, a living witness to man's capacity to upend himself without destroying himself. And even this thematic tension is at least as old as Hegel. *The Phenomenology of Mind*, especially the sections on Master and Slave

and the Unhappy Consciousness, is the best introduction to the philosophy of the absurd. Through the dark and thick tangle of German
metaphysics one sees burning the gem of Camus' thought. What
distinguishes his work and mission from that of Hegel and the philosophers is, paradoxically, best understood in terms of Hegel and the
philosophers. It is precisely that infoldment of consciousness in man
which makes him a witness to his time. Without a grounding in nineteenth century philosophy, most readers of Camus have felt this secret
attraction of his work. It is Camus himself that attracts us. At the end
of the absurd world he describes, we find him waiting for us.

The death of an artist can reverberate in the mind of his public.
He is missed in a special way. In the case of Camus, death is both part
of his thematic world, one of the central terms of his discourse, and
now closes out that world. Here is the prime example of the involution
of art and life: an artist whose theme is death dies. We must add this
to our list of illustrations of the absurd. But if we do, we must at the
same time attend to the moments of the absurd and be true to its
dialectical possibilities. An audience always survives an author, but it
is then the responsibility of that audience to recover the artist's
questions and enrich his dream. Camus leaves us at a time when we
can ill afford his death. Long after the tributes to him have completed
their course and the literary pickpockets have run their fingers through
his Nobel Prize address, it may be time to try to assess his gifts. We
shall, however, have to catch up with him, for he died *en route*.

PART THREE

HISTORY AND THE SOCIAL SCIENCES

13. A Study in Philosophy and the Social Sciences

My intention in this essay is not to survey either the historical or the structural relationships between philosophy and the social sciences, but rather to focus on a basic systematic problem in methodology: the philosophical character and implications of the methods of social-scientific inquiry. By "methodology" I understand the underlying conceptual framework in terms of which concrete studies in history, sociology, economics, and the like are carried out, and in terms of which they receive a general rationale. Therefore I am not concerned here with the nature of specific techniques that social scientists utilize, or with their evaluation. Instead, I am interested in what I take to be a distinctly philosophical task, the analysis of the underlying presuppositions of the conceptual systems employed by social scientists in virtue of which their scientific enterprise is carried out. Methodology in the sense in which I am using it thus implies a certain order of philosophical commitment.

The framework for my remarks is historically oriented, however, since I wish to begin with two major methodological approaches to the task of social-scientific inquiry. The approaches in question will provide us with a point of departure for a discussion of social-scientific methodology, its relationships with natural-scientific inquiry, and its general philosophical implications. Such a discussion looks toward the concrete problem of this paper, which is an analytic, critical comparison of naturalistic and phenomenological approaches to the methodology of the social sciences. It shall be my purpose to point out certain crucial inadequacies in the naturalistic interpretation of social science – inadequacies that can be overcome, it seems to me, by a phenomenological approach.

⟨ I ⟩

Let me begin, then, with a statement of two positions. I use the designation "naturalism" in this context to refer to that approach to social science which holds that the methods of the natural sciences, scientific method generally, are not only adequate for the understanding of social phenomena but indeed constitute the paradigm for all inquiry in this field. A conjoint thesis of naturalism is that of the qualitative continuum between problems of the natural and of the social sciences. William R. Dennes expresses this point quite clearly: "There is for naturalism no knowledge except that of the type ordinarily called 'scientific.' But such knowledge cannot be said to be restricted by its method to any limited field of subject matter – to the exclusion, let us say, of the processes called 'history' and the 'fine arts.'" [1]

Thelma Z. Lavine presents the thesis of naturalism in this way: "The naturalistic principle may be stated as the resolution to pursue inquiry into any set of phenomena by means of methods which administer checks of intelligent experiential verification in accordance with the contemporary criteria of objectivity. The significance of this principle does not lie in the advocacy of empirical method, but in the conception of the regions where that method is to be employed. That scientific analysis must not be restricted in any quarter, that its extension to any field, to any special set of phenomena, must not be curtailed – this is the nerve of the naturalistic principle. 'Continuity' of analysis can thus mean only that all analysis must be scientific analysis." [2]

It follows clearly that naturalistic methodology is held to be applicable to the problems of the social sciences – in fact, that a proper theory of the social sciences would have to be founded in these terms. In the words of Ernest Nagel, it would have to be a theory that, "in its method of articulating its concepts and evaluating its evidence," would be "continuous with the theories of the natural sciences." [3]

The second approach is radically different. It directly argues that the phenomena of the social sciences are not qualitatively continuous with those of the natural sciences, and that very different

---

[1] Dennes, W. R., "The Categories of Naturalism," in *Naturalism and the Human Spirit* (ed. by Yervant H. Krikorian), New York, 1944, 289.

[2] Lavine, T. Z., "Naturalism and the Sociological Analysis of Knowledge," *ibid.*, 184–85.

[3] Nagel, E., "Problems of Concept and Theory Formation in the Social Sciences," in *Science, Language, and Human Rights*, American Philosophical Association, Eastern Division, Philadelphia, 1952, 63.

methods must be employed to study social reality. Here it is maintained that what is needed above all is a way of looking at social phenomena which takes into primary account the intentional structure of human consciousness, and which accordingly places major emphasis on the meaning social acts have for the actors who perform them and who live in a reality built out of their subjective interpretation.

Obviously the label "phenomenological" is less than satisfactory for this total approach, since it neither derives directly from the philosophy of Edmund Husserl nor is always philosophically compatible with principles of Husserlian phenomenology. Nevertheless, I prefer the term "phenomenological" to the possible alternative "subjective," for although the former may be misunderstood, the latter is necessarily misinterpreted in the context of its present meaning if it is equated, as unfortunately it generally is, with personal or private or merely introspective, intuitive attitudes. I shall therefore use "phenomeno-logical" as a generic term to include all positions that stress the primacy of consciousness and subjective meaning in the interpretation of social action.

The clearest expression of this standpoint is offered by Max Weber: "Sociology ... is a science which attempts the interpretive understand-ing of social action in order thereby to arrive at a causal explanation of its course and effects. In 'action' is included all human behaviour when and in so far as the acting individual attaches a subjective meaning to it. Action in this sense may be either overt or purely inward or sub-jective; it may consist of positive intervention in a situation, or of deliberately refraining from such intervention or passively acquiescing in the situation. Action is social in so far as, by virtue of the subjective meaning attached to it by the acting individual (or individuals), it takes account of the behaviour of others and is thereby oriented in its course." [4]

Contemporary discussion of the problems of the social sciences has been dominated by the dialogue between representatives of the two camps. Most of the characteristic problems of social-scientific methodo-logy have been at issue: criteria of verification, the status of so-called introspective reports, the use of models in explanation, the applica-bility of mathematical or formalistic modes of description to social phenomena. But underlying all of these topics there is what I consider to be the root issue for the entire range of problems involved: the question of the nature and status of knowledge as such in science as

[4] Weber, M., *The Theory of Social and Economic Organization*, New York, 1947, 88.

such. At the basis of all methodological analysis there lies an essentially epistemological problem, that of the critique of knowledge. It is this problem I am interested in exploring at present. To carry out such an exploration requires that we turn to the epistemological grounding of the naturalistic and phenomenological approaches.

As we have seen, it is the central contention of the naturalistic school that the methods of natural science constitute the proper means for inquiring into social phenomena. Now if we distinguish between methods in the sense of concrete techniques and methods in the philosophical sense of conceptual instruments, it is clear that the naturalist's thesis is directed to a level concerned with the kind of knowledge involved in social science. In other words, the naturalist is suggesting that the concepts of the social sciences, as well as the theoretical matrix for those concepts, are identical or ought to be made identical with those of the natural sciences.

But at what level is this suggestion offered? Is the suggestion itself a proper part of scientific discourse? Is the analysis of the conceptual structure of a system within the province of science? Is the working out of a system of scientific explanation to take place within the framework of natural science? Are philosophical questions about natural science to be treated as problems within the methodology of natural science? All of these questions lead back to a foundational one: is an epistemological analysis of the kind of knowledge involved in natural-scientific discourse to be taken at the same level with natural-scientific problems, and therefore to be answered in terms of the criteria of explanation provided by natural science? The immediate question is then whether natural science can talk about itself philosophically in natural-scientific terms. But before turning to the paradox I think is involved here, let us glance at the epistemological problem relevant to the phenomenological approach.

To decide that the problems of the social sciences are first of all phenomenological means that social action is understood as founded on the intentional experience of the actors on the social scene. The kind of theoretical framework erected in accordance with this insight is distinctively philosophical, that is, questions about the nature and status of intentional experience may themselves be raised and resolved within the same framework. A phenomenological approach has then this unique characteristic: questions about its own methods and procedures are part of its structural content. Since a phenomenological system is not bound to criteria taken over from a non-philosophical or a supra-philosophical domain, it may consider immanent problems. For the same reason a philosophical system may, indeed must, consider its own procedures and articulation as part of its field for inquiry. The point is that a phenomenological approach lends itself completely to philosophical self-scrutiny.

At the conceptual level, then, the method of natural science and the method of social science are radically different; the former is rooted in a theoretical system that may never take itself as the object of its inquiry without transcending its own categories; the latter, in its phenomenological character, necessarily becomes self-inspecting yet remains within the conceptual system involved, that of philosophical analysis. Furthermore, whereas a phenomenological approach begins by raising the question of its own philosophical status, the naturalistic standpoint cancels out the possibility of self-inspection by its own claim that natural science provides the essential method for stating and evaluating philosophical claims.

It might appear that this analysis of naturalism does not do justice to its precisely philosophical character, that it fails to acknowledge the status of naturalism as a philosophy that reflects on nature and experience. Rather than replying to this caution directly, I prefer to consider it first in the context of a fairly recent statement by a philosopher in the naturalist tradition who approaches this criticism of naturalism in an especially forceful manner.

⟨II⟩

In a 1953 article Thelma Z. Lavine, herself a contributor to the earlier volume entitled *Naturalism and the Human Spirit*, reflects on certain problems raised in that volume concerning philosophical naturalism, and addresses herself to a criticism of the fundamental method of naturalistic inquiry.[5] Although her purpose is a reconstruction of naturalism in the light of her criticisms, rather than an abandonment of the position, her critical remarks are directly relevant to the present discussion.

Miss Lavine presents four basic charges that she thinks naturalism must face: "(1) naturalism's surrendering of the status of constructive philosophy for that of methodological principle; (2) its failure to raise the question of its own method as distinguished from that of science; (3) its neglect of elements other than the experimental

---

[5] Lavine, T. Z., "Note to Naturalists on the Human Spirit," *Journal of Philosophy*, L, February 26, 1953, 145–54.

in scientific method; (4) its omission of the problems of social science method." [6] Her statement of the first two charges will suffice for an account of her general argument:

The dominating concern with the unrestricted applicability of scientific method tends unfortunately to reduce naturalism itself to a mere uncompromising testimonial to the universal adequacy of that method. Naturalism is left with only a negative function: watchdog of scientific method, sniffing out interloping methods. A naturalism that is content to be defined by a principle of continuity of analysis conceived in terms of experiment and empirical verifiability must also be agreeable to forfeiting its status as a positive, i.e., constructive philosophy ... A related difficulty stems from the failure to distinguish at all times between the method stipulated by naturalism for inquiry into all types of subject matter and the method of naturalism itself. If naturalism views 'itself,' however, as nothing but a methodological principle, it is easy to see why more care was not devoted to distinguishing itself from the scientific method it recommends. Naturalism as mere 'controlling methodological principle' or as 'criticism' is in the limbo of methodology, concerning which methodological questions are rarely raised. The failure to raise clearly the question: '*What is the method of naturalism?*' even more than the failure to provide a clear answer, has two unhappy results. It has, firstly, suggested to some that the method of naturalism is the method of the sciences. Yet who should know better than a naturalist that only science uses scientific method? Secondly, an even less desirable result of not inquiring into the method of naturalism is that naturalists have thereby cut themselves off from that insight into their own philosophy which can lead them out of the *cul-de-sac* of a position which is nothing but a methodological principle. [7]

I have quoted here at length because I believe that this statement on its own account deserves more serious attention than it was given in Ernest Nagel's reply to it, [8] and because, coming from a naturalist, it is doubly interesting.

For Miss Lavine the way out of this naturalistic impasse is provided by a reconstructed "method of understanding" or *Verstehen*, which has, among other things, the "merit of designating the ... non-experimental elements in scientific and in philosophic theory." [9] "What is here being suggested," she writes, "is that those present difficulties of naturalism stemming from its incapacity to admit and to treat effectively the various non-experimental elements in inquiry may be resolved by a naturalistically reconstructed method of *Verstehen*. In this reconstruction the most important single task is working out a set of controls for the *verstehendes* element in philosophic and scientific theory which will serve, as do the controls in experimentation, as empi-

[6] *ibid.*, 153.

[7] *ibid.*, 146–47.

[8] Nagel, E., "On the Method of *Verstehen* as the Sole Method of Philosophy," *Journal of Philosophy*, L, February 26, 1953, 154–57.

[9] "Note to Naturalists on the Human Spirit," 150.

rical checks."[10] Of course, it is Miss Lavine's view that such a reconstruction *is* possible within the naturalistic framework. I would like to challenge this contention.

First, it is necessary to be clear about the meaning of *Verstehen*. The translation "understanding" is not a happy one, because *Verstehen* signifies a certain kind of understanding relevant primarily to human behavior. *Verstehen* is interpretive understanding. If we go back to Max Weber's conception of the subjective interpretation of meaning in social action, we will have a clearer notion of what is at issue here. Weber maintains that the primary task of the sociologist is to understand the meaning an act has for the actor himself, not for the observer. The kind of understanding involved is precisely that of *Verstehen*.

What is sought in such explanatory understanding is the total character of the intentional framework of the actor, which alone provides the key to the meaning of a specific act he performs. A particular act is referred back interpretively to the intentional matrix that is the ground of its meaning. "Thus," Weber writes, "for a science which is concerned with the subjective meaning of action, explanation requires a grasp of the complex of meaning in which an actual course of understandable action thus interpreted belongs. In all such cases, even where the processes are largely affectual, the subjective meaning of the action, including that also of the relevant meaning complexes, will be called the 'intended' meaning. This involves a departure from ordinary usage, which speaks of intention in this sense only in the case of rationally purposive action."[11] *Verstehen*, then, for Weber, is the operation concerned with explicating the structure of subjective interpretation of meaning. But this is not all that *Verstehen* signifies.

Alfred Schutz has pointed out that *Verstehen* has at least three different levels of application. It may be understood "as the experiential form of common-sense knowledge of human affairs ... as an epistemological problem, and ... as a method peculiar to the social sciences."[12] It is the failure to distinguish these different levels which explains, in part, much of the confusion involved in the criticisms directed against Weber's postulate of the subjective interpretation of meaning. These criticisms are usually generated by the following assumptions: first, that Weber is saying that a different kind of

[10] *ibid.*, 151–52.
[11] *op. cit.*, 95–96.
[12] Schutz, A., "Concept and Theory Formation in the Social Sciences," *Journal of Philosophy*, LI, April 29, 1954, 265.

knowledge is involved in understanding social phenomena from that involved in understanding natural phenomena; second, that the method of *Verstehen* consists in an empathic response to or imaginative reconstruction of another person's motivation in social action; third, that Weber's postulate of subjective interpretation involves a "subjectivism" that renders the method of *Verstehen* not only unscientific but even anti-scientific; and fourth, that the method of *Verstehen* offers no criteria for scientific explanation. As Ernest Nagel puts it, "the method of *Verstehen* does not, by itself, supply any *criteria* for the validity of conjectures and hypotheses concerning the springs of human action." [13]

All of these assumptions are false and completely misleading. A review of the three levels of *Verstehen* presented by Schutz will enable us to see what Weber *is* advocating. To say, in line with the first of those levels, that *Verstehen* is "the experiential form of common-sense knowledge of human affairs" means that as a matter of fact men in daily life do interpret one another's actions by seeking to grasp the meaning intended by fellow men. Consider some of the language involved at this level. "What did he really mean by that?" "Why don't you say what you mean?" "Who does he think he's fooling?" If overt statements and actions were always taken at face value, taken as true indicators of the speaker's opinions and attitudes, sincerity would be a meaningless term, politics would be without a subject matter, and history would be the chronicle of human vegetation. Common-sense interpretation turns out to be a highly complicated instrument. Motive, attitude, intent, and purpose are the primary structures looked to as the *real* basis for understanding overt behavior. *Verstehen* at the level of common sense is the actual mode of understanding utilized by actors in daily life to interpret one another's actions.

"As a method peculiar to the social sciences," another level of application formulated by Schutz, *Verstehen* is concerned with the typifications of interpretation found in common-sense life, and endeavors to provide a theoretical system suitable for their clarification. This theoretical system has as its guiding principle the subjective interpretation of meaning, but how this principle is utilized depends on the particular way in which the theoretical system is understood. There are two aspects to the system. First, it is the theoretical foundation for a method of interpreting social phenomena, that is, it provides the general concepts in terms of which the method of *Verstehen*

[13] *op. cit.*, 156.

is comprehensible. But second, it is a philosophical foundation for comprehending the intentional structure of social action.

For this reason it makes good sense to say, with Schutz, that *Verstehen* may be understood in a third application "as an epistemological problem." Here there are again two aspects to be grasped. *Verstehen* is concerned epistemologically with the cardinal philosophical problem of the social sciences, that of intersubjectivity; at this point it endeavors to pose the problem rather than to resolve it. But a second meaning of *Verstehen* involved here is that of philosophical method itself; in this sense it is synonymous with what might be termed metaphilosophical inquiry, that is, a necessarily *a priori*, dialectical, categorial analysis of philosophical procedures. Since philosophy is necessarily reflexive in character, since a philosopher must necessarily concern himself with the critique of his own enterprise (in its systematic rather than psychological context), it follows that metaphilosophy is an indispensable part of philosophical analysis. *Verstehen* is as essential to philosophical life as it is to common-sense life.

The misunderstandings involved in the criticisms of Weber presented before are now manifest. It is not that a different *kind* of knowledge is involved in the social sciences as compared with the natural sciences, but that the object of knowledge is different. The social sciences are concerned with the intentional dimension of social reality. Again, the "method" of *Verstehen* is not that of empathic or imaginative response, but rather a conceptual clarification of the interpretive understanding descriptively involved in the affairs of common-sense men in daily life. Furthermore, the "subjectivism" of Weber's postulate of interpretation does not mean that private, intuitive, unverifiable elements are involved in the understanding of social action, but that the very structure of social action is built out of the intentional character of human life.[14] Finally, to argue, as Nagel does, that "the method of *Verstehen* does not, by itself, supply any *criteria* for the validity of conjectures and hypotheses concerning the springs of human action"[15] is to confound several senses of "method" and to ignore what is distinctive about Weber's leading principle. *Verstehen* is not concerned at any level with providing empirical criteria for determining the validity of hypotheses; as a philosophically directed method it is concerned rather with the conceptual framework within which social reality may be comprehended.

Interestingly enough, this interpretation of the method of *Verstehen*

[14] Cf. Schutz, 269–70.
[15] *op. cit.*, 156.

as metaphilosophically oriented is in complete agreement with Miss Lavine's presentation of *Verstehen* as "designating the ... non-experimental elements in scientific and in philosophic theory."[16] Indeed, it is her claim that *"Verstehen* is the sole method of philosophy. Alternative philosophies cannot differ in the method they employ, but only in the types of terms they select as the objects of reflection."[17] But now it is Miss Lavine's contention that *Verstehen*, understood in this sense, may be appropriated by a reconstructed naturalism and thus provide what amounts to a philosophical grounding for the naturalistic position. I am in complete agreement with Miss Lavine's criticisms of naturalism, and with her conclusion that the method of *Verstehen* is needed to correct the central inadequacies she has indicated. I do not agree, however, that a reconstruction of *Verstehen* is possible in naturalistic terms. My reasons follow.

It seems to me, first of all, that Miss Lavine, having distinguished between methods of science and philosophical analysis, between "the method stipulated by naturalism for inquiry into all types of subject matter and the method of naturalism itself,"[18] lapses into the very evil she is attacking when she recommends a *Verstehen* reconstructed in such a way that empirical controls are built into it. It may be well, however, to quote her own conception of what such an empirically controlled *Verstehen* would involve:

A naturalistically reconstructed method of *Verstehen* would make possible the revising of the naturalistic methodological principle to incorporate *Verstehen* and would thus make this principle a more accurate statement of naturalistic aims. For naturalists do not so much seek to deny the fact of the various non-experimental elements in inquiry as they fear the uncontrolled philosophic vagaries which are apt to result from acknowledging them. Once naturalistic safeguards were provided for *Verstehen*, this new content might modify the form of the principle of continuity of analysis as follows: *The naturalistic principle is the resolution that inquiry into any area be subject to the single intellectual criterion of pertinent empirical checks upon the methods employed.* This is to say that *the nerve of the naturalistic position is not insistence upon a "single intellectual method" but upon a single intellectual criterion for whatever method may be feasible.* What is crucial, of course, is the concept of the pertinence of empirical checks to given methods.[19]

If *Verstehen* is offered by Miss Lavine as "the sole method of philosophy," which is then to be the method of naturalism, I do not see how it can be consistently suggested that "naturalistic safeguards" can be "provided for *Verstehen*." It was the philosophical status of naturalistic safeguards which was placed in question by Miss Lavine

16 "Note to Naturalists on the Human Spirit," 150.
17 *ibid.*, 153.
18 *ibid.*, 146.
19 *ibid.*, 152.

in her criticisms of naturalism. To reinvoke naturalistic criteria as correctives for a reconstructed naturalistic method is to take a step forward and follow with a step back. Moreover, Miss Lavine sacrifices the central point of her argument when, after making it clear that *Verstehen* is the essence of philosophical method, she reverts to a notion of *Verstehen* in the narrow sense of method as a conceptual device.

Verstehen in the broad sense cannot be "incorporated" into natural-istic methodology, because it is itself foundational; the meaning of methodological incorporation is part of the subject matter of *Verstehen*. What Miss Lavine wishes to do is quite clear. She wants to found naturalism philosophically without departing from naturalistic method. But her own placement of naturalism "in the limbo of methodology" should have warned her away from such an undertaking, and her insight into the character of *Verstehen* as the fundamental method of philosophical inquiry might have suggested a way out: the tran-scension of naturalism in favor of a phenomenological standpoint.

⟨III⟩

Thus far I have used the term "phenomenological" to designate a general style of social science which takes human consciousness and its intended meanings as the proper locus for the understanding of social action. In this sense such American social scientists as W. I. Thomas, Cooley, and G. H. Mead, in addition to the European school influenced directly by Max Weber, are all representatives of the phenomenological standpoint. Now, however, I wish to narrow my usage of the term to the technical meaning in contemporary philosophy given to it by Edmund Husserl, and suggest that Husserlian phenomenology not only is capable of providing a philosophical grounding for the social sciences but is distinctively suited to the philosophical task of *Verstehen*. Hus-serl's doctrine of the intentionality of consciousness provides an immediate entrance into the questions at issue.

All perceptual acts, in the broad Cartesian sense, have a directional character, an active movement that intends some object. Unlike the naive, real object of common sense or natural science, the intentional object is merely the correlate of the act of intending. The intentional object, or noema in Husserl's language, is the object as *meant*, as *intended* in the acts of thinking, remembering, willing, imagining, and the like. Phenomenology is a discipline concerned with the description of the phenomenon in so far as it is given to consciousness by way of the acts of intentionality. Since the entire range of intentional activity is taken as the subject matter for phenomenological investigation, the intentional life of actors in social reality is clearly included in the phenomenological domain. And here philosophical and sociological concerns merge into a single concordant venture: the attempt to comprehend social action in terms of the intentional meanings consciousness ascribes to its objects. Phenomenology is precisely, therefore, philosophical *Verstehen*.

In addition to its methodological rapport with the structure of social life, phenomenology is also a philosophy that claims to be self-founding. Determining whether it is truly a presuppositionless philosophy depends first on understanding in what sense that phrase is used by Husserl, a problem outside the province of this paper. But it is proper to suggest here that by a self-founding philosophy Husserl meant a position that attempts an absolute scrutiny of its own concepts, postulates, principles, and general procedures, by referring them back in each case to their experiential roots in the intentional life of consciousness. Therefore what distinguishes Husserlian phenomenology from all other positions is its insistence on a method that is reflexive, that places in radical question its own enterprise, and that seeks to found its results on a transcendental ground rendered apodictic by the instrument of phenomenological reduction. In contradistinction to naturalism, then, phenomenology not only is able to ground its own method but is defined by its insistence on doing so. Phenomenological philosophy is phenomenologically derived and phenomenologically realized.

Finally, the phenomenological approach to social reality fulfills the method of *Verstehen* since it offers a *philosophy* of the social world, rather than techniques or devices in the narrower methodological sense. And the social world at issue for the phenomenologist is the original, forceful, meaning-laden reality in which we exist. It is this world, the world of the natural attitude, which requires the interpretive understanding of *Verstehen*. When the naturalist approches social reality in terms of the methods of natural science, he forfeits his philosophical concern with a crucial dimension of reality and indeed reduces himself to limbo. Phenomenology claims to reconstruct social action by providing a fundamental clarification of its intentional structure within the framework of a comprehensive philosophy. It claims to return us to the social world in its full richness and urgent complexity. These are its claims. The demonstration of what is claimed involves another story, one much more difficult to tell.

14. Knowledge and Alienation:
Some Remarks on Mannheim's Sociology of Knowledge

There is a line of thought starting with the ancient sceptics, revitalized by Montaigne, and appropriated by certain modern thinkers, including Max Weber, which points to the root-incapacity of human reason and all theory to articulate an absolute conception of reality. Whether the argument starts with the divergence and variegation of sensory awareness, whether it points to the contingency of all human experience and its interpretation, or whether, in modern form, it advocates *positions* with respect to the Real instead of univocal solutions, the central direction of this theme is clear: it posits an alienation of the intellect from the grounds of assurance and certitude. The latest turn given this development is its historicization through the categories of sociology, and the clearest and most forceful expression of this style of analysis is Karl Mannheim's sociology of knowledge. I propose to take it as the framework for my remarks and to restrict myself to the epistemological aspect of Mannheim's work. What I have to say does not refer to his so-called substantive sociology.

My problem is the paradox of the relativization of thought as encountered in Mannheim's distinctive formulation of the sociology of knowledge.

The thinker [Mannheim writes] who sets out to relativize thought, that is, to subordinate it to supratheoretical factors, himself implicitly posits the autonomous validity of the sphere of thought while he thinks and works out his philosophical system; he thus risks disavowing himself, since a relativization of all thought would equally invalidate his own assertions as well.[1]

The way out of this paradox, Mannheim tells us, is the relativization of thought and the devaluation of the sphere of theoretical communica-

[1] Mannheim, K., *Essays on the Sociology of Knowledge*, New York, 1952, 137.

tion. This means concretely that the existential thinker, in Mannheim's phrase, by self-discipline and methodological decision discounts the world outlook into which he was born, which he shares with his fellow men, and discounts, even further, the very categories of knowledge which underly that outlook. That he discounts them permits him to utilize them with a purpose, but his purpose is not the uncovering of some specific inadequacy but rather the unmasking of a total ideology. The existential thinker emerges as the arch unmasker, and the immediate question arises, Is unmasking as a procedure itself a mask? Perhaps a more decisive formulation of the question might be, Is there anything behind the mask? If this question is pursued at the philosophical level and is not transposed into the realm of substantive sociology where it becomes an historico-empirical problem of a descriptive character, it leads, as Mannheim himself saw and admitted,[2] to metaphysics.

Let me try to formulate the relevant aspects of Mannheim's metaphysics. First, he denies the in-itself, purely immanent character of reality; second, the non-relative in respect to which relativized thought is relative is itself a function of a particular *Weltanschauung:* we are left with relational structures leading to non-relational centers which are themselves moulded by the fundamental perspectives and presuppositions of an epoch or tradition. It is not foolish or facetious to speak here of a relative certitude. But if this description is fair to Mannheim's position, we have here a metaphysical conception of whole and part which is both historical and methodological in its implications. It is historical to the extent that revolutions and major transitions in thought witness to *some* order of change from a totality to a radical segment which stands in a dialectical relation to the totality. It is methodological, however, in quite a different way. Here we are told that the true comprehension of our *Weltanschauung* requires that we step outside it by rejecting, for purposes at hand, the quality and status of theoretical thought. And this, Mannheim urges, has been done and is repeatable.

The movement from whole to part was intended to avoid the reflexivity of the thesis of the existential determination of knowledge. Has it succeeded? I think not. First of all, the movement from whole to part is predicated on the abandonment of the immanence of thought. The devaluation of the sphere of theoretical communication requires precisely an abandonment, as Mannheim puts it, of thinking only

---

[2] *ibid.*, 175.

"within thought." [3] With this abandonment goes the possibility of a rationale for a theoretical explication of the procedures of devaluation as well as for a coherent explanation of its metaphysical justification. What is left is a series of *positions*, intellectual camping sites, which are the variant loci of the existential thinker. The point is not that the existential determination of knowledge requires at least one proposition which is true – the thesis itself, but rather that the way of transcending the immanence of thought leaves the existential thinker with no basis for evaluating his own movement of transcendence or its internal implications for the metaphysical status of his intellectual activity.

The existential thinker is left with temporary determinations not because of a generalized fallibilism or historicism or some evolutionary point of view, but because systematically each position is in its very nature, for Mannheim, merely a fulcrum for the displacement of ideologies. It must be emphasized that when Mannheim stresses the existential nexus of epistemology, his emphasis is not historicistic but metaphysical: "epistemology," he writes, "is as intimately enmeshed in the social process as is the totality of our thinking." [4] And this is the case, for Mannheim, because the existential thinker alone can view the pre-formed structuration of his own thought in the very act in which he transcends it by devaluating it and partializing it. The metaphysical corollary of such partialization is what I would call, appropriating Mannheim's language, the unmasking of the object of knowledge and the event in which that object is given to consciousness. The existential thinker moves from the object and the event to the conditions of thought which structure them. In a special sense, the existential thinker concerns himself with the conditions of knowledge:

Just that which one perceives in 'phenomenological immediacy,' [Mannheim writes] is, in fact, already shaped by the historical process; it is already permeated by the form-giving categories of a new 'reason,' or a new 'psyche.' In every event, then, there is something other than the event itself. The event is moulded by a totality, either in the sense of a law patterning or in the sense of a principle of systematization. [5]

What is unusual about this interest in the conditions of knowledge and what distinguishes it from, let us say, the transcendental method of Kant is the very conditionality of the entire enterprise. Instead of a transcendental concern with the necessary conditions for the possibi-

---

[3] *ibid.*, 138.
[4] Mannheim, K., *Ideology and Utopia*, New York, 70.
[5] *Essays on the Sociology of Knowledge*, 89.

lity of knowledge, the sociology of knowledge interprets conditions as masks to be penetrated. Metaphysically, the movement is from the object and event to their source in knowledge, and since sources of knowledge demand transcension, the existential thinker is left without foundation or the hope of self-resolution. It is in this sense exactly that I speak of his alienation from certitude as thematic of a tradition of scepticism which leads in modern form to the minimal assertion of *positions* with respect to knowledge rather than solutions. A position is a decisional modality, it is purely heuristic in function and requires no ultimate philosophical commitment; it is a neutral mechanism designed to facilitate insights and interpretations which might otherwise be obscured. Its utility is measured purely in pragmatic terms. The dependence upon positions, then, amounts to a declaration of the bankruptcy of pure reason.

In return for his alienation from certitude, the existential thinker has the advantages of a nomadic existence in the historical realm. Bound by no formal commitments, he can move lightly through traditional formulations of social causation, control, and prediction. But the price Mannheim pays for the originality of his concrete investigations in the sphere of substantive sociology is epistemological and metaphysical fragmentation. The release from the wheel of analysis offered by Hegel and Marx is closed to Mannheim. His existential thinker must remain an unhappy consciousness.

Our thesis may now be formulated explicitly: the paradox of the relativization of thought turns out to be, in our interpretation of Mannheim, the alienation of the existential thinker. The sociology of knowledge has, then, as at least one of its major implications the problematic role of the sociologist of knowledge. As unmasker, penetrator of lies and ideologies, as relativizer and devaluator of immanent thought, as disintegrator of *Weltanschauungen*, he is the agent of a theory that seeks metaphysical justification and epistemological adequation but which, in principle, is committed to the impossibility of both. The transcendence of theoretical thought to partial existential determinations is a transcension of philosophy itself; what remains is the illumination of mistakes and blunders. In this sense it may be suggested that there can be no sociology of knowledge; there can be only a sociology of error.

I would like to extend my thesis by analyzing the concept of alienation more closely. To say that the existential thinker is alienated from certitude means several things: first, that he has given up the dream of absolute truth; second, that he is an oppositional thinker, an intellectual mercenary in the service of dialectic; third, that he allies himself with the sceptic tradition and finds his placement in philosophy as a definer of limits and positions. Beyond this, alienation means that the existential thinker is an antagonizer of orthodoxies and has a marginal role to play within society. His alienation is a function of his self-awareness of the historical process in which his marginal role is constituted. But the more profound character of alienation arises, I think, at a different level and derives from another source. To say that the existential thinker is alienated means that he is divorced in virtue of his own position from the sphere of theoretical thought. The relativization of thought creates a paradox which is resolved only, it must be recalled, by transcending the immanence of thought. Existential determination is not an influence, however powerful, but a mode of reality. It is within supratheoretical thought that the existential thinker lives. His alienation here is defined by his commitment to the principles of relativization: that all determinations are historicized, that all determinations are ideologized, that all determinations are, if not ultimately disintegrated, at least partialized and devalued. These principles, themselves relational, define the existence of the sociologist of knowledge and are the reasons for and the very meaning of his alienation. They lead to a final remark.

If commitment is decisional and therefore neutral, there would appear to be at least as much to argue against as there is to argue for Mannheim's epistemology. What accounts for his reasons for moving in one direction rather than the other may itself be a problem of the sociology of knowledge, but it is unfair to dismiss the issue by suggesting, as has been done,[6] that Mannheim's position is itself merely an expression of the times in which he lived. The decision to become, to be, and to remain an existential thinker is at issue, and it is that decision which the sociology of knowledge does not explain by appealing to procedural or methodological decision. Much more is involved in making such a decision than articulating a formal device. Nor is the problem a topic for motivational psychology, psychoanalysis, or statistics. I would assign it to a philosophical anthropology, in the Continental sense, which considers styles of being. The meaning of alienation might find its statement in such a critique.

---

[6] "Could *Ideology and Utopia* have been written anywhere save in Germany between 1919 and 1933?" asks Frank E. Hartung, "Problems of the Sociology of Knowledge," *Philosophy of Science*, XIX, 1952, 23.

15. *History as a Finite Province of Meaning*

The man bent over his guitar,
A shearsman of sorts. The day was green.
They said, "You have a blue guitar,
You do not play things as they are."
The man replied, "Things as they are
Are changed upon the blue guitar ..."

Wallace Stevens

The history of civilizations and cultures, and of the monumental deeds
of heroes, the history of Hegel, Spengler, and Toynbee, we shall call
"Big history"; the history of ordinary people in the everyday, working
world, living their lives, involved in the daily web of obscure
projects and minor skirmishes, the history of the unknown, the
unsung, and the easily forgotten, we shall call "little history."
Our theme is the relationship between the two, and our thesis is
that investigating this problem is decisively relevant for the philosophy of history. Indeed, a study of "little history" may lead
to the clarification of an entire dimension of the philosophy of history
which has generally been overlooked or obscured. A preliminary
indication of this dimension will bring whatever we have to say into
immediate focus.

Men living in the everyday common-sense world are not only aware of
"Big history" but, in their actual existence, take up attitudes and
positions with regard to it. The realm of experience involved here is
composed not of the overt actions and statements of actors in the
historical world but of the subjective interpretations men in the world
of daily life give to their own actions and attitudes as they deem them
relevant to the domain of history. Our question is: What is presupposed
and involved in the common-sense individual's interpretation of his
own situation with respect to history? Following the general line of
argument suggested in the writings of Max Weber, we may distinguish,
on the one hand, between those completely valid but only partial
aspects of philosophy of history which deal with the nature of the
historical process and of the methodological problems involved in the
historian's knowledge of that process and, on the other hand, those

questions related to the actor in the common-sense world who is not only a performer within history but also a self-conscious agent who, as a matter of fact, interprets his own actions and beliefs and lives within the cosmion created out of those very interpretations.[1] Our central problem in what follows is to explore this dimension of philosophy of history and to endeavour to illuminate its significance.

⟨ I ⟩

To say that the individual lives in the common-sense world in which he interprets the meaning of his own acts suggests the possibility of other worlds of meaning in which he also has status and evidences interest. There are, indeed, as William James indicated,[2] "multiple realities" in which human beings live: the world of everyday life is called by James the "sub-universe" of "sense, or of physical 'things' as we instinctively apprehend them," and in addition he lists "the world of science," of "ideal relations, or abstract truths," "the world of 'idols of the tribe,' illusions or prejudices common to the race," "the various supernatural worlds, the Christian heaven and hell, the world of Hindoo mythology," "the various worlds of individual opinion," and "the worlds of sheer madness and vagary."[3] James has brilliantly analyzed these realities at the psychological level; more recently, however, the problem of "sub-universes," or "finite provinces of meaning" as we may now call them, has been given a more distinctively philosophical examination by Alfred Schutz in his article "On Multiple Realities," which provides a phenomenological framework for the consideration of our subject.[4] The present paper is an application of that framework to the problem of history.

In order to comprehend history as a finite province of meaning, however, we must first state the essential features of the common-sense world which, as the paramount reality, is the model for all other worlds.[5] The paramount reality of daily life is the intersubjective world into which we are all born, in which we work, and in which we die. It is a world that involves those who lived before ourselves, as well as our contemporaries, and our anonymous successors. This world is characterized by our "attention to life," to use Bergson's phrase, and

---

[1] Cf. Eric Voegelin, *The New Science of Politics*, Chicago, 1952, 27.
[2] *Principles of Psychology*, New York, 1893, Vol. II, Ch. XXI.
[3] *ibid.*
[4] *Philosophy and Phenomenological Research*, V, June 1945, 533–576.
[5] *ibid.*

by our particular concern for what we deem to be relevant to some purpose at hand. In addition, it is a world whose existence we do not fundamentally doubt and whose reality we experience under a specific time perspective. But most important, to say that the world of daily life is the paramount reality means that all other finite provinces of meaning are oriented about it, and that a shift to another finite province is comprehensible as a transposition in the placement of the "accent of reality."

The shift to the historical world is established by a bestowal of the accent of reality upon this particular province of meaning. And this new placement is in turn occasioned by a specific form of suspension of belief (*epoché*, in Husserl's language) [6] in the central importance of the individual's personal life. Under this suspension, the world ceases to be centered about *me* and I instead become defined within what I take to be *its* center. This kind of suspension has its prototype in daily life where I continually move from central to marginal positions (and the reverse), depending on the situation. A student asks me for an appointment; I ask my Dean for an appointment. My child asks me for a nickel; I ask my bank for somewhat more. And so on. The point is, however, that there is a specific style of suspension which dislocates my importance in the historical realm. I now take up new positions, attitudes, and interpretations with regard to my own "situation" in history; i.e., my own interpretation of how I figure in a world in which my individuality is a minor, subordinate, or even insignificant moment in a process evolving about other persons and their activities. Such a radical shift in the accent of reality from the everyday world to the historical one is an indication of the corresponding change in the structure of relevance in the new province of meaning. What is relevant to the historical world depends on a number of other aspects of that province of meaning which can only be summarily indicated here:

First, the time perspective changes from both the *durée* and standard time to the dimensions of past, present, and future of historical reality; second, there is what might be termed a "distance" element introduced which distinguishes the events of history as no longer "at hand" as are the occurrences of the ordinary world; third, there is a fundamental factor of ambiguity respecting all actions and interpretations of events in the historical realm; finally, the historical world is grasped in a fragmentary fashion by the common-sense interpreter who is aware of but a fraction of the past and a narrow segment of the present. Time,

[6] *ibid.*

distance, ambiguity, and fragmentation are aspects of the individual's finite province of history as they are of his daily life, though they take concrete forms in both worlds as a result of the mode of suspension of belief characteristic of each. A more detailed examination of the idea of fragmentation may provide us with a clue to the difference and similarity between both provinces as well as to the essential structure of the historical microcosm.

⟨ II ⟩

For the professional historian, "little history" is lived within "Big history"; but for the man in daily life the reverse is true: "Big history" is known and interpreted within a subjective schema. The deeds, events, movements, and implications of "Big history" are refracted through the prism of relevance, and the emergent qualities are the fragments which constitute the individual's historical awareness. On closer examination, however, we may distinguish between three aspects of the idea of fragmentation: the historical fragment of which the individual is aware, the fragmentary character of his awareness itself, and fragmentation as the style of the microcosm.

"The" event in history of which the individual is aware is usually an interpreted phenomenon built up from the evidence of traces or reports of traces. The event is presented through the proxies that report it. What the individual is aware of, then, is *an* interpretation or *a* report; the event "itself" is a limiting concept which remains transcendent to the halo of accounts which announce it. In this sense, the historical event is known as a fragment which points to its source but reveals only a partial image.

The awareness of this fragment is itself fragmentary because awareness is always relevance-directed. My awareness of the conflict engaging the efforts of the forces of the North and South in the United States from 1861–65 is pre-interpreted at the outset, for example, depending on whether I refer to that struggle as the "Civil War" or the "War between the States." A fragmentary awareness is situated and committed in its very nature because the question involved in such awareness is not what is significant for history, but what is historically significant for me. I organize my world in the very interpretation of it, and my awareness is both an affecting and affected agency in this process.

Finally, the historical microcosm is a fragmented one in the very style of its being. Fragmentation is understood here as the overwhelm-

ing disjunction between the multitude of discrete elements given
for historical interpretation and the integral and selective character of
the judgment about them expected of the observer. Involved in the
complexity of data, the individual seeks to interpret himself with
clarity; caught between insight and impotence, he lives self-enchanted
and self-distressed in the world of his own limits and possibilities.

The fragment, the fragmentary, and the fragmented in the historical
microcosm provide a clue to the nature of this province of meaning, for
taken together they point to one of its dominant features: the referent
of the historical process, that of which there are fragments, is beyond
the control and manipulation of the individual. The historical past is
inaccessible to the craft of the interpreter in daily life. It is this fact
that explains the suspension of belief in his own dominant importance
which is the basis for the reality of the historical microcosm. At the
same time, the transcendence of the historical past differentiates it
from the accessible world of daily life which is in its very nature
manageable and alterable. In "little history" the individual is the self-
acknowledged master of his plans and projects; in "Big history" he is
the instrument of others. Yet the decisive point here is that "little
history" is completely aware of this very situation: the common-sense
individual acts within a world he knows is dominated by others; but he
lives within a world defined by his attitudes toward domination. The
meaning his action has for him is the crucial realm of signification in
which the individual lives. History as a finite province of meaning is
the microcosm created by the subjective interpretation of actors in
daily life who place the accent of reality upon their own interpretations
of the "Big history" which remains transcendent to the world of
"little history" in which they live.

But the contrast between the realities of history and daily life also
reveals their fundamental similarity. To say that daily life is the
paramount reality, the model for all other finite provinces, is to
appreciate the analogous structures of fragmentation in the common-
sense world. Though I gear into daily life, alter its circumstances and
help shape its design, I am also aware that my centrality and independence in this world are limited and ultimately ill-defined. My
success and power depend on typical mechanisms of authority and
control which may be dislocated or lost as a result of conditions or
forces unknown to me. The accessible, understandable world of daily
life has its "fringes" of strangeness and futility, and it is only within
segments of the common-sense world that my "formulas" for results of

various kinds work. The events of daily life also have their fragmentary character, and human existence is qualified at its root by the incertitude of social action. In both the province of history and daily life I find myself as a being in a situation whose ultimate conditions transcend my existence; and whether I react to this fact with resignation or anger, I live within a microcosm defined by the choice I make. Whether it be "Big" or "little," it is not history but ourselves who are ambiguous and fragmented.

⟨ III ⟩

The suggestion that history, understood as a finite province of meaning, is a proper object of analysis for the philosophy of history has been presented in terms of a phenomenological approach which takes the "natural attitude" (in Husserl's sense) as itself open to reflective treatment. The individual's subjective interpretation of his acts is understood, therefore, not through the causal-genetic categories of psychological inquiry but rather by way of a direct inspection of the essential features of experience as they are known to the experiencer himself, not to the detached observer who describes them from "without." The possibility of viewing this dimension of history, then, turns upon the achievement of a reflective standpoint internal to human experience. The justification of such a standpoint and general method is obviously beyond the limits of a paper which intends merely to recommend the relevance of such an approach for the philosophy of history; still, a final word may be offered toward clarifying the nature of our position.

Man is not only a being who lives in the world; he is a being who *has* a world, and even further, we may say, he is a being who *is* a world. Whatever is given to him in experience, therefore, is transposed and translated into the fabric of his cognitive and conative life and becomes restructured and reformed into an aspect of his self-awareness. Born into a world "already there," we nevertheless define it, illuminate it, and live within the confines of the meaningful structure thus established. "The" world is only a shorthand for the paramount reality of everyday life which is the model for the other worlds; but as James says, "each world *whilst it is attended to* is real after its own fashion." [7] It is in this sense that the finite province of history is to be comprehended. Its reality is the reality of the subjectivity that creates and defines it, that bears its meaning, and that is witness to its truth.

[7] *op. cit.*, 293.

16. History, Historicity, and the Alchemistry of Time

⟨ I ⟩

Suicide notes have a rather dubious status in the list of materials of the historian's craft, but their intrinsic fascination can hardly be denied. In recent times the death of President Vargas of Brazil has presented the contemporary historian with a paradigm case of the suicide note whose content and purpose are historically defined, defined not by the annalist but by the actor on the historical scene, by Vargas himself. This is what he wrote to his people:

I offer my life in the holocaust. I choose this means to be with you always. When they humiliate you, you will feel my soul suffering at your side. When hunger beats at your door, you will feel inside you the energy to fight for yourselves and your children. ... To hatred I respond with pardon. And to those who think they have defeated me I reply with victory. I was the slave of the people, and today I free myself for eternal life. But this people to which I was a slave will not longer be a slave to anyone. My sacrifice will remain forever in your soul, and my blood will be the price of your ransom. I fought against the looting of Brazil. I fought against the looting of the people. I have fought bare-breasted. The hatred, infamy and calumny did not beat down my spirit. I gave you my life. Now I offer my death. Nothing remains. Serenely I take the first step on the road to eternity, and I leave life to enter history.[1]

The peculiar texture of this note, its flamboyant style, its passionate cry can, of course, be waved aside as merely a product of Latin American histrionics, as the rhetoric of an unbalanced mind. The state of Brazilian politics which occasioned this note is of no interest to me at this point. It is not the suicide of Vargas which is relevant here but his interpretation of suicide as an historical act. What does it mean to "enter history"? Or more specifically, what does it mean for Vargas to "enter history"? These questions have indeed a strange ring. Pre-

[1] *Time*, September 6, 1954, 29.

sumably, they are problems for some psychological inquiry into the subjective attitudes of historical figures, or else they are puzzles for metaphysical speculation. But are they the sort of issues proper for strict historical investigation? Are they materials for the historian's craft? These questions constitute the starting point for an inquiry into the relationship of philosophy and history.

Definitions of history suffer from a curious ailment: the subject matter they seek to locate depends on the character of the apparatus for location. Judgments about what is relevant or irrelevant to the discipline of history presuppose not only criteria of relevance but some conception of the very meaning of relevance, a subject of the most difficult philosophical character. But there is an additional problem. The subject matter of history is events or states of affairs whose epistemic nature is either presupposed by a particular historical school or else interpreted in a committed fashion. The difference between Ranke and Collingwood is a clear illustration of more than a disagreement about methods or techniques; it is a distinctively philosophical opposition which distinguishes them. How does one get back to things as they happened? What is at issue in the effort to reconstruct the past? Often we are told that whatever methods historians use, they are eager to get at the facts, that although they may disagree about philosophical approaches, they are at one with regard to the search for the truth. And the truth seems to point back to what there was. The historian, then, endeavours to be true to what there was. Examine this more closely.

"What there was" is composed of states of affairs whose elements are ordinarily called facts, and facts are the prime data, it would appear, for the historian's reconstructive task. Here is one, rather standard, report of what the historian understands by "fact":

A historical 'fact' [Gottschalk writes] may be defined as a particular derived directly or indirectly from historical documents and regarded as credible after careful testing in accordance with the canons of historical method. An infinity and a multiple variety of facts of this kind are accepted by all historians: e.g., that Socrates really existed; that Alexander invaded India; that the Romans built the Pantheon ... Simple and fully attested 'facts' of this kind are rarely disputed. They are easily observed, easily recorded (if not self-evident like the Pantheon ...), involve no judgments of value ... contradict no other knowledge available to us, seem otherwise logically acceptable, and, avoiding generalization, deal with single instances.[2]

What is "fact" here? *That* Alexander invaded India? *That* Socrates

[2] Gottschalk, L., *Understanding History*, New York, 1950, 140.

really existed? Is Alexander's invasion of India the fact or is it the fact *that* Alexander invaded India? The difference is not insignificant, for we are interested in determining whether fact is the event itself or a predicate of some order regarding the event. When we say it is a fact *that* Socrates really existed we are, it would seem, reporting *about* a state of affairs, the actual life of Socrates, but we are not saying that the actual life of Socrates is the historical datum. If facts are reports about states of affairs, then they are not equivalent to what they report, and they must not be confused with events. Does the historian deal with events or with reports about events? Again, answers by methodologists of history are not hard to find.

The historian, we are told, is destined to locate the past indirectly, through traces of what has occurred or what has been. Even when we have monuments, tombs, diaries, letters, documents, first-hand accounts, etc., we are still left with the problem of relating them to their original time, place, and to the intentions of those who made them or wrote them or transcribed them. In fact, there is no return to "what there was" as it was. The primary characteristic, then, of historical procedure, as Marc Bloch puts is, "is the fact that knowledge of all human activities in the past, as well as of the greater part of those in the present, is, as Francois Simiand aptly phrased it, a knowledge of their tracks. Whether it is the bones immured in the Syrian fortifications, a word whose form or use reveals a custom, a narrative written by the witness of some scene, ancient or modern, what do we really mean by *document*, if it is not a 'track,' as it were – the mark, perceptible to the senses, which some phenomenon, in itself inaccessible, has left behind?" [3] In these terms, the historian's "facts" are not even the traces or tracks of what has occurred but a judgment in the form of a proposition about what occurred. The "fact," then, is twice removed from the event. There is the event, there is the trace of that event, and there is the judgment of the historian about the trace. It is only the last that is termed "fact," and this means that not only are historians concerned with the past in a most indirect manner but that their judgments are rooted in the interpretive apparatus of the observer, the practicing historian. The certitude of fact, the objectivity of fact, the apodictic status of fact are all pieces of a single deeply rooted illusion, the illusion that in getting the facts the historian's own subjectivity, his own philosophic attitudes or lack of them, and his own value-world are methodologically set aside in the practice of his craft. This illusion

---

[3] Bloch, M., *The Historian's Craft*, New York, 1953, 54–55.

is itself part of a larger attitude which many historians share with the naive realism of the common-sense world. The world and our experience of it is, for common sense, simply *there*, and though we may doubt aspects of it for certain restricted purposes at particular times, we cannot conceivably doubt the fundamental truth of its being there in much the way in which it appears to normal perceivers. Thus, " 'fact is the material of experience; it is the solid datum which experience must accept and may come to understand. In experience facts are accepted, analyzed and coordinated, but they may not be tampered with. Facts are observed, remembered and combined; they are material, not the result of judgment. Fact is coercive because it cannot be questioned, infallible because from it there is no appeal, and both because it is given. The furthest reach of experience is the collection and reflective consideration of unalterable facts.' "

This caricature of the historian as naive realist is, unfortunately, not too far from the truth. The author of the caricature, Michael Oakeshott, presents its refutation:

This melancholy doctrine [he writes] as common as it is crude, suffers from obvious disabilities. Fact, whatever else it may be, is experience; without thought there can be no fact. Even a view which separates ideas from things must recognize that facts are ideas. Fact is what has been made or achieved; it is the product of judgment. And if there be an unalterable datum in experience, it certainly cannot consist of fact. Fact, then, is not what is given, it is what is achieved in experience. Facts are never merely observed, remembered or combined; they are always made. We cannot 'take' facts, because there are none to take until we have constructed them. And until a fact is established, that is, until it has achieved a place in a coherent world, it is not more than an hypothesis or a fiction.[4]

The "coherent world" in which facts find placement is the historian's projection of reality, his interpretive schema for organizing the elements of his experience. But to talk in these terms is to stress the importance of interpretation, awareness, judgment, attitude, and analysis. In short, the historian's craft is rooted in the soil of his subjectivity. Far from having to avoid what are ordinarily called "psychological" or "metaphysical" questions, the historian can hardly exist professionally without them. When he thinks he is avoiding them, his discipline suffers concretely. When he faces them, he moves toward the fulfillment of his calling.

There are at least two kinds of reasons for the disjunction between history and philosophy – for that is exactly what is meant by the

[4] Oakeshott, M., *Experience and Its Modes*, Cambridge, England, 1933, 41–42.

historian's turning away from problems of subjectivity. First, the field of philosophy of history is shared in certain ways by both philosophers and historians. When historians do philosophy of history, they frequently are working in the domain of historiography. Philosophers have different interests. I would suggest that historiography is properly concerned with the underlying problems of the writing of history. Canons of historical method, questions of research and procedure are all part of the subject matter of historiography. To the historian as historiographer the study of philosophies of history is the study of the problems involved, methodologically, in the activities of the historian. To be sure, philosophers of history can be studied as part of history. What they said becomes the subject matter for inquiry. But there is a qualitative difference between studying what was said and studying the essential concepts which taken together articulate a philosophical position. For a philosopher, philosophy of history is concerned with the problems of philosophy of history. And this means that the student as philosopher is called upon to examine not merely what Hegel said but the problems with which Hegel worked. These problems become, in turn, the data for the student of philosophy. The question is not how Hegel wrote philosophy of history but the issues with which his philosophy of history are concerned. There are, in these terms, historians who are doing philosophy of history, not historiography, and philosophers who are doing historiography, not philosophy of history. I have presented logical, not descriptive categories.

The second reason for the disjunction between history and philosophy involves the question of the scientific status of the historian's craft. Very simply, for some historians involvement with philosophy in any professional sense lends suspicion to the historian's product. Philosophy in this view represents everything that is not scientific, everything that is subjective in the pejorative sense of that term. To become a science history must attend to its own business, to the location, organization, compilation of facts into larger patterns of order. Philosophy represents a threat to that enterprise. For such an outlook philosophy of history can only validly mean historiography, and historiography is translated into the training of the student of history, introducing him to research techniques, library procedures, and the general apparatus of fact gathering. Both reasons for avoiding the union or encounter of history and philosophy are, I believe, unfortunate. Among lesser losses, this disjunction has obscured the problem of subjectivity for the historian. Whatever else may not convince him of the importance of a truly philosophical approach to history, there is one thing which the historian must face or risk a profound lacuna in his professional life, and that is the radical status of his own existence, his own being in the historical world. History, let us say, is characterized by the remarkable fact that the historian's study of it is part of it. Ranke's study of the past is no less a part of the content of history than the original object of his investigation. The subjectivity of the historian is a prime historical datum. To avoid subjectivity in history is to negate its very meaning.

⟨ II ⟩

Unfortunately, the term "subjectivity" is charged with a variety of almost hopelessly confused connotations which involve everything from psychological to mystical references. Unambiguous usage requires more than stipulated definitions. By "subjectivity" I understand the intrinsic relatedness of experience to consciousness, of the elements of action and understanding to the essential structure of awareness. Consciousness in these terms is not a neurological affair nor a psychological structure; it is instead a purely formal and immanent stream of intentional directedness, having its own *a priori* nature and its own constitutive dynamics. I am concerned with a phenomenological rather than a naturalistic or behavioral view of the mental. And this means that the study of consciousness is primarily an epistemological, not a psychological task. To speak of the subjectivity of the historian in this context is to turn to the relatedness of events or whatever the historical phenomena are taken to be to the conditions for the possibility of knowledge. It is not the actual empirical mind or thinking of the historian which is in question but the essentially logical structure of his awareness, of his historical consciousness. Perhaps a change in terms might be of help to mark the movement from talking about psychological to phenomenological affairs. Instead of the psychological variations or peculiarities of the mind of the individual historian concerned with what is ordinarily called history, we are interested in the formal structure of the historian's awareness of history as he grasps or intends it, with what we shall call historicity. History is distinguished from historicity in the same way as natural events are demarcated from acts of intellection. If history is the study of what there was, historicity is the historian's conceptual experience of what there was. In short, the historian who is professionally concerned with the meaning of his own historical existence is implicitly concerned with historicity.

The task before us then is a study of historicity, and this appears as a distinctive problem for a philosophy of history. I doubt that the issue can even be formulated in terms of traditional historiography. And in turning to philosophy of history, it is necessary to consider the epistemic dimension rather than what is overtly called philosophy of history. The concept of historicity, for example, would be missed if we looked for it only in Hegel's lectures on the philosophy of history. For Hegel's insights into the realm of the historicistic we must turn to his *Phenomenology of Mind*. And since we have taken Hegel as our illustration of a philosopher concerned with historicity we may well begin with his kind of philosophy.

Hegelian phenomenology is committed to a dialectical account of the evolution of experience from its immediate and primordial givenness in the lowest range of sensory awareness to its highest manifestation in conceptual life. A "phenomenology" in this sense is a survey of the modalities of consciousness in their logical unfolding. For Hegel, the history of concepts is to be located in their logical genesis, not in their chronological development. Chronology presupposes temporality, and the study of temporality is necessarily the survey of the dialectics of consciousness. The relationship between consciousness and its objects is an integral one, but the relationship can be explicated only by the reflexive activity of consciousness concerned with itself. The possibilities and perplexities of awareness are rooted in the original paradox of consciousness operative in a reality which it both discovers and constitutes. The dialectic of consciousness is expressed by Hegel in his typical stylistic extravagance:

This dialectic process which consciousness executes on itself [he writes], on its knowledge as well as on its object – in the sense that out of it the new and true object arises, is precisely what is termed Experience. In this connection, there is a moment in the process just mentioned which should be brought into more decided prominence, and by which a new light is cast on the scientific aspect of the following exposition. Consciousness knows something; this something is the essence or what is *per se*. This object, however, is also the *per se*, the inherent reality, *for consciousness*. Hence comes ambiguity of this truth. Consciousness, as we see, has now two objects; one is the first *per se*, the second is the existence *for consciousness* of this *per se*. The last object appears at first sight to be merely the reflection of consciousness into itself, i.e., an idea not of an object, but solely of its knowledge of that first object. But, as was already indicated, by that very process the first object is altered; it ceases to be what is *per se*, and becomes consciously something which is *per se* only *for consciousness*. Consequently, then, what this real *per se* is for consciousness is truth: which, however, means that this is the essential reality, or the object which consciousness has. This new object contains the nothingness of the first; the new object is the *experience* concerning that first object.[5]

One advantage in quoting Hegel is that it is never necessary to say "unquote." By the same token, we seem to have a splendid example of everything scientific historians seek to avoid. Is it conceivable that anything very crucial for the study of history could emerge from the forest of such language? The answer will have to be "yes." And this "yes" is itself an eminent historical datum, for out of Hegelian metaphysics there has come not only a philosophy of history of decisive importance for our time but a concept of historicity which may be considered beyond the matrix of Marxist thought. However difficult Hegel's language may be, it is necessary to come to terms with his heritage. We are not done with that quotation.

The paradox of duality Hegel is describing is not unfamiliar in a different guise to common sense. In daily life we worry about the relationship between what we know of a man and what he is apart from our understanding or interpretation of him. We distinguish implicitly between objects and our experience of an object and subsequent interpretations of that experience. There is my knowledge of a person and my later interpretation of my knowledge. Examples could be multiplied without profit, for what is at issue is an epistemic relationship which underlies all illustrations and which must be grasped if the illustrations are truly to illustrate. The object, for Hegel, is absorbed in the act of knowing, and what is gained in knowledge is, in a way, lost in return. We gain knowledge of the object, we lose the object as it stood prior to the cognitive act which places it in the range of experience. We may feel little loss with respect to common objects – tables and chairs – but there is something more important involved when the object is a fellow man or ourselves. Here the dialectic becomes overpowering.

Just as there is a qualitative difference between my understanding of an object and my understanding of a fellow man, so there is an analogous difference between my understanding of a fellow man and my understanding of myself. Fellow men are observed, but I hardly can be said to "observe" myself in the ordinary current of life. It is only on special occasions that I step out of my routine of awareness and formally "observe" some aspect of my behavior. For the most part, I simply live in the stream of my continuous action, aware in a naive

[5] Hegel, G. W. F., *The Phenomenology of Mind*, London, 1931, 142–143.

way of that stream and its contents. Philosophy might be understood as a deliberate, self-conscious movement out of that taken for granted current of life, a movement which succeeds in rendering the assumed and presupposed an explicit object for inquiry. In a related but still radical way, art is an effort to explore the familiar by exhibiting its structure in forms which make of the taken for granted unique moments in aesthetic contemplation. Philosophy and art are divergent modes of handling our world by pointing to its transcendental conditions. Such activity involves the inquirer in his inquiry. To be philosophically or aesthetically committed is to locate oneself as philosopher or artist as a cardinal aspect of the subject matter for study. And this means necessarily that self-awareness, subjectivity in its broadest reference, is inescapably part of the experiential structure of our lives. Philosophy is the discipline of subjectivity.

Hegel's statement has led to its most urgent application, the dual aspect of consciousness in the experience of the individual concerned with comprehending himself. Here object and subject receive a strange dialectical status precisely because the individual subject aware of himself renders himself object for himself in his act of reflection and yet remains at the same time subject for all activities of consciousness. The epistemological implications of these problems are overwhelming in their complexity, but there is one feature of Hegelian subjectivity which lends itself to a more limited treatment, and that is historical subjectivity or, in the term we have chosen, historicity. The self-conscious, deeply reflective actor on the historical scene makes of the events of the historical world the historicistic component of consciousness. He interprets not only the events of history but his own evaluation and ordering of those events. And he finds that concern with history hides within itself a double face: on one side, the subject's awareness of historical events is reflected in his historicistic consciousness; on the other side, historicity has its own history in the development of the individual factor on the historical scene. The play between these double facets of the historical leads to a dialectical embarrassment which Hegel calls the "Unhappy Consciousness."

The paradoxical dualism of subject and object with respect to ordinary phenomena returns in intensified form in the dualism of consciousness seeking to grasp itself, liberate itself from its cognitively transposing activities, and achieve the unity it senses within itself. There is a direct historical counterpart to this beleaguered subjectivity. Hegel's views on the Master and Bondsman in *The Phenomenology of*

Mind, his hidden conception of revolt as rooted in philosophical alienation, is the clue to the analogue of this conceptual movement at the historical and historicistic level. Struggling at all of these strata, individual and historical, is the effort of consciousness to ground itself, to free itself from the bondage of epistemic dualisms. "Thus we have here," Hegel writes, "that dualizing of self-consciousness within itself, which lies essentially in the notion of mind; but the unity of the two elements is not yet present. Hence the *Unhappy Consciousness (unglückliches Bewusstsein)*, the Alienated Soul which is the consciousness of self as a divided nature, a doubled and merely contradictory being." [6]

Again, it would appear that little of scientific worth could follow from such speculation. Certainly, if history is to concern itself with this kind of talk, the results are not especially promising for anyone whose philosophic grounding is empiricistic or positivistic. Wouldn't it be better to leave to philosophers the gift of Hegel's madness? The answer is interrupted by the fact that these problems have not been left entirely to philosophers, or at least those who have engaged them as purposeful issues have refused to consider their philosophic concern to be isolated from the total historical and cultural scene. I propose to consider an example of such refusal, one in historical politics. Through it I hope to explore the living testimony that lies secreted in Hegel's view of human subjectivity.

⟨ III ⟩

The Moscow Trials of 1938 received great notoriety in all quarters of the world and were discussed by intellectuals of all political faiths. The fascination of the Trials went beyond the drama of political courtrooms; what was at issue in the proceedings was a logical development of Marxism working itself out in the field of historical action. The central theme of the Trials was the necessity of counter-revolutionary activity for the party in power as well as for those who lost power. And nowhere was this theme more evident than in the case of the defendant, Nicholai Bukharin, theoretician and revolutionary. The game of the trial was obvious: that Bukharin was innocent of the crimes of which he was accused was clear to the Court, to the Prosecutor Vyshinsky, to Bukharin's co-defendants, to the people, and to himself. The comedy of the Trial was constituted out of these mutual recognitions, and all roles

[6] *ibid.*, 251.

had to be played within the limits of those recognitions. But unlike his less insightful co-defendants, Bukharin accepted the role of tactical guilt but insisted on historical justification. He pleaded guilty to the charge that inevitably would bring about his execution, but insisted on defending his ideological position. For three months Bukharin remained silent in prison, refusing to "confess." Suddenly he changed. It is impossible to understand his transformation in terms of torture; everything in his story points back to an interior theoretical abandonment of a position of refusal in favor of fulfilling what was for him a necessary historical role, that of conceptual revolt as a moment in the unfolding of the dialectic. In the skein of charges and refutations, denial and feverish assertions, one thing emerges which is unavoidable: the Hegelian theme of subjectivity working itself out in trans-political terms. And with an irony beyond irony, Hegel's theme becomes explicit in Bukharin's testimony.

Throughout his trial Bukharin taunted Vyshinsky, the prosecutor, with philosophic jibes. All of them rest on a more serious contention, the claim that the issue of the Trial is ideological, that the question of guilt must be tied to ideological grounds, that practical acts of subversion are beside the point. "I want first," Bukharin testified, "to deal with ideological positions." [7] And he persisted throughout the Trial in an effort to establish not his innocence but the character of his historical guilt. His theoretical jests were merely the fringes to his purpose. At one point in the Trial Vyshinsky says to Bukharin, "You have already reached the year 1933. Bukharin: The reason I wanted to refer to his question is that it is connected with the practical preparations ... Vyshinsky: So speak of the practical preparations, instead of telling us why this or that did not take place. The Court is interested in knowing what took place, and why. Bukharin: Yes, but every negation contains an affirmation, Citizen Procurator. Spinoza once said that in the sphere of determination ... Vyshinsky: Speak concretely: how were you preparing the seizure of power, with whose aid, by what means, with what aims and objects in view?" [8] A little later in the Trial, the following encounter takes place between the examiner and the defendant: "Vyshinsky: Accused Bukharin, is it a fact or not that a group of your confederates in the North Caucasus was connected with Whiteguard emigré Cossack circles abroad? Is that a fact or not?

[7] Report of Court Proceedings in the Case of the Anti-Soviet "Block of Rights and Trots-kyites," Verbatim Report, Moscow 1938, 379.
[8] ibid., 394.

Rykov says it is, Slepkov says it is. Bukharin: If Rykov says it is, I have no grounds for not believing him. Vyshinsky: Can you answer me without philosophy? Bukharin: This is not philosophy. Vyshinsky: Without philosophical twists and turns. Bukharin: I have testified that I had explanations on this question. Vyshinsky: Answer me 'No.' Bukharin: I cannot say 'No,' and I cannot deny that it did take place. Vyshinsky: So the answer is neither 'yes' nor 'No'? Bukharin: Nothing of the kind, because facts exist regardless of whether they are in anybody's mind. This is a problem of the reality of the outer world. I am no solipsist." [9] Still another example. "Vyshinsky: Accused Bukharin, were you with Khodjayev at his country place? Bukharin: I was. Vyshinsky: Did you carry on a conversation? Bukharin: I carried on a conversation and kept my head on my shoulders all the time, but it does not follow from this that I dealt with the things of which Khodjayev just spoke; this was the first conversation ... Vyshinsky: It is of no consequence whether it was the first or not the first. Do you confirm that there was such a conversation? Bukharin: Not such a conversation, but a different one, and also secret. Vyshinsky: I am not asking you about conversations in general, but about this conversation. Bukharin: In Hegel's 'Logic' the word 'this' is considered to be the most difficult word ... Vyshinsky: I ask the Court to explain to the accused Bukharin that he is here not in the capacity of a philosopher, but a criminal, and he would do better to refrain from talking here about Hegel's philosophy ... Bukharin: A philosopher may be a criminal. Vyshinsky: Yes, that is to say, those who imagine themselves to be philosophers turn out to be spies. Philosophy is out of place here. I am asking you about that conversation of which Khodjayev just spoke; do you confirm it or do you deny it? Bukharin: I do not understand the word 'that.' " [10] Vyshinsky's ultimate reply to these thrusts comes in his summation before the Court of the State's case when he says, "I know of no other instances – this is the first instance in history of a spy and murderer using philosophy, like powdered glass, to hurl into his victim's eyes before dashing his brains out with a footpad's bludgeon."[11] So far, however, we have explored the comedy of the Trial at its most superficial level. The philosophical weight lies below.

Bukharin, we have said, chooses to argue his case on ideological grounds. Legal guilt is no issue in the Trial. It is obvious to everyone

[9] *ibid.*, 400–401.
[10] *ibid.*, 420–421.
[11] *ibid.*, 628.

that death is the only possible conclusion. Within these limits the philosophical drama of the Trial unfolds. The climax is reached in Bukharin's last plea to the Court. Direct quotation here is worth more than any explanation or commentary. Even Koestler's literary portrait of Bukharin in *Darkness at Noon* does not excel the almost fictive quality of his speech. I must quote at length. Bukharin is speaking:

I want briefly to explain the facts regarding my criminal activities and my repentance of my misdeeds. I already said when giving my main testimony during the trial, that it was not the naked logic of the struggle that drove us, the counter-revolutionary conspirators, into this stinking underground life, which has been exposed at this trial in all its starkness. This naked logic of the struggle was accompanied by a degeneration of ideas, a degeneration of psychology, a degeneration of ourselves, a degeneration of people ... it seems to me probable that every one of us sitting here in the dock suffered from a peculiar duality of mind, an incomplete faith in his counter-revolutionary cause. I will not say that the consciousness of this was absent, but it was incomplete. Hence a certain semi-paralysis of the will, a retardation of reflexes. And this was due not to the absence of consistent thought, but to the objective grandeur of socialist construction. A dual psychology arose. Each of us can discern this in his own soul, although I will not engage in a far-reaching psychological analysis. Even I was sometimes carried away by the eulogies I wrote of socialist construction, although on the morrow I repudiated this by practical actions of a criminal character. There arose what in Hegel's philosophy is called a most unhappy mind. This unhappy mind differed from the ordinary unhappy mind only by the fact that it was also a criminal mind. ... It seems to me that when some of the West European and American intellectuals begin to entertain doubts and vacillations in connection with the trials taking place in the U.S.S.R., this is primarily due to the fact that these people do not understand the radical distinction, namely, that in our country the antagonist, the enemy, has at the same time a divided, a dual mind. And I think that this is the first thing to be understood.[12]

Bukharin is contemptuous of the easy explanation in the West for his confession and admission of guilt. He sharply criticizes the idea that he was drugged or hypnotized. To another possible explanation he devotes an interesting rebuttal:

This repentance is often attributed to the Dostoyevsky mind, to the specific properties of the soul ('l'âme slave' as it is called), and this can be said of types like Aloysha Karamazov, the hero of the 'Idiot' and other Dostoyevsky characters, who are prepared to stand up in the public square and cry: 'Beat me, Orthodox Christians, I am a villain!' But that is not the case here at all. 'L'âme slave' and the psychology of Dostoyevsky characters are a thing of the remote past in our country, the pluperfect tense. Such types do not exist in our country, or exist perhaps only on the outskirts of small provincial towns, if they do even there. On the contrary, such a psychology is to be found in Western Europe.[13]

---

12 *ibid.*, 775–777.
13 *ibid.*, 777.

And finally Bukharin comes to his personal confession, to the elements which defined his role in the Trial:

I shall now speak of myself, of the reasons for my repentance. Of course, it must be admitted that incriminating evidence plays a very important part. For three months I refused to say anything. Then I began to testify. Why? Because while in prison I made a revaluation of my entire past. For when you ask yourself: 'If you must die, what are you dying for?' – an absolutely black vacuity suddenly rises before you with startling vividness. There was nothing to die for, if one wanted to die unrepented. And, on the contrary, everything positive that glistens in the Soviet Union acquires new dimensions in a man's mind. This in the end disarmed me completely and led me to bend my knees before the Party and the country. And when you ask yourself: 'Very well, suppose you do not die: suppose by some miracle you remain alive, again what for? Isolated from every-body, an enemy of the people, in an inhuman position, completely isolated from everything that constitutes the essence of life. ...' And at once the same reply arises. And at such moments, Citizen Judges, everything personal, all the personal incrustation, all the rancour, pride, and a number of other things, fall away, disappear ... I am about to finish. I am perhaps speaking for the last time in my life. ... The point, of course, is not this repentance, or my personal repentance in particular. The Court can pass its verdict without it. The confession of the accused is not essential. The confession of the accused is a medieval principle of jurisprudence. But here we also have the internal demolition of the forces of counter-revolution. And one must be a Trotsky not to lay down one's arms.[14]

⟨IV⟩

The movement from history to historicity is a discovery of the dynamic of time as the underlying agency of man's social evolution. In addition to what might be termed public or external time, in Bergson's classifi-cation, there is personal or inner time consciousness. The same duality holds at the historical level. Hegel's bequest to Marx was more than the dialectical method Marxists insist on as the valid content of Hegelian philosophy; what is truly radical in Hegel is a messianic conception of history wedded to an historical phenomenology of human subjectivity. The doctrine of the Unhappy Consciousness gives way in Marx to the concept of alienation, the reification of subjectivity in the object of production. And the inner meaning of dialectic is posed in terms of class struggle and the privileged potential of the proletariat precisely because an historical eschatology requires a subjectivity capable of transforma-tion within historical time. History gives way to historicity because the chronology of historical events in turn gives way to the temporality of the historical process. Time becomes the engine of history.

Although it is obvious that historians are concerned with phenomena

---

[14] *ibid.*, 777-778.

whose time dimension is of central importance, the study of time itself does not appear to be considered universally as part of the historian's craft. Events which occur *in* time are the objects of study, or perhaps, more exactly, traces of occurrences which are time-bound are studied, but time itself is more often than not presupposed in historical method and left unexamined. To argue, as I have, that subjectivity is the axial datum for a historicistic conception of methodology is to be committed to a concern with time and temporality as the "object-matter" of history. But the mode of study must be attuned to its object. Historicistic time cannot be studied by the techniques of natural scientific method, nor can the problem of historical time even be posed in terms of naturalistic categories. A chemistry of time will not do; we must search for a more magical instrument of divination, and that is why I choose to speak of an "alchemistry" of time. My clue is taken from Thomas Mann's *Magic Mountain*. At one point Hans Castorp says, "There is such a thing as alchemistic-hermetic pedagogy, transubstantiation, from lower to higher, ascending degrees ..." [15] The education of the individual, assuming he has a little something to start with, advances toward the fulfillment of an entelechy which is partly defined by what he makes of his epoch, how he attends to his mentors, what risks he manages within the promises of an age. Magic makes of the Mountain an hermetic microcosm, but it is a monad whose structure and content mirror the forces and possibilities of the historical order. Transubstantiation is an historical event, and its product is an historicized consciousness. The happy illusions of Settembrini and the bitter prophecies of Naphta are *aufgehoben* in the destiny of Castorp. The seven years he spends at Davos are the distillation of time's alchemy.

The application of such a conception of time and subjectivity to the concrete activity of historians is at best problematic. But there is one field of contact which seems to me inescapable, the life of the historian has a reflexive dimension; he necessarily becomes the object of his own inquiry. It is in this necessity that the study of history locates its alchemic properties. Self-study is, in principle, beyond the possibility of behavioristic explanation. The historian's decision to study some phase of history is an act whose significance depends largely on his own interpretation of his own choice. Here action becomes not an external event but an intentional phenomenon. The discipline which concerns itself with such phenomena, among others, is a philosophically conceived history, one whose dominant effort is the

15 Mann, T., *The Magic Mountain*, New York, 1955, 596.

location, ordering, and interpretive understanding of the historistic. Such a discipline does not replace history as ordinarily comprehended. Instead, to the extent that historians recognize the alchemic dimension of their enterprise, they restore to its proper level the status of philosophy as the foundation of historical methodology.

A different way of seeing the relevance of philosophy for the study of history is to consider again the question of what constitutes the realm of historical fact. When we distinguish between the event, its trace, and the historian's attempt to reconstruct events through the study of traces, we suggest, really, that there is a major problem with respect to the reality of which events are a part. To question the logical status of the event is to question, ultimately, the logical status of reality itself. To the extent to which the historian operates as a naive realist, epistemologically, he presupposes that of course reality is a subsistent affair, composed of elements whose independent status is much the same as the status of facts ordinarily located in the external world. And it is precisely here that the real trouble begins, for it is not enough for the historian to assume that his object of concern is philosophically neutral or obvious or to be taken for granted. It is instead necessary to acquaint himself with the philosophic issues and to commit himself to consistency, clarity, and as much sophistication as he can manage. If pushed far enough such claims lead to a pedagogic impasse.

What is it the student of history must do? Must he settle the problems of metaphysics and epistemology before he can write his dissertation or monograph on the Lost State of Franklin? The answer is "yes," but I don't believe in the answer. Rather, I maintain that a reconstruction of the history of the Lost State of Franklin involves, in principle, every major issue one can locate in the methodology and philosophy of history. The point is that judging accomplishments in the writing of history necessarily involves the pathos of relative failure. The same thing holds in philosophy, except possibly in more intensified form. And the problem is not only what one is able to accomplish, but what questions one dares to formulate. Philosophic concern in this sense can be understood as a commitment to honesty, that kind of honesty which admits freely but responsibly that the initial limits one places on a project reflect not only the kinds of results that can be looked for but the kinds of embarrassments that are implicitly avoided. We should be judged not only on what we have done but on what we have attempted.

It is time to conclude the argument. The awareness of events, I have maintained, is no less an historical datum than the study of historical phenomena, traditionally understood. Historicity is the plenum of all intentional action in the historical scene. The actor in history is a subjectivity concerned with the meaning of his own action. It is the task of the historian to comprehend not only the action of fellow men but his own existence. To the extent that he strives for interpretive understanding of the historicistic world, he encroaches on the domain of magic, and the logic of his inquiry leads him to the prime datum of temporality as the essential stuff of our lives. To profess a concern with history as historicity is necessarily to utilize the instrumentality of magic, to participate in conceptual alchemy. Such is the argument. Those who are bent upon interpreting such terms as "subjectivity," "temporality," "magic," and "alchemy" as the vocabulary of Satan are free to proceed as they wish. One can hardly keep them from the appointment they have made from the outset of this paper. As they depart for their rendezvous, however, I offer a final caution. In addition to the historian's career there is the historian's life. Reflectively or not, he projects a certain style of existence. Profession and person are not isolated terms. Taken integrally they lead to at least the possibility of responsible commitment; splintered apart, the study of history becomes what Spengler called "ant work."

17. Causation as a Structure of the Lebenswelt

> "All visible objects, man, are but as pasteboard
> masks. But in each event – in the living act, the
> undoubted deed – there, some unknown but still
> reasoning thing puts forth the mouldings of its
> features from behind the unreasoning mask. If man
> will strike, strike through the mask!"
>
> Herman Melville

⟨ I ⟩

Whatever radical insights existentialism and phenomenology have
occasioned in philosophy as well as in science, an implicit consequence
of their intellectual vitality is the question they raise regarding the
nexus between philosophy and science. Nowhere is this question more
clearly found than in contemporary psychiatry. The recent stir in many
quarters over existential psychoanalysis is only the surface disturbance
of a much deeper problem, for underlying the publicity that has
attended this movement is the more important, more insistent issue of
the relationship between philosophical viewpoints and systems and the
role of psychiatric theory in the matrix of knowledge. What is at issue,
ultimately, is the very meaning of theory itself. I am interested in
exploring theory in terms of a particular perspective, that of a fundamental problem for all science, the problem of causation. In a way, the
choice of causation is less than necessary, for I could as well turn to
the status of "fact" or "law" or "hypothesis" as a way into the difficulties I wish to engage. But if "causation" is a half-arbitrary choice, it
is no less the case that it will do very well for the purposes at hand.
Causation, I trust, will prove to be the threshold to the domain of
theory as well as a clue to the meaning of the contribution of existential
and phenomenological philosophy to science in general and to psychiatry in particular.

   The notion of "theory" is especially exasperating. Not only are
there divergent connotations for the term, but there is little agreement
within a single discipline as to proper usage. For some, theory means
the formulation of general principles, the location of guiding lines for
inquiry. For others, the very term has a rather pejorative inflection.
Theory is opposed to practice, and that very opposition tends to make

of theory an abstract survey of concepts which may be relevant for philosophers but may prove hazardous for more concretely oriented practitioners. Theory, as I propose to treat it, has a very different placement. I am interested in examining the basic presuppositions of natural science, of the common-sense world, and of all attitudes which are derivative from them. To the extent that philosophy is a critique of presuppositions, it has a theoretical orientation. The clarification and ordering of all basic concepts taken for granted in scientific and common-sense life is the specific task of theory. In this sense, theory means the rationale of science as well as existence; it is the logos of all phenomena.

But treating theory as logos does not liberate it from philosophic difficulties. To begin with, there are at least two qualitatively different approaches to the meaning of theory in the history of thought. One division goes back to Francis Bacon and to the idea that the legitimation of theory lies essentially in practice, in the uses to which theory is put. Contemporary pragmatism is a child of this ancient parent. The emphasis here is on what theory does, what it produces, what its applications are, how it functions in the practice of science and of daily life. A kind of fundamental value judgment is brought to bear on theory, for according to its fruits the theory is judged valid, weak, or impotent. The acid test, then, is performance, and performance is itself judged in accordance with the canons of standard scientific method. A good theory must be able to predict accurately, generate theorems which not only hold for the empirical world but which are interconsistent with each other, and merge with cognate disciplines and their findings. In Baconian terms, knowledge is validated in its capacity to transform the world. Knowledge is indeed power.

The other way of looking at theory has a very different lineage. From Plato through St. Thomas Aquinas to more recent thinkers we will discuss a little later comes the fundamental idea that knowledge is understanding and that understanding is self-validating. The task of theory is comprehension; and not comprehension for the sake of something else, but comprehension for the sake of comprehension. The criteria for a good theory are its internal coherence, its capacity to illuminate the structure of reality, its power to transform not the world but the theorist, to make of him a wise man. Theory is concerned with that order of question which is reflexive, which is able to turn back upon itself. Thus, if one asks the empiricist why he wishes to change the world, to dominate and control it, his answer must be in terms of some predicate of value which he must, at some point, take as intrinsically good. But one cannot judge the status of intrinsic good in terms of empirical criteria. A pragmatist may judge something good in terms of its product, but his judgment of that product as good cannot itself become a further object of inquiry without the danger of an infinite regress. For those, however, who look to understanding as self-validating and to theory as essentially philosophic comprehension, the dialectical examination of intrinsic goods is quite possible. A reflexive concern with the very notion of good is a proper part of the meaning of this order of theory. The kinds of questions we raise, what we presuppose as a meaningful question, will in fact stem from what tacitly or explicitly we grasp as theory.

There is one kind of question which is endemic to symposia in which philosophers meet with scientists. The latter very often want to know how a particular philosophy or approach to philosophical problems will help them concretely in their own work. This is a very fair question, but it is often posed in such a way that it presupposes a Baconian conception of theory. Presumably, if an idea will not be of any concrete aid to a scientist, his time may not be wasted but the symposium will then not have professional significance for him. I should like to ask for a special favor, a psychiatric boon. For once, let us set aside the question, How will all this help me in the practice of psychiatry? Without underestimating the importance of therapy, let this be one time when that question does not arise. In a way, the question is pointless, for all its good will and decency. If it would require a philosopher to make out a detailed case for the practical implications of what he says, then there is hardly any real hope of turning to him for help. What he has to offer lies in a completely different dimension, one which I propose to explore. But for the time being, then, we will have a moratorium on such questions. And while we are making preliminary arrangements, we may as well turn to the initial problem of relative areas of competence.

For the most part, psychiatrists are not philosophers and philosophers are not psychiatrists. There are notable exceptions, but this hardly helps the general situation. Individual psychiatrists may have a sophisticated background in philosophy without posing as professional philosophers; in return, some philosophers have more than an amateur's appreciation of some of the concrete problems of psychiatry. Most of us, unfortunately, fall between these camps. It seems reasonable to me to be frank in announcing our mutual illiteracies and to be appreciative of our efforts to understand what the other may take for granted. The whole point of our holding a symposium in common, it seems to me, is that we are not professing to appropriate the other's specialized domain, but rather to explore certain areas which present challenges to all of us. Those areas are precisely theoretical in nature, and our task, our common task, is to approach theory with all the candor philosophy and science demand if they are to hold truth dear.

⟨II⟩

Causation is without doubt a central term of all scientific discourse. Its methodological status reveals a double aspect. First, causation refers to the orderly interrelatedness of all events; second, causation denotes a procedural dimension of scientific method. It is a cardinal presupposition of all scientific inquiry that the world can, in principle, be known. This means that it bears an inherent order of connectedness, a causal order, of such a nature that scientific observers can come to terms with what they study. Although the causal order may in fact escape us temporarily, we must suppose that such escape is only temporary, that ideally all of nature exhibits causal structure throughout. Science in this sense is a persistent and controlled effort to exhibit the order of events in nature. "Why" questions in science are answered typically in terms of organized accounts of antecedent states of affairs. We know "why" a muscle contracts when we know something about a complex set of antecedent states of affairs in body chemistry and physics. If we persist, like children, in further "why" questions regarding these antecedent events, we must turn to still other, still broader states of affairs which in turn, we expect, will show the causal relationship between the event in question and what produced it. So far the stress is on the object of inquiry, the structure of events in nature and their causal order. But if we turn to the mode of causal explanation, to the character of scientific method itself, we transpose our inquiry to another dimension of the problem. We, in effect, turn to the causal way of explaining, to what may be termed genetic method in scientific analysis. Here we meet the concept of causation on very different though related terrain. And it is here that my own proper inquiry begins.

The causal or genetic mode of investigation projects a particular conception of explanation as well as a particular view of the datum to be explained. Explanation consists in tracing back causal relationships to the springs of action. What is given in experience cannot be understood in its givenness; it must be referred back to antecedent states, to prior conditions, to origins from which it derived. A full account of such a causal chain seen in its gigantic complexity constitutes an explanation. Of course, there are criteria for plausible accounts. For the moment, however, I am not concerned with how we know whether an explanation explains, but what explaining consists in. Quite apart from whether, for example, we can predict successfully on the basis of a particular explanation, there is the very meaning of what is involved in explanation as such. In these terms, explanation, for the genetic approach, is generated out of the delineation of causal structure. So deeply ingrained is this notion that a scientist or researcher or student almost automatically commences the effort to explain by searching out the causal linkage of events that eventually will lead to a relatively complete picture of the phenomena under investigation. Were the causal mode of examination stricken from scientific procedure, we would be left with a corpse.

Explanation, then, is causal ordering, but what about the datum observed, the phenomenon to be explained? What is its status? For the genetic method, the phenomenon given is merely a starting point for further searching. What is given is not a qualitative unity as much as a point of departure backward toward roots and antecedent conditions. Givenness in these terms cannot provide a datum which may be analyzed out of itself, so to speak; it is always the case that givenness is a clue to a sphere of order that is its ground. *What* is explained, the object of explanation, comes into focus only after the causal order has been established. Until then what is given is, we might say, merely "loaned." Stated differently, the datum for genetic explanation is a disguised entity. The task of the observer is to penetrate its disguise, to unmask its appearance and locate its reality. The datum cannot stand alone. Givenness *qua* givenness is not a proper object for scientific scrutiny. In so far as its method is essentially genetic, science is committed to penetrate the manifestation of the datum by securing its place in the schema of causation.

Apparently this situation pertains to the discipline of psychiatry. Symptoms are quite exactly symptomatic of something. What appears, what presents itself, is caused by, produced by, occasioned by other states of affairs, and other states of affairs are in turn generated out of broader explanatory syndromes which include the forces of heredity, environment, childhood experiences, unconscious and subconscious styles of influence, and patterns of social and cultural character. To understand a single event one must, ideally, understand the total structure of a life or of a style of life. What manifests itself appears over against a latent background which it is the task of the psychiatrist to reconstruct in its essential outlines. Understanding a patient means penetrating the disguises of his appearance in order to comprehend the true nature of those appearances. Psychiatry might be defined as systematic distrust. It would seem, then, that the given cannot be taken as it is given, the datum cannot be explicated out of itself, and the methodological character of psychiatric explanation requires a transcension of the object in favor of an account of what produced it.

Thus far the model of explanation in science has implicitly been that of the exact sciences; physics is perhaps the paradigm case. And it appears that some schools of psychiatry in following the ideal of natural scientific explanation tend to build their own image of method after that of the natural sciences. But there is a rather crucial difficulty here, one that has been clearly recognized by many workers in psychiatry. The datum for psychiatric study is, generally taken, the human being. Whatever aspect of his behavior happens to be the explicit object of study, it is a concrete man always who is studied. Clinical categories are not reified; they have meaning only in so far as there are individual people who exemplify them in some fashion. But if this is so, then the psychiatric datum is a being who is not only an object for the causal placement of the scientist studying him or the psychiatrist trying to help him, he is, above all, primarily a creature who has his own causal reality, a being who interprets his own world in terms of his own causal categories. This datum is very much alive, and his life is originally self-projected and self-interpreted. The psychiatrist is looking in on a reality that is looking out.

If it is commonplace to suggest that human beings are self-aware creatures who are different from molecules or window shades, I must confess to a concern for the obvious. But the obvious is by no means simple or trivial. To the contrary, as the phenomenologist Alfred Schutz has shown, the structure of the taken for granted world of daily life with its apparent obviousness is in reality the most complex and philosophically subtle of all the phenomena with which we have to deal. The apparent certitude of daily life is a prime datum for our investigation. So to say that men are self-reflective beings who interpret their own reality and project a causal schema of their own making is to recommend a fundamental distinction between the datum traditionally conceived in scientific terms with its causal apparatus of explanation and the datum presented to us as actors in daily life, enmeshed in the world as we interpret it. In this way, we come to the problem of causation in the Life-world or *Lebenswelt*, as Husserl called it. In my opinion, it is one of the richest "finds" ever made in contemporary thought. Its appreciation, then, becomes our special responsibility.

⟨ III ⟩

The *Lebenswelt* is the world of concrete existence as projected and lived by men in daily life. My own immediate awareness of my surroundings, the familiarity of home and neighborhood, relations and friends, all refer to a taken for granted horizon of reality as experienced through the events of ordinary life. The *Lebenswelt* is characterized by the fact that within it there arise no distinctively philosophical problems. My own existence, the existence of fellow men, communication with others, the very being of the external world are all assumed naively; they present no distinctive issues of any problematic order for men in action in the public world. Moreover, everything experienced in *my* world is taken as roughly similar to what is experienced in the world of all normal fellow men. In short, *we* live in the same world, experience its typical aspects in a similar way, and act in a reality which we can then dominate in common. This is *our* world and we live *our* lives within its limits. The naive realism of the *Lebenswelt* consists in the way in which its taken for granted structures are lived rather than rendered objects of inspection. As long as I exist within the ongoing stream of my awareness of the world of daily life, I presuppose its philosophical dimension. Philosophy lies concealed within the *Lebenswelt* as its interior possibility.

The philosophical discovery of the *Lebenswelt* theme is a recognition of the order of daily life as a constitutive product of consciousness. The quality of the *Lebenswelt* as taken for granted in our experience is something achieved by subjectivity, something that arises as a result of the relatedness of consciousness to its objects. The phenomenological description of the structures of the *Lebenswelt*, then, is an attempt to account for its constitutive history, for its coming into being as a meaningful unity. Rather than assume that reality simply *has* such and such a typical structure, the phenomenologist endeavours to turn directly to the essential forms of the activity of consciousness building the meanings of its world. The constructive activity of consciousness is not taken as a product of experience but as a transcendental condition for experience. The orientation is Kantian to the extent that it is not the world that is to be explained but our experience of the world. One looks to natural science for an explanation of the world; one looks to philosophy for an account of man's experience of the world. The location of the *Lebenswelt* is, above all, the recognition that daily life is neither produced by nature nor fashioned after the conceptual models of the natural sciences. The problem of the *Lebenswelt* is that of attending to the givenness of existence as it is directly appreciated by men in action living their lives within the naive schemas of explanation they construct for themselves in daily life.

Just as familiarity is a thematic assumption of ordinary existence, so causation is taken for granted within the *Lebenswelt*. Again, there are two facets of the problem. Causation as a *Lebenswelt* concept may refer to the order of experience as men live it or it may denote the way in which interpretation of daily life is structured. But the objective and subjective aspects of causation are qualitatively different from their counterparts which we examined in discussing causality in the domain of the natural sciences. For within the *Lebenswelt* the very meaning of causation remains largely indeterminate, implicit, and generally vague. Both the object of causal analysis and the mode of analysis remain relatively obscure to the consciousness of ordinary men involved in their jobs. To be sure, there are areas within the taken for granted world of daily life which are rather expertly interpreted. The causal pattern there is somewhat different. The diesel engineer undoubtedly has a much more sophisticated notion of locomotive engineering than the average person whose job is everything but diesel engineering. The physician has a profound understanding of the operation of the heart compared to the man who waits on tables or runs a bookstore or teaches Latin in a secondary school. But it is not difficult to see that areas of special competence are themselves only fragments of the public world, and that in ordinary life each of us, no matter what his specialty, is a novice at dozens of other fields. There is nothing new in all of this, but there is something to be understood about the familiar. Causation is, for the most part, naively taken for granted in a completely inexpert way by men operating within the *Lebenswelt*. Nor will degrees of civilization be any solution to the situation. In some ways, less advanced peoples know a great deal more about the causal structure of their world than we do about ours. Max Weber makes this point quite forcefully in his essay on "Science as a Vocation." Do we today, he asks, have a greater knowledge of the conditions of life under which we exist than has an American Indian or a Hottentot? Hardly. Unless he is a physicist, one who rides on the streetcar has no idea how the car happened to get into motion. And he does not need to know. He is satisfied that he may "count" on the behavior of the streetcar, and he orients his conduct according to this expectation; but he knows nothing about what it takes to produce such a car so that it can move. The savage knows incomparably more about his tools. ... How does it happen that one can buy something for money – sometimes more and sometimes less? The savage knows what he does in order to get his daily food and which institutions serve him in this pursuit. The increasing intellectualization and rationalization do not, therefore, indicate an increased and general knowledge of the conditions under which one lives. It means something else, namely, the knowledge or belief that if one but wished one *could* learn it at any time.[1]

It is an endemic feature of the Life-world, then, that all of us, more or less advanced in civilized life, are destined to interpret its causal structure in a fragmentary manner. And the structure thus interpreted is not an image or a reflection of causation in natural science or in expert areas of knowledge, but causation as the indeterminate horizon of human action.

I have suggested that there is a double aspect to causation as a structure of the *Lebenswelt*. On the one hand, the elements observed in the Life-world are taken to be causally ordered; on the other hand, the way in which men in daily life experience their immediate reality involves a causal ordering. In both cases, however, I have insisted that the kind of causation operative in the *Lebenswelt* is qualitatively different from that at issue in the natural sciences. This contention must now be supported in greater detail. The best procedure, I think, is to turn to an extended example. But before doing this, I wish to introduce a methodological note which perhaps will set the example in its proper context. The approach I am both following and trying to explain is the phenomenological method originated by Edmund Husserl. The very location of the *Lebenswelt* is itself a phenomenological act. In these terms, the object located in phenomenological description as well as the activity of consciousness involved in investigating that object is a meaning-structure. We are not interested here in object in the physical sense but rather in the logical sense. The object is any element *meant* by the activity of consciousness. The physical properties or geographical location of the object in the ordinary sense of that term are not at issue here. They are bracketed from our procedure. This does not mean that they are denied or disregarded; instead, we set our traditional attitude

[1] Weber, M., "Science as a Vocation," in *Sociological Analysis* (ed. by Logan Wilson and William L. Kolb), New York, 1949, 7–8.

or belief toward them in methodological abeyance. Objects, then, are directly given to the acts of consciousness, to intentional consciousness, in Husserl's language, precisely as consciousness thinks them, treats them, places them, believes them, fears them, or considers them. The object, furthermore, is not given to us, but to *me* the inquirer. And as a phenomenologist, I do not presuppose the historical, natural, cultural, or common-sense character of the object given for description. I turn to the object ideally in perfect neutrality. I attend to what presents itself. I make myself available to the stream of experience in its sheer givenness. And in doing this, I gain access to the intentional data of consciousness independent of any causal schema or preconceived doctrine of causation. Causality, then, is bracketed, and I attend to the given in a causation-free attitude. The result, indeed, seems strange to both natural science and common sense. How is it possible to understand the structure of the *Lebenswelt* by means of a method that frees itself of traditionally conceived naturalistic categories? And more particularly, how is it possible to study causation as a structure of the *Lebenswelt* by means of a method that begins by bracketing causation? We shall turn to the resolution of this paradox later. For the present, it is first necessary to examine causation within the *Lebenswelt* by means of some illustration that will enable us to see the issues in question in concrete form. I propose to use as my example the encounter with the Absurd, taking the Absurd as a central category of existential philosophy.

⟨ IV ⟩

The man who suddenly loses control of the stable image of the world is a familiar symbol. We encounter him in life as often as we meet him in literature. We say that in facing the Absurd he has been transformed. Spatial metaphors often announce such changes. We crack up or we break down. In the ecstasy of the Absurd we are beside ourselves. But the metaphor transcends the spatial and introduces what might be termed the spatiality of inner life, the space of the "I" moving through the corridors of consciousness. Kafka's Joseph K. undertakes his defense in a world in which defense is indicative of guilt. The first act of the guilty man is to affirm his innocence. Another of Kafka's heroes suddenly locates himself metamorphosed into the insect whose life he had all along lived in utter unconcern. Camus' stranger murders the lucidity of a day and advances himself from the backdrop of reality into the focus of mundane destruction. In Sartre's *Nausea* the protagonist encounters the sheer quality of facticity, the pure is-ness of experience; he becomes the Absurd. In all of these remarkable instances, some facet of an essential structure of inner life is transposed; the world remains stable perhaps, but our experience of it shifts into the horizon of a new vision, a new sense of awareness in which subject and object are no longer traditionally conceived. Within the interior space of consciousness the Absurd moves and waits; its domain is bounded only by the reach of awareness. We may define the Absurd as the intrinsic questionability of all order. The Absurd is causation turned inside out.

Rather than choose an example from literature, the poor man's equivalent of the psychiatrist's cases, I propose to consider the Absurd in terms of an Ideal Type in Max Weber's sense. My illustration for the encounter with the Absurd will be a construction, one which relates to empirical and literary phenomena but which transcends any of their possible exemplifications or actualizations. As Ideal Type, the Absurd is a composite of person, situation, and action. Let us then imaginatively project an encounter with the Absurd and look to the causal structure of both the object of awareness, what is given, and the noetic aspect of the awareness, what we may call the Absurd consciousness. The given as Absurd presents itself in packets. It were as though the totality of what there is announced itself in sudden, finite charges. *This* bed, *this* ceiling, *this* room are not parts of anything; they are themselves units whose inner and outer horizons form an immanent circle. Perspective is fractured at its causal root. Instead of seeing things *in* ordinary frames, we appropriate them as they give themselves not in isolation but in a modality of consciousness in which relatedness itself is displaced. Isolation means isolation *from* something; these givens are neither isolated nor related. They stand free of all connectedness, all order, all causal reference beyond themselves. And if perspective is bracketed, one may move in closer and closer to the unity given, explore its givenness in overpowering detail. *This* ceiling, then, may become mine not as part of anything but simply as there-for-me. My room's ceiling is not identical with *this* ceiling I have presented to me here and now in my room. From outside the circle of awareness the two may be identified; within the circle they have no necessary connection. Indeed, "connection" is an abortive concept. The Absurd object steps out of the country of its birth, it calls me to its explicit and stark presence.

Moving from the object aspect of the Absurd to the subjective or noetic side, I attend now to the awareness of what I have termed *this* ceiling. There is a glance of consciousness that intends this object. It is a kind of this-ceiling-attending that becomes thematic here. But no relatedness manifests itself between this act of consciousness and the mainstream of what I call my awareness. Nor do I intend *this* ceiling as the noematic unity for a series of possible acts of awareness. For the Absurd consciousness there is no repetition of acts all of which point toward the same meaning. Each intending has its fixed label, its inimitable and unrepeatable texture. Moreover, it is that specific texture that captivates me. The ceiling is the same ceiling for my ordinary predications as well as for my ordinary perceptions. But in Absurd consciousness it is in every instance a new moment of consciousness that arises in perceptual experience. Causation has been flushed out of consciousness; the remainder is the overpowering particularity of the world. Absurdity has afflicted the intentional structure of consciousness, and the Absurd man is, in a strange way, analagous to some of the aphasic patients described in the work of Kurt Goldstein.[2]

I hope the last point will not be misunderstood. A phenomenology of the Absurd is not a pathology of the Absurd. There is no issue here of disfunction. Rather, the Absurd is a metaphysical modality, and it requires direct inspection. Seeing the world in a certain way, possessing the world in a certain way, bearing the reality of the world in a certain way are, I am suggesting, more than interpretations of the Real. They *are* the reality with which we have to deal and with which we must come to terms. The causal analysis of particular styles of existence, the examination of the Absurd, for instance, must first respect the full quality and status of its metaphysical object. It is not even enough to attempt to gain an appreciative and sympathetic understanding of the way in which the Absurd man sees his world. It is above all demanded of us, philosophers and psychiatrists alike, that we view his reality in full depth, not as the product of distortion but as a conceivable and conceivably valid permutation of experience. To be sure, it may

[2] Of course, the Absurd has a horizon of universality as well as of specificity. In addition to the delimitation of reality to "thises," unique packets of awareness, it is possible to point to a plethora of possible causal relata. In place of the minimal order and relatedness we assume as normal for daily life, there may be posited an almost infinitely detailed schema of causation. The Absurd in this manifestation approaches some forms of schizophrenic consciousness. Everything has its secret connection. The world is dominated by mysterious linkages, endless chains of implication, a subtle apparatus of forces and hidden controls. Far from appreciating only the specific intention, the individual is led to the Hegelian disaster of total, absolute causation pulsing in every living act and implicit in nature itself. The world is rendered Absurd either way, with the shattering of causation or its pathological magnification to the point of unbearable Gnostic design.

later be the professional task of the psychiatrist to categorize the Absurd in his own terms. His scientific delineation looks forward to therapy. But any change presupposes the original status of that which is to be changed. If the datum escapes us, we move ahead in conceptual danger.

Exactly what has my illustration of the Ideal Type of the Absurd really illustrated? Essentially, the explosion of causal relatedness in the *Lebenswelt*. That I have chosen an extreme case does not prevent the application of the same ideas to the more nearly normal character of the Life-world. The application must, of course, be modified radically, for in the normal scheme of things in ordinary life there *is* a causal pattern operative. But causation remains largely implicit in its meaning and function. As Alfred Schutz once suggested, the notion of "likelihood" which Aristotle develops in his *Topics* is a possible approach to the meaning of the kind of causation that operates in the *Lebenswelt*. Men in daily life deem innumerable events "likely" to follow from the performance of certain actions. There is no systematic concept involved. As a common-sense man, I simply take it for granted that certain types of actions will follow from other types of actions. Causation has been thoroughly typified. Alfred Schutz writes:

I take it for granted that my action (say putting a stamped and duly addressed envelope in a mailbox) will induce anonymous fellowmen (postmen) to perform typical actions (handling the mail) in accordance with typical in-order-to motives (to live up to their occupational duties) with the result that the state of affairs projected by me (delivery of the letter to the addressee within reasonable time) will be achieved.[3]

All of us as common-sense men operate within the horizon of such typifications. Social reality is largely possible in virtue of this order of *Lebenswelt*-causation.

In choosing to explore the problem of causation in terms of the radical example of the Absurd, I have moved away from the typification of the normal toward the environs of the abnormal. This movement is purposeful for several reasons. First, the stronger, stranger case of the Absurd delimits more dramatically the region of the Life-world from that of the models constructed by the genetic method of the natural sciences. Second, the Absurd dramatizes the problem of a social reality built up out of the typifications of common sense. For if we are destined to live within such constructs, we find necessarily that

[3] Schutz, A., "Common-Sense and Scientific Interpretation of Human Action." *Philosophy and Phenomenological Research*, XIV, September, 1953, 19.

portions of our daily world are reified or rendered paradoxical in virtue of their typically constructive character. The Absurd man is not as far off from the center of normalcy as we supposed. Both the object he intends and the quality of his intending are perhaps the limit points of typified existence. The genetic method is not free to attend to such problems, but it is exactly such problems that form the nucleus of our lives. The phenomenological approach endeavours to remain true to the texture of human reality. Paradoxically, a method that brackets causal analysis is utilized to describe causation as a structure of the *Lebenswelt*. It is time to attend to that paradox.

⟨ V ⟩

The phenomenological procedure requires that the phenomenologist place in abeyance his ordinary believing in the world, his causal and valuational appreciation of reality. Bracketing is not denying; it is a methodological device (though I believe it has more generalized philosophical implications) to overcome the naive committedness of men within the natural attitude. Setting aside causation, then, in this methodological sense, does not involve denying or ignoring causation. Indeed, causation instead may be rendered an explicit object for description. But the phenomenologist does not pursue that description in causal terms. It is not necessary to write in green ink in order to describe a green table. One does not "greenly" call the table green. We recognize that the descriptive process may have independence from the objects for description. Similarly, but in a much more radical mode, the phenomenologist disconnects his ordinary naive believing in causal order in the hope of being able to "catch" that causal order in neutral terms. The paradox is only apparent. Having taken care of one paradox, however, we find that another rises in its place.

For the natural standpoint, that not only of mundane existence but of natural science, the phenomenologist's non-causal treatment of causation presents a paradox because a certain relationship is pre-supposed between the sensory order and the physical order. Naturalism in all of its forms simply assumes that there is a nexus between sensory events and the physical world of such a nature that causality is properly to be located in terms of that nexus. Consciousness is viewed as, at best, an epiphenomenon to neurological events. The causal order of the nervous system grounds the resultant events in consciousness. As long as such a view is held either explicitly or, worse, implicitly, the phenomenologist's conception of consciousness as a sovereign domain will appear paradoxical, and causality must remain a fugitive concept. From the phenomenological side, however, the paradox arises only if we make the presuppositions which the naturalist insists on. "Causality," Husserl writes, "belongs in principle to the system of the constituted intentional world, and has no meaning except in this world..." [4] The paradox of causation arises for phenomenology only if we ignore the conception of intentional consciousness that phenomenology projects.

If causation does not serve as a naturalistic nexus between the "objective" world and the "subjective" states of consciousness – and this is the view explicitly denied by phenomenologists – then description of reality is an integral project. Phenomenology is a movement beyond traditional realisms and idealisms; it refuses to accept the common-sense distinction between subject and object. The prize of that refusal is a radical vision of man in his Life-world. It is this achievement of phenomenology together with its existential implications which has attracted so many creative minds in contemporary psychiatry, especially in Europe, to its possibilities within the domain of psychiatric theory. And it is here that the relevance of philosophy for psychiatry may be observed. Whether we are common-sense men operating in ordinary life or philosophers bracketing the natural attitude in order to comprehend it, or psychiatrists attempting to understand the patient's world in its integral unity, we are committed at multiple levels to *seeing* the world. If we presuppose that the cardinal philosophical features of reality are obvious and to be taken for granted as being largely what they naively appear to be, we waive our right to locate a more neutral conception of the Real as well as a more exciting one. The moral is that we must never assume that we don't pay for what we take for granted. Philosophical ingenuousness may be another name for scientific arrogance. I have argued that both are out of place in modern psychiatry, and that existentialism and phenomenology have largely been responsible for teaching us the profits of openness and humility.

A final problem remains within the limits of this essay. Earlier I suggested that psychiatry is concerned with an aspect of the relationship between appearance and reality. To the extent that the psychiatrist seeks to penetrate disguises, to unmask disguises, he is attempting to transcend appearance and gain reality. The reality is the living unity of the person, his inwardness, in Kierkegaard's language. But to locate

---

[4] Husserl, E., *Ideas*, 162.

that essential person it is necessary, in cases of mental pathology, to evaluate what appears as a clue to what does not manifest itself. Appearance is not reality, but how is it possible for a psychiatrist to explore reality without precisely that genetic method of causal analysis we have been criticizing from the outset? Isn't an appearance-reality dualism destined to utilize causal procedures? I should like to clarify, not qualify, my position. Phenomenological method is not in conflict with genetic procedures. Phenomenology and science can never contradict each other because, as Husserl clearly pointed out in his essay on "Philosophy as a Rigorous Science," they operate at qualitatively different levels and have different spheres of experience for their subject matter. There is nothing in phenomenology which demands that scientific method disqualify itself from the study of man and nature. Rather, the situation is this: genetic method is untrue to itself if it assumes naively that phenomenological description, uncovering of the data of experience, is unnecessary or a mere philosophical luxury. It is above all the nature of the given that is the prime problem of any science that seeks interpretive understanding of human reality. The necessity of phenomenology must then be understood as a propaedeutic to any later inquiry. In a more generalized sense, philosophy has an analogous role to play. Its aim is to achieve that synoptic unity without which all disciplines would remain fragmentary and isolated efforts to come to terms with the world. If psychiatry is systematic distrust, philosophy is creative persistence.

It may appear that the conclusion to my argument is a call to some sort of truce between science and philosophy, a call to cooperative harmony. Since they don't contradict each other, genetic and phenomenological method can get along tidily. I'm afraid such a claim would be as hopeless with respect to practical operations as it would be false on more theoretical grounds. There is no need to underestimate the distance between naturalistic and positivistic and existential and phenomenological categories. But it is critically important to recognize the legitimacy of phenomenological procedures with respect to a causally inspired natural science. With respect to psychiatry my claim has been that there are epistemic and metaphysical dimensions to the reality with which psychiatrists are concerned. To assume that the philosophical problem here is of only limited practical significance is to miss not only the meaning of the impact of existentialism and phenomenology on contemporary psychiatry but to abandon any hope of establishing the outlines of theory in the discipline of psychiatry.

Phenomenology does not entail a denial of the appearance-reality motif; indeed, to the contrary, it offers a remarkable methodological apparatus for probing that duality. It urges that we attend to the tension between what there is and what there seems to be, but that we remain true to the experiential givenness through which both person and *persona* achieve expression.

18. Death and Situation

⟨ I ⟩

As an "essay in phenomenological ontology" [1] Sartre's *L'Être et le néant* is concerned with the structures of Being in so far as Being presents itself, i.e., in so far as it is given in experience. As a phenomenology, *Being and Nothingness* deals only with presentations, and as a descriptive enterprise, it cannot handle metaphysical problems. Thus Sartre gives us extensive descriptive analyses of the self, the body, the various concrete relations with the alter ego (love, language, desire, etc.), but he does not attempt to analyze questions of the ultimate origin, purpose, or meaning of reality. Since the character of his investigation is descriptive, and since Sartre's method takes the standpoint of the individual consciousness, the question of what is within and outside *our* experience becomes transposed into the problem of what is within and outside *my* experience, *I* as experiencing consciousness. What is within the experience of my fellow man may be in principle inaccessible to my direct experience and vice versa. A crucial case in point is the problem of the experience of death. My experience of death is always my experience of the death of the Other, the death of a fellow man. The experience of my death as a phenomenon, Sartre claims, can only be a phenomenon for the experience of the Other, whether that Other is friend, relation, associate, stranger, or part of the anonymous "public." If "my" death is thus outside my possible experience, in what sense is my death a possible object for my phenomenological investigation?

In endeavouring to consider this question, I believe that an analysis of Sartre's philosophy of death may be of interest and of value in several ways: first, we may clarify a vital point of difference between

[1] the subtitle of Jean-Paul Sartre's *L'Être et le néant*, Paris, 1943.

the thought of Sartre and Heidegger, philosophers sometimes taken as expressing equivalent positions; second, we may come to a more careful understanding of the fundamental Sartrean concept of "situation" with which his idea of death is connected; third, we may implicitly come to a more penetrating appreciation of the problem of death as a theme of phenomenological philosophy. I propose, then, to turn to a brief exposition of Sartre's views on death, to proceed to an examination of the correlated but more fundamental concept of "situation," to offer certain critical remarks on Sartre's treatment of the problem in the light of his total ontology, and finally to turn to the larger theme of a phenomenological approach to the meaning of death in human experience.

〈 II 〉

Although it is well known that Heidegger has made much of his idea of *Sein zum Tode*, of the emergence of the authentic person from the condition of anonymity (*das Man*), it is pertinent to note that in this regard Sartre does not follow Heidegger; to the contrary, he clearly and thoroughly dissents from the Heideggerian position. Sartre's dissent is occasioned by a rejection of Heidegger's underlying thesis that *my* death may become, in a direct sense, a phenomenon in *my* experience. To understand his reasons for rejecting Heidegger's philosophy of death, it is necessary to summarize Sartre's general conception of death.[2]

For Sartre (1) *my* death is not an experience of which I can ever be aware, for awareness is a life-characteristic: death means absolute and final cessation of my awareness; (2) my death, as phenomenon, is a possible experience only for a fellow man: it is a structure of "being-for-the-Other"[3]; (3) I cannot meditate on my life from the standpoint of death, since that standpoint would have to be that of a fellow man, a standpoint denied me in principle[4]; (4) I can meditate on my possible future death from the standpoint of my life, but such meditation fails to reveal my death, it only refers me to the existence of the Other, of some fellow man for whom that possible future death will be a possible

---

[2] *L'Être et le néant*, 615–638.
[3] *ibid.*, 631.
[4] According to Sartre, I can know the Other only as object for my subjectivity or I may experience myself as object for the Other's subjectivity, but I cannot know the Other as subjectivity for my subjectivity; hence I cannot take the standpoint of the Other as subjectivity. See *ibid.*, 327–328.

experience; (5) my finitude and my death must be differentiated: the former is an ontological structure (which does not derive from death) and so is an object for my phenomenological investigation; the latter is not.

Sartre has defined "being for-itself" (*l'être pour-soi*) or, most simply, the self, as a principle of negativity. The self, understood from different aspects as human subjectivity, consciousness, etc., is the "being for which being is in question in its being," [5] i.e., the being which is constantly, ceaselessly undergoing a nihilating transition and alteration which places its very nature in question. My past, what I have done and been, is, so long as I live, continually being reconstructed and reinterpreted by me as well as by others in terms of a present self which is itself undergoing change in the light of an anticipated future which shapes and conditions the intentions underlying my present projects. The self is *pro*-jected, it is, temporally, a forward moving structure whose present being is a "nihilation" (*néantisation*) defined by the anticipated future, so that without that future the present has no status. Most simply: the self *is* only to the extent that what it tends toward establishes the very condition of that "is." Thus, Sartre says, it is because the self is the being which always claims an after, that there is no place for death in the being which the self is.[6] As a self my being exists in the stream of life activities moving toward the future: my death cannot be any part of this structure of being.

"My project toward *a* death is comprehensible (suicide, martyrdom, heroism)," Sartre writes, "but not the project toward *my* death." [7] *My* death would mean the unfulfillment or the collapse of my projects, it would place my projects in the hands of Others whose standpoint I cannot take; *a* death is a meaningful aspect of my projects, for it is only the concept of death as such that is involved. But is not the difference between *my* death and *a* death Heidegger's problem of the distinction between authenticity and anonymity? Here we come to Sartre's specific criticism of Heidegger's philosophy of death. Sartre writes:

Heidegger ... begins by individualizing the death of each of us, by indicating to us that it is the death of a *person*, of an individual, the 'only thing that nobody can do for me'; then he utilizes this incomparable individuality which he has conferred upon death from the 'Dasein' in order to individualize the 'Dasein' itself: it is by projecting itself freely toward its ultimate possibility that the 'Dasein'

[5] *ibid.*, 624.
[6] *ibid.*
[7] *ibid.*

will reach authentic existence and will break away from the everyday banality in order to attain the irreplaceable oneness of the person. But there is a circle here; how, in effect, prove that death has this individuality and the power to confer it.[8]

The "circle" indicated is really this: the experience of my death is the ground of my authenticity; the authentic I replaces the I of anonymity, *das Man*, yet the individuality of death presupposes my capacity to recognize it as unique. How is the I of *das Man*, the inauthentic banal self, able to appreciate the uniqueness of the experience of its own death? Sartre concludes that the phenomenon of *my* death, in so far as it can be entertained at all as an idea, is meaningful only in the same sense in which *my* love, *my* vows, or *my* emotions are *mine*, i.e., as defined by my subjectivity. "Thus, from this point of view," Sartre writes, "the most banal love is, like death, irreplaceable and unique, no one can love for me." [9] *My* death remains then, for Sartre, the possible experience of the Other, an experience beyond my consciousness, and to me forever inaccessible.

⟨III⟩

But Sartre's rejection of Heidegger's philosophy of death is not, in itself, his major concern. Indeed, Sartre's own analysis of death is not an independent topic of inquiry nor a fundamental theme of *Being and Nothingness*. It is introduced as a clarifying agent for a broader problem, one to which Sartre has devoted a considerable amount of attention, the problem of "situation." The analysis of death will, in part, he writes, "permit a clearer conception of what a 'situation' is." [10] To be a self, according to Sartre, is to be in a "situation": the self *is* its situation. As self I am: first, "an existent in the midst of other existents" [11]; second, an existent born into a world which has a history, societal organization, etc.[12]; third, an existent who determines the rapport of utensility or of adversity of the realities which surround me in the world; fourth, an existent who constitutes my situation through the selection of the goals toward which my projects are aimed; fifth, an existent who *is* only in the face of the not-yet future which conditions as a limit what is given in my experience.

[8] *ibid.*, 617.
[9] *ibid.*, 618.
[10] *ibid.*, 633.
[11] *ibid.*
[12] Cf. Sartre's *Anti-Semite and Jew*, New York, 1948, 59–60.

My situation is, therefore, a complex dialectically generated out of both objective and subjective conditions: "the situation cannot be subjective, for it is neither the sum nor the unity of the *impressions* which things make upon us; it is the *things themselves* and myself among the things." [13] But the situation "can no more be objective, in the sense in which it would be a pure given which the subject would verify without being in any way engaged in the system thus constituted." [14] Rather, the situation is a *"relation of being"* [15] between the facticity of the world and the "illumination" [16] of that facticity by the subject. In this manner, situation is defined by the self in a double sense: by the actual being of the self and also by that which the self has not yet become.

⟨ IV ⟩

We have stated that Sartre treats the experience of death as subordinate and contributive to the larger problem of "situation." Let us now reverse his procedure and see the relationship between the two, taking the problem of death as primary. In what way does his idea of "situation" clarify his idea of death?

My situation is always *concrete*. The universal ends I choose for my life are chosen from my particular standpoint, they reflect *my* ambition, *my* hope, *my* struggle. The very selection of the "life of a professional man," for example, is made in the light of *my* conception of what such a life implies and involves. But in addition, the degree to which I realize the "life of a professional man" is expressed in the concrete situations of my existence. In this manner we come to the relationship of death and situation within the context of the concrete events of my life.

Sartre recalls Kafka's story of the merchant who comes to plead a case at the castle: "a terrible guard bars his entrance. He dares not pass beyond, waits and dies in waiting. At the hour of death, he asks the guardian: 'How does it happen that I was the only one to wait?' and the guardian answers him: 'This gate was made only for you.' " [17] And Sartre adds: "each one makes for himself his own gate." [18] As self I do not choose my own death (though I may choose *a* death, as we have

[13] *L'Être et le néant*, 633.
[14] *ibid.*, 634.
[15] *ibid.*
[16] *ibid.*
[17] *ibid.*, 635.
[18] *ibid.*

seen), for *my* death is an ontologically transcendent phenomenon available only to the Other; rather, death as such is an *a priori* condition of the human reality, the sheer facticity of what is given in the human condition: "it is absurd that we are born," Sartre writes, "it is absurd that we die." [19] But every general objective aspect of my situation, death included, is constituted in so far as the self "makes a human reality exist as species." [20] Though I do not "create" death as an *a priori* facticity of the human situation, there *is* a human situation only to the extent that there are selves who constitute such worlds. The *a priori* of death, then, is the condition not of *my* death but of my finitude. To be finite is to choose one end to the exclusion of others, for the very conception of "exclusion" involves the choice of *this* and no other, a choice that establishes my self as defined by the irreversibility of temporality.[21] Thus death is an *a priori* condition defining my situation as finite, but I choose my situation and that choice is within the situation of my choosing. I cannot choose the objective condition of finitude, but without my self-constituted world that *a priori* would remain abortive.

<V>

Taken together, then, death and situation, for Sartre, are mutually revealing structures which illuminate man's being; but situation transposes death into the phenomenological givenness of finitude. My death is a phenomenon for the situation of *Others*, of a situation that transcends my existence. And if we now add that finitude cannot be derived from the conception of death we are left with Sartre's reduction of the problem: man, as *pour-soi*, is a being whose finitude defines his situation and whose situation defines his finitude; death remains only as an *a priori* limit of the human condition.

This reduction of death to finitude is open, I would suggest, to a number of criticisms. First, to speak of the phenomenon of death is necessarily to locate those meanings which present themselves directly to my awareness as observer of the Other's death. Even if the Other dies-for-me, his death is independent, as phenomenon, of the causal categories that make up the physical or medical definition of death. My friend's death does not consist for me in the biological fact of cessation

[19] *ibid.*, 631.
[20] *ibid.*, 636.
[21] *ibid.*, 631.

of heartbeat or respiration or the decay of his tissues; it is my friend who has died, not his body. If the phenomenon of my friend's death is the complexus of meanings signified by his dying, then those meanings are available to me with respect to my own death. I need not be the witness of my death, the guardian of my corpse, to locate the phenomenon of my death. But there is a second point to be made: it is not possible, I think, to derive the meaning of finitude from the self alone, apart from the structure of death. For the self to be finite means that it must move forward temporally to a point of cessation that is more than the end of a formal series: that point of cessation which is the terminus of consciousness is my death. To be finite is to be limited by death; to derive finitude from man's being alone is to conceive of an "end" without that ground which makes the very conception of man's "end" possible. There is, finally, a third point of criticism: Sartre makes of death an *a priori* limit of man's situation. But this device merely returns us to the problem of the constitution of the situational *a priori*. Since the self ultimately constitutes the way in which its situation is structured, death as an *a priori* is returned, full circle, to the immanence of consciousness. Death and situation, in my own view, are comprehensible as aspects of an integral experiential reality which is phenomenologically given. In this respect, I think Heidegger is closer to the truth than Sartre. But rather than play one doctrine against the other, I think it more profitable at this time to turn to the completely valid question implicitly raised by both philosophers: In what sense is a phenomenology of death possible? Perhaps the best way of approaching this question is to abandon the special, often tangled, terminology of Sartre and Heidegger and turn directly to the phenomena themselves.

As soon as we are born, Heidegger recalls in *Sein und Zeit*, we are old enough to die. The awareness of death may come for the child through the death of a pet, the sight of an animal killed on the road, or through the experience of a death in the family. However it comes, there comes along with it the uncanny, almost insidious realization that the child too will die. Thus, death enters the world and gives a shock to innocence from which innocence can never recover. The child's questions about death are the adult's questions more honestly stated and the philosopher's questions naively discovered. "Will I die too?" asks the child; "Why must I die?" "What does it mean to die?" And the simple truth is that there are no final answers to these questions, though there are myths and dreams and desperate hopes evinced in the answers children get. Our evasions are decisive evidence of our metaphysical illiteracy.

But death for the adult world is no less the ambivalent problematic of our daily lives. It is not necessary to turn to Heidegger to locate the immediacy of the issues. Heidegger himself makes reference to Tolstoi's remarkable story "The Death of Ivan Ilyich." We could trace the problem in quite other directions as well. Writing in 1915, twelve years before the publication of *Sein und Zeit*, one investigator discusses the spiritual atmosphere of Europe at the time of the First World War:

a factor to which I attribute our present sense of estrangement in this once lovely and congenial world [he writes] is the disturbance that has taken place in our attitude towards death, an attitude to which hitherto we have clung so fast. This attitude was far from straightforward. We were of course prepared to maintain that death was the necessary outcome of life, that everyone owes a debt to Nature and must expect to pay the reckoning – in short, that death was natural, undeniable and unavoidable. In reality, however, we were accustomed to behave as if it were otherwise. We displayed an unmistakable tendency to 'shelve' death, to eliminate it from life. We tried to hush it up ... at bottom no one believes in his own death.[22]

The author of this statement is not an existential philosopher but a psychoanalytic philosopher, Sigmund Freud.

From childhood through our adult lives, then, the problem of making sense of life by making sense of death is a primary obligation in a purely descriptive sense; for whether we like it or not, death is the horizon of our being. And it is perhaps as horizon that we can interpret it phenomenologically. When I come to terms with reality, I admit the overpowering truth of my total human situation: that I am a being born into a world in which I am destined to grow older and to die. My being in this world is along a horizon of action and belief that includes my death in a world that transcends me. The first evidence, pheno-menologically, that is given to me of this horizon of death is, I would suggest (though I cannot develop it here), a sense of *uncanniness* which haunts the experienced elements of my familiar surroundings.[23] The uncanny is appresented, we might say, with the familiar. Each familiar object, person, or event carries with it the possibility of the sinister and the strange. If the familiar is rooted in life, the uncanny is its *Doppelgänger*. And though it may be perfectly "natural" that plants

---

[22] Freud, S., "Thoughts on War and Death," in *Collected Papers*, Vol. IV, London, 1949, 304–305.

[23] Again, Freud's essay on "The 'Uncanny'," *ibid.*, pp. 368–407, is remarkably suggestive, although he does not consider the implications of the problem with respect to death.

and animals and other human beings die, it remains strange beyond comparison that this will *really* happen to me. Here, then, I believe is a root meaning of the experience of death; the uncanny thrusts us instantaneously within the horizon of death.

These remarks lead to no special conclusion. As Landsberg says in his essay on "The Experience of Death," the question of the meaning of death to the human being as a person admits of no conclusion, "for we are dealing with the very mystery of man, taken from a certain aspect." [24] And he adds: "every real problem in philosophy contains all the others in the unity of mystery." [25] Our effort has been directed to the articulation of a problem rather than to its solution. In this sense, the central contribution of Sartre and Heidegger to the clarification of these issues is their recovery of a philosophical problem that has been almost lost to contemporary thought in a scientific age. Whatever their technical inadequacies, they have succeeded not only in relocating an authentic problem but in directing our attention to its living urgency. It has been a long time since Montaigne reminded us of Cicero's injunction that to philosophize is to learn how to die. In our age the same truth is expressed by Rilke:

"Lord, give to each man his own death."

[24] Landsberg, P.-L., *The Experience of Death & The Moral Problem of Suicide*, New York, 1953, 1.
[25] *ibid.*